ECONOMICS

CFA® Program Curriculum
2024 • LEVEL PREREQUISITE READING • VOLUME 2

©2023 by CFA Institute. All rights reserved. This copyright covers material written expressly for this volume by the editor/s as well as the compilation itself. It does not cover the individual selections herein that first appeared elsewhere. Permission to reprint these has been obtained by CFA Institute for this edition only. Further reproductions by any means, electronic or mechanical, including photocopying and recording, or by any information storage or retrieval systems, must be arranged with the individual copyright holders noted.

CFA®, Chartered Financial Analyst®, AIMR-PPS®, and GIPS® are just a few of the trademarks owned by CFA Institute. To view a list of CFA Institute trademarks and the Guide for Use of CFA Institute Marks, please visit our website at www.cfainstitute.org.

This publication is designed to provide accurate and authoritative information in regard to the subject matter covered. It is sold with the understanding that the publisher is not engaged in rendering legal, accounting, or other professional service. If legal advice or other expert assistance is required, the services of a competent professional should be sought.

All trademarks, service marks, registered trademarks, and registered service marks are the property of their respective owners and are used herein for identification purposes only.

ISBN: 978-1-953337-82-5

CONTENTS

How to Use the CFA Program Curriculum   vii
    Errata   vii

Economics

Learning Module 1   **Topics in Demand and Supply Analysis**   3
    Introduction   3
    Demand Concepts   4
    Price Elasticity of Demand   6
        Extremes of Price Elasticity   9
    Predicting Demand Elasticity, Price Elasticity, and Total Expenditure   9
    Income Elasticity of Demand, Cross-Price Elasticity of Demand   11
        Cross-Price Elasticity of Demand   11
    Substitution and Income Effects; Normal Goods, Inferior Goods, and Special Cases   14
        Normal and Inferior Goods   15
    Supply Analysis: Cost, Marginal Return, and Productivity   17
        Marginal Returns and Productivity   17
    Marginal Revenue, Marginal Cost and Profit Maximization; Short-Run Cost Curves: Total, Variable, Fixed, and Marginal Costs   22
        Understanding the Interaction between Total, Variable, Fixed, and Marginal Cost and Output   24
    Summary   29
    Practice Problems   31
    Solutions   34

Learning Module 2   **Introduction to the Firm and Market Organization**   37
    Analysis of Market Structures   37
        Analysis of Market Structures   38
    Perfect Competition   40
        Demand Analysis in Perfectly Competitive Markets   41
    Other Factors Affecting Demand   42
    Consumer Surplus: Value minus Expenditure   43
    Supply Analysis, Optimal Price, and Output in Perfectly Competitive Markets   45
        Optimal Price and Output in Perfectly Competitive Markets   47
    Long-Run Equilibrium in Perfectly Competitive Markets   50
    Monopoly Markets: Demand/Supply and Optimal Price/Output   52
        Demand Analysis in Monopoly Markets   54
        Supply Analysis in Monopoly Markets   55
        Optimal Price and Output in Monopoly Markets   56
    Price Discrimination and Consumer Surplus   58
    Monopoly Markets: Long-Run Equilibrium   60
    Summary   61
    References   63
    Practice Problems   64

indicates an optional segment

	Solutions	66
Learning Module 3	**Aggregate Output, Prices, and Economic Growth**	**67**
	Introduction	68
	Aggregate Output and Income	69
	Gross Domestic Product	70
	The Components of GDP	77
	Relationship among Saving, Investment, the Fiscal Balance and the Trade Balance	79
	Aggregate Demand and Aggregate Supply	82
	Aggregate Demand	83
	Aggregate Supply	87
	Shifts in the Aggregate Demand Curve	89
	Equilibrium GDP and Prices	102
	Economic Growth and Sustainability	111
	The Production Function and Potential GDP	112
	Sources of Economic Growth	114
	Measures of Sustainable Growth	119
	Measuring Sustainable Growth	122
	Summary	*124*
	References	*128*
	Practice Problems	*129*
	Solutions	*134*
Learning Module 4	**Introduction to Business Cycles**	**137**
	Introduction	137
	Consumer Behavior	138
	Consumer Confidence	138
	Measures of Consumption	138
	Income Growth	139
	Saving Rates	140
	Housing Sector Behavior	141
	Available Statistics	141
	Sensitivity to Interest Rates and Relationship to Credit Cycle	141
	The Role of Demographics	141
	Impact on the Economic Cycle	142
	External Trade Sector Behavior	142
	Cyclical Fluctuations of Imports and Exports	143
	The Role of the Exchange Rate	143
	Overall Effect on Exports and Imports	144
	Unemployment	145
	The Unemployment Rate	146
	Overall Payroll Employment and Productivity Indicators	147
	Inflation	149
	Deflation, Hyperinflation, and Disinflation	150
	Measuring Inflation: The Construction of Price Indexes	150
	Price Indexes and Their Usage	151
	Explaining Inflation	155
	Summary	*161*

◘ indicates an optional segment

	Practice Problems	165
	Solutions	*169*

Learning Module 5 Monetary and Fiscal Policy   171

Introduction to Monetary and Fiscal Policy   171
Money: Functions, Creation, and Definition   173
    The Functions of Money   173
    Paper Money and the Money Creation Process   174
    Definitions of Money   177
Money: Quantity Theory, Supply and Demand, Fisher Effect   178
    The Demand for Money   178
    The Supply and Demand for Money   180
    The Fisher Effect   182
The Costs of Inflation   183
Summary   *184*
Practice Problems   *186*
Solutions   *188*

Learning Module 6 International Trade and Capital Flows   189

Introduction & International Trade: Basic Terminology   189
    International Trade   190
Patterns and Trends in International Trade and Capital Flows   191
Comparative Advantage and the Gains from Trade: Absolute and Comparative Advantage   195
    Gains from Trade: Absolute and Comparative Advantage   195
Ricardian and Heckscher–Ohlin Models of Comparative Advantage   198
Balance of Payments: Accounts and Components   200
    Balance of Payments Accounts   200
    Balance of Payments Components   201
National Economic Accounts and the Balance of Payments   204
Summary   *208*
References   *211*
Practice Problems   *212*
Solutions   *214*

Learning Module 7 Currency Exchange Rates   217

Introduction & The Foreign Exchange Market   217
Market Functions   218
Exchange Rates and the Trade Balance: The Elasticities Approach   223
Exchange Rates and the Trade Balance: The Absorption Approach   226
Summary   *230*
Practice Problems   *233*
Solutions   *234*

Glossary   G-1

◨ indicates an optional segment

How to Use the CFA Program Curriculum

The CFA® Program assumes basic knowledge of Economics, Quantitative Methods, and Financial Statements as presented in introductory university-level courses in Statistics, Economics, and Accounting. CFA Level I candidates who do not have a basic understanding of these concepts or would like to review these concepts can study from any of the three prerequisite-reading volumes as follows:

- Prerequisite reading volume 1: Quantitative Methods
- Prerequisite reading volume 2: Economics
- Prerequisite reading volume 3: Financial Statement Analysis

ERRATA

The curriculum development process is rigorous and includes multiple rounds of reviews by content experts. Despite our efforts to produce a curriculum that is free of errors, there are instances where we must make corrections. Curriculum errata are periodically updated and posted by exam level and test date online on the Curriculum Errata webpage (www.cfainstitute.org/en/programs/submit-errata). If you believe you have found an error in the curriculum, you can submit your concerns through our curriculum errata reporting process found at the bottom of the Curriculum Errata webpage.

Economics

LEARNING MODULE 1

Topics in Demand and Supply Analysis

by Richard V. Eastin, PhD, and Gary L. Arbogast, PhD, CFA.

Richard V. Eastin, PhD, is at the University of Southern California (USA). Gary L. Arbogast, PhD, CFA (USA).

LEARNING OUTCOMES

Mastery	The candidate should be able to:
☐	calculate and interpret price, income, and cross-price elasticities of demand and describe factors that affect each measure
☐	compare substitution and income effects
☐	contrast normal goods with inferior goods
☐	describe the phenomenon of diminishing marginal returns
☐	determine and interpret breakeven and shutdown points of production

INTRODUCTION

In a general sense, *economics* is the study of production, distribution, and consumption and can be divided into two broad areas of study: macroeconomics and microeconomics. **Macroeconomics** deals with aggregate economic quantities, such as national output and national income, and is rooted in **microeconomics**, which deals with markets and decision making of individual economic units, including consumers and businesses.

Microeconomics classifies private economic units into two groups: consumers (or households) and firms. These two groups give rise, respectively, to the theory of the consumer and the theory of the firm as two branches of study. The *theory of the consumer* deals with consumption (the demand for goods and services) by utility-maximizing individuals (i.e., individuals who make decisions that maximize the satisfaction received from present and future consumption). The *theory of the firm* deals with the supply of goods and services by profit-maximizing firms.

It is expected that candidates will be familiar with the basic concepts of demand and supply. In this reading, we will explore how buyers and sellers interact to determine transaction prices and quantities.

2. DEMAND CONCEPTS

☐ calculate and interpret price, income, and cross-price elasticities of demand and describe factors that affect each measure

The fundamental model of the private-enterprise economy is the demand and supply model of the market. In this section, we examine three important topics concerning the demand side of the model: (1) elasticities, (2) substitution and income effects, and (3) normal and inferior goods.

The quantity of a good that consumers are willing to buy depends on a number of different variables. Perhaps the most important of those variables is the item's own price. In general, as the price of a good rises, buyers will choose to buy less of it, and as its price falls, they buy more. This is referred to as the **law of demand**.

Although a good's own price is important in determining consumers' willingness to purchase it, other variables also influence that decision. Consumers' incomes, their tastes and preferences, and the prices of other goods that serve as substitutes or complements are just a few of the other variables that influence consumers' demand for a product or service. Economists attempt to capture all these influences in a relationship called the **demand function**. (A function is a relationship that assigns a unique value to a dependent variable for any given set of values of a group of independent variables.)

Equation 1 is an example of a demand function. In Equation 1, we are saying, "The quantity demanded of good X depends on (is a function of) the price of good X, consumers' income, and the price of good Y":

$$Q_x^d = f(P_x, I, P_y) \tag{1}$$

where

Q_x^d = the quantity demanded of some good X (such as per household demand for gasoline in liters per month)

P_x = the price per unit of good X (such as € per liter)

I = consumers' income (as in €1,000s per household annually)

P_y = the price of another good, Y. (There can be many other goods, not just one, and they can be complements or substitutes.)

Often, economists use simple linear equations to approximate real-world demand and supply functions in relevant ranges. Equation 2 illustrates a hypothetical example of our function for gasoline demand:

$$Q_x^d = 84.5 - 6.39P_x + 0.25I - 2P_y \tag{2}$$

where the quantity of gasoline demanded $\left(Q_x^d\right)$ is a function of the price of a liter of gasoline (P_x), consumers' income in €1,000s (I), and the average price of an automobile in €1,000s (P_y).

The signs of the coefficients on gasoline price (negative) and consumers' income (positive) reflect the relationship between those variables and the quantity of gasoline consumed. The negative sign on average automobile price indicates that if automobiles go up in price, fewer will likely be purchased and driven; hence, less gasoline will be consumed. As discussed later, such a relationship would indicate that gasoline and automobiles have a negative cross-price elasticity of demand and are thus complements.

Demand Concepts

To continue our example, suppose that the price of gasoline (P_x) is €1.48 per liter, per household income (I) is €50,000, and the price of the average automobile (P_y) is €20,000. In this case, this function would predict that the per-household monthly demand for gasoline would be 47.54 liters, calculated as follows:

$$Q_x^d = 84.5 - 6.39(1.48) + 0.25(50) - 2(20) = 47.54$$

recalling that income and automobile prices are measured in thousands. Note that the sign on the "own-price" variable (P_x) is negative; thus, as the price of gasoline rises, per household consumption would decrease by 6.39 liters per month for every €1 increase in gas price. **Own price** is used by economists to underscore that the reference is to the price of a good itself and not the price of some other good.

In our example, there are three independent variables in the demand function and one dependent variable. If any one of the independent variables changes, so does the quantity demanded. It is often desirable to concentrate on the relationship between the dependent variable and just one of the independent variables at a time. To accomplish this goal, we can hold the other independent variables constant and rewrite the equation.

For example, to concentrate on the relationship between the quantity demanded of the good and its own price, P_x, we hold constant the values of income and the price of good Y. In our example, those values are 50 and 20, respectively. The equation would then be rewritten as

$$Q_x^d = 84.5 - 6.39P_x + 0.25(50) - 2(20) = 57 - 6.39P_x \qquad (3)$$

The quantity of gasoline demanded is a function of the price of gasoline (6.39 per liter), per household income (€50,000), and the average price of an automobile (€20,000). Notice that income and the price of automobiles are not ignored; they are simply held constant, and they are "collected" in the new constant term, 57 [84.5 + (0.25)(50) − (2)(20)]. Notice also that we can solve for P_x in terms of Q_x^d by rearranging Equation 3, which gives us Equation 4:

$$P_x = 8.92 - 0.156 Q_x^d \qquad (4)$$

Equation 4 gives the price of gasoline as a function of the quantity of gasoline consumed per month and is referred to as the **inverse demand function**. Q_x in Equation 4 must be restricted to be less than or equal to 57 so that price is not negative. The graph of the inverse demand function is called the **demand curve** and is shown in Exhibit 1.[1]

---

1 Following usual practice, we show linear demand curves intersecting the quantity axis at a price of zero. Real-world demand functions may be non-linear in some or all parts of their domain. Thus, linear demand functions in practical cases are approximations of the true demand function that are useful for a relevant range of values.

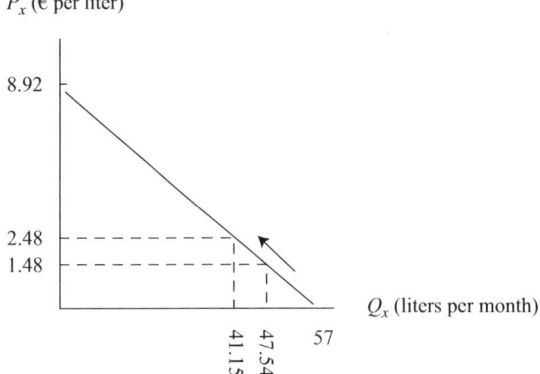

Exhibit 1: Household Demand Curve for Gasoline

The demand curve represents the highest quantity willingly purchased at each price as well as the highest price willingly paid for each quantity. In this example, this household would be willing to purchase 47.54 liters of gasoline per month at a price of €1.48 per liter. If price were to rise to €2.48 per liter, the household would be willing to purchase only 41.15 liters per month.

This demand curve is drawn with price on the vertical (y) axis and quantity on the horizontal (x) axis. It can be correctly interpreted as specifying *either* the highest quantity a household would buy at a given price *or* the highest price it would be willing to pay for a given quantity. In our example, at a price of €1.48 per liter, households would each be willing to buy 47.54 liters per month. Alternatively, the highest price they would be willing to pay for 47.54 liters per month is €1.48 per liter. If the price were to rise by €1, households would reduce the quantity they each bought by 6.39 units, to 41.15 liters. The slope of the demand curve is measured as the change in price, P, divided by the change in quantity, Q ($\Delta P/\Delta Q$, where Δ stands for "the change in"). In this case, the slope of the demand curve is $1/-6.39$, or -0.156.

The general model of demand and supply can be highly useful in understanding directional changes in prices and quantities that result from shifts in one curve or the other. Often, though, we need to measure how sensitive quantity demanded or supplied is to changes in the independent variables that affect them. This is the concept of **elasticity of demand** and **elasticity of supply**. Fundamentally, all elasticities are calculated in the same way: They are ratios of percentage changes. Let us begin with the sensitivity of quantity demanded to changes in the own price.

3. PRICE ELASTICITY OF DEMAND

☐ calculate and interpret price, income, and cross-price elasticities of demand and describe factors that affect each measure

In Equation 1, we expressed the quantity demanded of some good as a function of several variables, one of which was the price of the good itself (the good's "own price").

In Equation 3, we introduced a hypothetical household demand function for gasoline, assuming that the household's income and the price of another good (automobiles) were held constant. That function was given by the simple linear expression

$Q_x^d = 57 - 6.39P_x$. Using this expression, if we were asked how sensitive the quantity of gasoline demanded is to changes in price, we might say that whenever price changes by one unit, quantity changes by 6.39 units in the opposite direction; for example, if price were to rise by €1, quantity demanded would fall by 6.39 liters per month. The coefficient on the price variable (–6.39) could be the measure of sensitivity we are seeking.

There is a drawback associated with that measure, however. It is dependent on the units in which we measured Q and P. When we want to describe the sensitivity of demand, we need to recall the specific units in which Q and P were measured—liters per month and euros per liter—in our example. This relationship cannot readily be extrapolated to other units of measure—for example, gallons and dollars. Economists, therefore, prefer to use a gauge of sensitivity that does not depend on units of measure. That metric is called **elasticity**. Elasticity is a general measure of how sensitive one variable is to any other variable, and it is expressed as the ratio of percentage changes in each variable: $\%\Delta y/\%\Delta x$. In the case of **own-price elasticity of demand**, that measure is illustrated in Equation 5:

$$E_{P_x}^d = \frac{\%\Delta Q_x^d}{\%\Delta P_x} \tag{5}$$

This equation expresses the sensitivity of the quantity demanded to a change in price. $E_{P_x}^d$ is the good's own-price elasticity and is equal to the percentage change in quantity demanded divided by the percentage change in price. This measure is independent of the units in which quantity and price are measured. If quantity demanded falls by 8% when price rises by 10%, then the elasticity of demand is simply –0.8. It does not matter whether we are measuring quantity in gallons per week or liters per day, and it does not matter whether we measure price in dollars per gallon or euros per liter; 10% is 10%, and 8% is 8%. So the ratio of the first to the second is still –0.8.

We can expand Equation 5 algebraically by noting that the percentage change in any variable x is simply the change in x (Δx) divided by the level of x. So, we can rewrite Equation 5, using a few simple steps, as

$$E_{P_x}^d = \frac{\%\Delta Q_x^d}{\%\Delta P_x} = \frac{\frac{\Delta Q_x^d}{Q_x^d}}{\frac{\Delta P_x}{P_x}} = \left(\frac{\Delta Q_x^d}{\Delta P_x}\right)\left(\frac{P_x}{Q_x^d}\right) \tag{6}$$

To get a better idea of price elasticity, it might be helpful to illustrate using our hypothetical demand function: $Q_x^d = 57 - 6.39P_x$. When the relationship between two variables is linear, $\Delta Q_x^d/\Delta P_x$ is equal to the slope coefficient on P_x in the demand function. Thus, in our example, the elasticity of demand is –6.39 multiplied by the ratio of price to quantity. We need to choose a price at which to calculate the elasticity coefficient. Using our hypothetical original price of €1.48, we can find the quantity associated with that particular price by inserting 1.48 into the demand function as given in Equation 3:

$Q = 57 - (6.39)(1.48) = 47.54$

and we find that $Q = 47.54$ liters per month.

The result of our calculation is that at a price of 1.48, the elasticity of our market demand function is $-6.39(1.48/47.54) = -0.2$. How do we interpret that value? It means, simply, that when price equals 1.48, a 1% rise in price would result in a fall in quantity demanded of 0.2%.

In our example, when the price is €1.48 per liter, demand is not very sensitive to changes in price because a 1% rise in price would reduce quantity demanded by only 0.2%. In this case, we would say that demand is **inelastic**. To be precise, when the magnitude (ignoring algebraic sign) of the own-price elasticity coefficient has a value of less than one, demand is said to be inelastic. When that magnitude is greater than one, demand is said to be **elastic**. And when the elasticity coefficient is equal to negative one, demand is said to be **unit elastic**, or unitary elastic. Note that if the law of demand holds, own-price elasticity of demand will always be negative because a rise in price will be associated with a fall in quantity demanded, but it can be either elastic (very sensitive to a change in price) or inelastic (insensitive to a change in price). In our hypothetical example, suppose the price of gasoline was very high, say, €5 per liter. In this case, the elasticity coefficient would be −1.28:

$Q = 57 − (6.39)(5) = 25.05$

and

$−6.39 (5/25.05) = −1.28$

Because the magnitude of the elasticity coefficient is greater than one, we know that demand is elastic at that price.[2] In other words, at lower prices (€1.48 per liter), a slight change in the price of gasoline does not have much effect on the quantity demanded, but when gasoline is expensive (€5 per liter), consumer demand for gas is highly affected by changes in price.

- elastic good: the quantity demanded is sensitive to changes in price
- inelastic good: the quantity demanded is not very sensitive to changes in price

By examining Equation 6 more closely, we can see that for a linear demand curve the elasticity depends on where on the curve we calculate it. The first term, $\Delta Q/\Delta P$, which is the inverse of the slope of the demand curve, remains constant along the entire demand curve. But the second term, P/Q, changes depending on where we are on the demand curve. At very low prices, P/Q is very small, so demand is inelastic. But at very high prices, Q is low and P is high, so the ratio P/Q is very high and demand is elastic. Exhibit 2 illustrates a characteristic of all negatively sloped linear demand curves. Above the midpoint of the curve, demand is elastic; below the midpoint, demand is inelastic; and at the midpoint, demand is unit elastic.

Exhibit 2: The Elasticity of a Linear Demand Curve

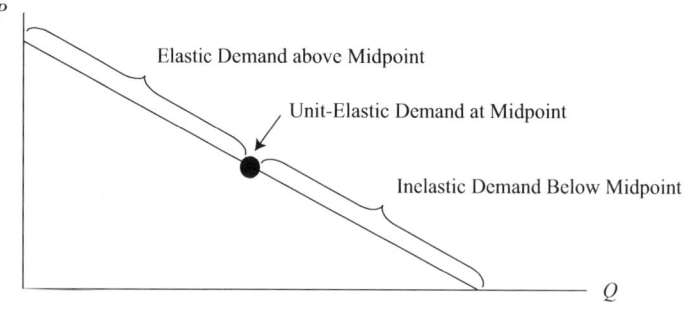

Note: For all negatively sloped, linear demand curves, elasticity varies depending on where it is calculated.

---

[2] If interested, evidence on price elasticities of demand for gasoline can be found in Molly Espey, "Explaining the Variation in Elasticity Estimates of Gasoline Demand in the United States: A Meta-analysis," *Energy Journal*, vol. 17, no. 3 (1996): 49–60. The robust estimates were about −0.26 for short-run elasticity—less than one year—and −0.58 for more than a year.

Extremes of Price Elasticity

There are two special cases in which linear demand curves have the same elasticity at all points: vertical demand curves and horizontal demand curves. Consider a vertical demand curve, as in Panel A of Exhibit 3, and a horizontal demand curve, as in Panel B. In the first case, the quantity demanded is the same, regardless of price. There is no demand curve that is perfectly vertical at all possible prices, but it is reasonable to assume that, over some range of prices, the same quantity would be purchased at a slightly higher price or a slightly lower price. Thus, in that price range, quantity demanded is not at all sensitive to price, and we would say that demand is **perfectly inelastic** in that range.

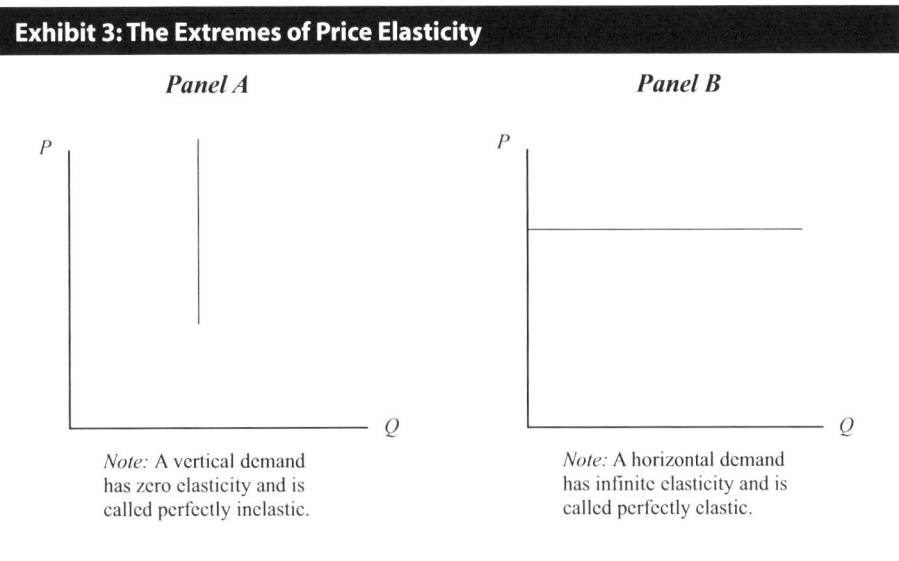

Exhibit 3: The Extremes of Price Elasticity

Panel A

Note: A vertical demand has zero elasticity and is called perfectly inelastic.

Panel B

Note: A horizontal demand has infinite elasticity and is called perfectly elastic.

In the second case, the demand curve is horizontal at some given price. It implies that even a minute price increase will reduce demand to zero, but at that given price, the consumer would buy some large, unknown amount. This situation is a reasonable description of the demand curve facing an individual seller in a perfectly competitive market, such as the wheat market. At the current market price of wheat, an individual farmer could sell all she has. If, however, she held out for a price above market price, it is reasonable to believe that she would not be able to sell any at all; other farmers' wheat is a perfect substitute for hers, so no one would be willing to buy any of hers at a higher price. In this case, we would say that the demand curve facing a seller under conditions of perfect competition is **perfectly elastic**.

PREDICTING DEMAND ELASTICITY, PRICE ELASTICITY, AND TOTAL EXPENDITURE

☐ calculate and interpret price, income, and cross-price elasticities of demand and describe factors that affect each measure

Own-price elasticity of demand is a measure of how sensitive the quantity demanded is to changes in the price of a good or service, but what characteristics of a good or its market might be informative in determining whether demand is highly elastic? Perhaps the most important characteristic is whether there are close substitutes for the good in question. If there are close substitutes for the good, then if its price rises even slightly, a consumer would tend to purchase much less of this good and switch to the less costly substitute. If there are no substitutes, however, then it is likely that the demand is much less elastic. Consider a consumer's demand for some broadly defined product, such as bread. There really are no close substitutes for the entire category of bread, which includes all types from French bread to pita bread to tortillas and so on. So, if the price of all bread were to rise, perhaps a consumer would purchase a little less of it each week, but probably not a significantly smaller amount. Now, consider that the consumer's demand is for a particular baker's specialty bread instead of the category "bread" as a whole. Surely, there are close substitutes for Baker Bob's Whole Wheat Bread with Sesame Seeds than for bread in general. We would expect, then, that the demand for Baker Bob's special loaf is much more elastic than for the entire category of bread.

In addition to the degree of substitutability, other characteristics tend to be generally predictive of a good's elasticity of demand. These include the portion of the typical budget that is spent on the good, the amount of time that is allowed to respond to the change in price, the extent to which the good is seen as necessary or optional, and so on. In general, if consumers tend to spend a very small portion of their budget on a good, their demand tends to be less elastic than if they spend a very large part of their income. Most people spend only a little on toothpaste each month, for example, so it really does not matter whether the price rises 10%. They would probably still buy about the same amount. If the price of housing were to rise significantly, however, most households would try to find a way to reduce the quantity they buy, at least in the long run.

This example leads to another characteristic regarding price elasticity. For most goods and services, the long-run demand is much more elastic than the short-run demand. For example, if the price of gasoline rises, we probably would not be able to respond quickly to reduce the quantity we consume. In the short run, we tend to be locked into modes of transportation, housing and employment location, and so on. With a longer adjustment period, however, we can adjust the quantity consumed in response to the change in price by adopting a new mode of transportation or reducing the distance of our commute. Hence, for most goods, long-run elasticity of demand is greater than short-run elasticity. Durable goods, however, tend to behave in the opposite way. If the price of washing machines were to fall, people might react quickly because they have an old machine that they know will need to be replaced fairly soon anyway. So when price falls, they might decide to go ahead and make a purchase. If the price of washing machines were to stay low forever, however, it is unlikely that a typical consumer would buy more machines over a lifetime.

Knowing whether the good or service is seen to be discretionary or non-discretionary helps to understand its sensitivity to a price change. Faced with the same percentage increase in prices, consumers are much more likely to give up their Friday night restaurant meal (discretionary) than they are to cut back significantly on staples in their pantry (non-discretionary). The more a good is seen as being necessary, the less elastic its demand is likely to be.

In summary, own-price elasticity of demand is likely to be greater (i.e., more sensitive) for items that have many close substitutes, occupy a large portion of the total budget, are seen to be optional instead of necessary, or have longer adjustment times. Obviously, not all these characteristics operate in the same direction for all goods, so elasticity is likely to be a complex result of these and other characteristics.

INCOME ELASTICITY OF DEMAND, CROSS-PRICE ELASTICITY OF DEMAND

☐ calculate and interpret price, income, and cross-price elasticities of demand and describe factors that affect each measure

Elasticity is a measure of how sensitive one variable is to change in the value of another variable. Up to this point, we have focused on price elasticity, but the quantity demanded of a good is also a function of consumer income.

Income elasticity of demand is defined as the percentage change in quantity demanded $(\%\Delta Q_x^d)$ divided by the percentage change in income $(\%\Delta I)$, holding all other things constant, as shown in Equation 7:

$$E_I^d = \frac{\%\Delta Q_x^d}{\%\Delta I} \qquad (7)$$

The structure of this expression is identical to the structure of own-price elasticity given in Equation 5. (All elasticity measures that we will examine have the same general structure; the only thing that changes is the independent variable of interest.) For example, if the income elasticity of demand for some good has a value of 0.8, we would interpret that to mean that whenever income rises by 1%, the quantity demanded at each price would rise by 0.8%.

Although own-price elasticity of demand will almost always be negative, *income* elasticity of demand can be negative, positive, or zero. Positive income elasticity means that as income rises, quantity demanded also rises. Negative income elasticity of demand means that when people experience a rise in income, they buy less of these goods, and when their income falls, they buy more of the same good.

- normal goods: positive income elasticity
- inferior goods: negative income elasticity

In our discussion of the demand curve, we held all other things constant, including consumer income, to plot the relationship between price and quantity demanded. If income were to change, the entire demand curve would shift one way or the other. For normal goods, a rise in income would shift the entire demand curve upward and to the right. For inferior goods, however, a rise in income would result in a downward and leftward shift in the entire demand curve.

Cross-Price Elasticity of Demand

We previously discussed a good's own-price elasticity. However, the price of another good might also have an impact on the demand for that good or service, and we should be able to define an elasticity with respect to the other price (P_y) as well. That elasticity is called the **cross-price elasticity of demand** and takes on the same structure as own-price elasticity and income elasticity of demand, as represented in Equation 8:

$$E_{p_y}^d = \frac{\%\Delta Q_x^d}{\%\Delta P_y} \qquad (8)$$

Note how similar this equation is to the equation for own-price elasticity. The only difference is that the subscript on P is now y, where y indicates some other good. This cross-price elasticity of demand measures how sensitive the demand for good X is to changes in the price of some other good, Y, holding all other things constant. For some pairs of goods, X and Y, when the price of Y rises, more of good X is demanded; the cross-price elasticity of demand is positive. Those goods are referred to as **substitutes**. In economics, if the cross-price elasticity of two goods is positive, they are substitutes, irrespective of whether someone would consider them "similar."

This concept is intuitive if you think about two goods that are seen to be close substitutes, perhaps like two brands of beer. When the price of one of your favorite brands of beer rises, you would probably buy less of that brand and more of a cheaper brand, so the cross-price elasticity of demand would be positive. For substitute goods, an increase in the price of one good would shift the demand curve for the other good upward and to the right.

Alternatively, two goods whose cross-price elasticity of demand is negative are said to be **complements**. Typically, these goods tend to be consumed together as a pair, such as gasoline and automobiles or houses and furniture. When automobile prices fall, we might expect the quantity of autos demanded to rise, and thus we might expect to see a rise in the demand for gasoline.

Although a conceptual understanding of demand elasticities is helpful in sorting out the qualitative and directional effects among variables, using an empirically estimated demand function can yield insights into the behavior of a market. For illustration, let us return to our hypothetical individual demand function for gasoline in Equation 2, duplicated here for convenience:

$$Q_x^d = 84.5 - 6.39 P_x + 0.25 I - 2 P_y$$

The quantity demanded of a given good $\left(Q_x^d\right)$ is a function of its own price (P_x), consumer income (I), and the price of another good (P_y).

To derive the market demand function, the individual consumers' demand functions are simply added together. If there were 1,000 individuals who represented a market and they all had identical demand functions, the market demand function would be the individual consumer's demand function multiplied by the number of consumers. Using the individual demand function given by Equation 2, the market demand function would be as shown in Equation 9:

$$Q_x^d = 84,500 - 6,390 P_x + 250 I - 2,000 P_y \tag{9}$$

Earlier, when we calculated own-price elasticity of demand, we needed to choose a price at which to calculate the elasticity coefficient. Similarly, we need to choose actual values for the independent variables—P_x, I, and P_y—and insert these values into the "estimated" market demand function to find the quantity demanded. Choosing €1.48 for P_x, €50 (in thousands) for I, and €20 (in thousands) for P_y, we find that the quantity of gasoline demanded is 47,543 liters per month. We now have everything we need to calculate own-price, income, and cross-price elasticities of demand for our market. Those elasticities are expressed in Equation 10, Equation 11, and Equation 12. Each of those expressions has a term denoting the change in quantity divided by the change in each respective variable: own price, $\Delta Q_x/\Delta P_x$; income, $\Delta Q_x/\Delta I$; and cross price, $\Delta Q_x/\Delta P_y$.

As we stated in the discussion of own-price elasticity, when the relationship between two variables is linear, the change in quantity $\left(\Delta Q_x^d\right)$ divided by the change in own price (ΔP_x), income (ΔI), or cross price (ΔP_y) is equal to the slope coefficient on that other variable. The elasticities are calculated by inserting the slope coefficients from Equation 9 into the elasticity formulas.

Own-price elasticity:

$$E_{P_x}^d = \left(\frac{\Delta Q_x^d}{\Delta P_x}\right)\left(\frac{P_x}{Q_x^d}\right) = (-6,390)\left(\frac{1.48}{47,542.8}\right) = -0.20 \tag{10}$$

Income elasticity:

$$E_I^d = \left(\frac{\Delta Q_x^d}{\Delta I}\right)\left(\frac{I}{Q_x^d}\right) = (250)\left(\frac{50}{47,542.8}\right) = 0.26 \qquad (11)$$

Cross-price elasticity:

$$E_{P_y}^d = \left(\frac{\Delta Q_x^d}{\Delta P_y}\right)\left(\frac{P_y}{Q_x^d}\right) = (-2000)\left(\frac{20}{47,542.8}\right) = -0.84 \qquad (12)$$

In our example, at a price of €1.48, the own-price elasticity of demand is −0.20; a 1% increase in the price of gasoline leads to a decrease in quantity demanded of about 0.20% (Equation 10). Because the absolute value of the own-price elasticity is less than one, we characterize demand as being *inelastic* at that price; for example, an increase in price would result in an increase in total expenditure on gasoline by consumers in that market. The income elasticity of demand is 0.26 (Equation 11): A 1% increase in income would result in an increase of 0.26% in the quantity demanded of gasoline. Because that elasticity is positive (but small), we would characterize gasoline as a normal good. The cross-price elasticity of demand between gasoline and automobiles is −0.84 (Equation 12): If the price of automobiles rose by 1%, the demand for gasoline would fall by 0.84%. We would, therefore, characterize gasoline and automobiles as complements because the cross-price elasticity is negative. The magnitude is quite small, however, so we would conclude that the complementary relationship is weak.

EXAMPLE 1

Calculating Elasticities from a Given Demand Function

An individual consumer's monthly demand for downloadable e-books is given by the equation $Q_{eb}^d = 2 - 0.4P_{eb} + 0.0005I + 0.15P_{hb}$, where Q_{eb}^d equals the number of e-books demanded each month, I equals the household monthly income, P_{eb} equals the price of e-books, and P_{hb} equals the price of hardbound books. Assume that the price of e-books is €10.68, household income is €2,300, and the price of hardbound books is €21.40.

1. Determine the value of own-price elasticity of demand for e-books.

Solution to 1:

The own-price elasticity of demand is given by $\left(\Delta Q_{eb}^d / \Delta P_{eb}\right)\left(P_{eb}/Q_{eb}^d\right)$. Notice from the demand function that $\Delta Q_{eb}^d / \Delta P_{eb} = -0.4$. Inserting the given variable values into the demand function yields $Q_{eb}^d = 2 - (0.4)(10.68) + (0.0005)(2,300) + (0.15)(21.4) = 2.088$. So at a price of €10.68, the own-price elasticity of demand equals $(-0.4)(10.68/2.088) = -2.046$, which is elastic because in absolute value the elasticity coefficient is greater than 1.

2. Determine the income elasticity of demand for e-books.

Solution to 2:

Recall that income elasticity of demand is given by $\left(\Delta Q_{eb}^d / \Delta I\right)\left(I/Q_{eb}^d\right)$. Notice from the demand function that $\Delta Q_{eb}^d / \Delta I = 0.0005$. Inserting the values for I and Q_{eb}^d yields income elasticity of $(0.0005)(2,300/2.088) = 0.551$, which is positive, so e-books are a normal good.

3. Determine the cross-price elasticity of demand for e-books with respect to the price of hardbound books.

Solution to 3:

Recall that cross-price elasticity of demand is given by $(\Delta Q_{eb}/\Delta P_{hb})(P_{hb}/Q_{eb})$, and notice from the demand function that $\Delta Q_{eb}/\Delta P_{hb} = 0.15$. Inserting the values for P_{hb} and Q_{eb} yields a cross-price elasticity of demand for e-books of $(0.15)(21.40/2.088) = 1.537$, which is positive, implying that e-books and hardbound books are substitutes.

6. SUBSTITUTION AND INCOME EFFECTS; NORMAL GOODS, INFERIOR GOODS, AND SPECIAL CASES

☐ compare substitution and income effects
☐ contrast normal goods with inferior goods

The law of demand states that if nothing changes other than the price of a particular good or service itself, a decrease in that good's price will tend to result in a greater quantity of that good being purchased. Simply stated, it is the assumption that a demand curve has negative slope; that is, where price per unit is measured on the vertical (y) axis and quantity demanded per time period is measured on the horizontal (x) axis, the demand curve is falling from left to right, as shown in Exhibit 4.

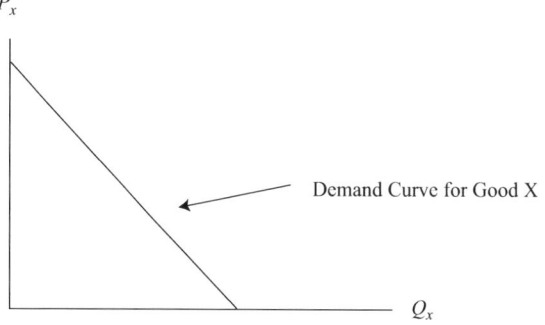

Exhibit 4: A Negatively Sloped Demand Curve—The Law of Demand

There are two reasons why a consumer would be expected to purchase more of a good when its price falls and less of a good when its price rises. These two reasons are known as the substitution effect and the income effect of a change in price. We address these two effects separately and then examine the combination of the two.

When the price of something—say, gasoline—falls, that good becomes relatively less costly compared with other goods or services a consumer might purchase. For example, gasoline is used in driving to work, so when its price falls, it is relatively cheaper to drive to work than to take public transportation. Hence, the consumer is likely to substitute a little more driving to work for a little less public transportation.

On its own, the substitution effect suggests that when the price of something falls, consumers tend to purchase more of that good. But another influence is often at work as well—the income effect. Consider a consumer spending all of her "money income" on a given combination of goods and services. (Her money income is simply the quantity of currency available to spend in any given time period.) Now suppose the price of something she was regularly purchasing falls while her money income and the prices of all other goods remain unchanged. Economists refer to this as an increase in purchasing power or **real income**. For most goods and services, consumers tend to buy more of them when their income rises. So when the price of a good—say, beef—falls, most consumers would tend to buy more beef because of the increase in their real income. Although the consumer's money income (the number on her paycheck) is assumed not to have changed, her real income has risen because she can now buy more beef—and other goods, too—as a result of the fall in the price of that one good. So, quite apart from the substitution effect of a fall in a good's price, the income effect tends to cause consumers to purchase more of that good as well.

Substitution and income effects work the other way, too. If the price of beef were to rise, the substitution effect would cause the consumer to buy less of it and substitute more chicken for the now relatively more expensive beef. Additionally, the rise in the price of beef results in a decrease in the consumer's real income because now she can buy less goods with the same amount of money income. If beef is a good that consumers tend to buy more of when their income rises and less of when their income falls, then the rise in beef price would have an income effect that causes the consumer to buy less of it.

Normal and Inferior Goods

Economists classify goods on various dimensions, one of which relates to how consumers' purchases of a good respond to changes in consumer income. Earlier, when discussing income elasticity of demand, we introduced the concept of normal goods and inferior goods. For most goods and services, an increase in income would cause consumers to buy more; these are called **normal goods**. But that does not hold true for all goods: There are goods that consumers buy less of when their income rises and goods that they buy more of when their incomes fall. These are called **inferior goods**. This section will contrast normal goods with inferior goods.

We previously discussed income and substitution effects of a change in price. If a good is normal, a decrease in price will result in the consumer buying more of that good. Both the substitution effect and the income effect are at play here:

- A decrease in price tends to cause consumers to buy more of this good in place of other goods—the substitution effect.
- The increase in real income resulting from the decline in this good's price causes people to buy even more of this good when its price falls—the income effect.

So, we can say that for normal goods (restaurant meals, for example, as most people tend to eat out more often when their incomes rise), the substitution and the income effects reinforce one another to cause the demand curve to be negatively sloped.

For inferior goods (cheaper cuts of meat or generic beverages, for example, which most people buy less of as their incomes rise), an increase in income causes consumers to buy less, not more, and if their incomes fall, they buy more, not less. "Inferior" does not imply anything at all about the quality of the good; it is simply used to refer to a good for which an increase in income causes some people to buy less of it.

The same good could be normal for some consumers while it is inferior for others. Consider a very low-income segment of the population. For those consumers, an increase in their income might very well result in their buying more fast-food meals.

They might take some of that added income and enjoy eating out at a fast-food restaurant a little more often. Now consider a high-income group. If their income rises, they might be much less inclined to eat at fast-food restaurants and instead do their dining out at a fashionable French bistro, for example. So, fast-food meals might be a normal good for some people and an inferior good for others.

Let us now consider the substitution and income effects of a change in the price of normal and inferior goods. The substitution effect says that if the price of a good falls, the consumer will substitute more of this good in the consumption bundle and buy less of some other good. The substitution effect is true for both normal and inferior goods.

Exhibit 5 summarizes the substitution and income effects for normal and inferior goods.

Exhibit 5: The Substitution and Income Effects of a Price Decrease on Normal and Inferior Goods

	Substitution Effect	Income Effect
Normal good	Buy more because the good is relatively cheaper than its substitutes.	Buy more because the increase in purchasing power raises the total consumption level.
Inferior good	Buy more because the good is relatively cheaper than its substitutes.	Buy less because the increase in real income prompts the consumer to buy less of the inferior good in favor of its preferred substitutes.

EXAMPLE 2

Income and Substitution Effects of a Decrease in Price

Monica has a monthly entertainment budget that she spends on (a) movies and (b) an assortment of other entertainment items. When the price of each movie is $8, she spends a quarter of her budget on six movies a month and the rest of her budget on other entertainment. Monica was offered an opportunity to join a movie club at her local theater that allows her to purchase movies at half the regular price, and she can choose each month whether to join the movie club or not. There is a membership fee she must pay for each month she belongs to the club. Monica is exactly indifferent between (a) not buying the membership and, therefore, paying $8 for movies and (b) buying the membership and paying $4 per movie. So, she flips a coin each month to determine whether to join the club that month. In months that she does join the club, she sees eight movies. For her birthday, a friend gave her a one-month club membership as a gift, and that month she saw 12 movies.

1. If there were no club and the price of movies were to simply fall from $8 to $4, how many more movies would Monica buy each month?

Solution to 1:

Six movies. When her friend gave her a club membership, she bought 12 movies instead of her usual 6. With the gift of the club membership, Monica could buy movies at a price of $4 without paying for that privilege. This is the same as if the price of each movie fell from $8 to $4.

2. Of the increased number of movies Monica would purchase if the price were to fall from $8 to $4, determine how much of the increase would be attributable to the substitution effect and how much to the income effect of that price decrease.

Solution to 2:

When Monica pays the club membership herself, she buys eight movies, two more than usual. Because Monica is equally well off whether she joins the club for a monthly fee and thereby pays half price or whether she does not join the club and pays full price, we can say that the income effect of the price decrease has been removed by charging her the monthly fee. So the increase from six movies to eight is the result of the substitution effect. When Monica's friend gave her the gift of a club membership, allowing her to pay half price without paying for the privilege, Monica bought 12 movies, 6 more than usual and 4 more than she would have had she paid the membership fee. The increase from 8 movies to 12 is the result of the income effect.

3. For Monica, are movies a normal or inferior good?

Solution to 3:

When the price fell from $8 to $4, Monica bought more movies. Additionally, because the substitution effect and the income effect are in the same direction of buying more movies, they are a normal good for Monica. The substitution effect caused her to buy two more movies, and the income effect caused her to buy an additional four movies.

SUPPLY ANALYSIS: COST, MARGINAL RETURN, AND PRODUCTIVITY

7

☐ describe the phenomenon of diminishing marginal returns

To fully comprehend the supply side of a consumer goods market, an analyst must understand the firm's costs.

The firm's marginal cost is the foundation of the firm's ability and willingness to offer a given quantity for sale, and its costs depend on both the productivity of its inputs and their prices. In this section, we will describe the firm's cost curves—total, average, and marginal costs in both the short run and in the long run—paying special attention to what economists call the **law of diminishing marginal returns**. We will then use this information to explore the conditions under which a firm would find it beneficial to continue operation, even if its economic profits are negative, and at what levels of production its shutdown and breakeven points occur. Long-run costs will be examined in the context of economies and diseconomies of scale.

Marginal Returns and Productivity

There is an economic phenomenon known as **increasing marginal returns**, in which **marginal product**—the productivity of each additional unit of a resource—increases as additional units of that input are employed.

Initially, a firm can experience increasing returns from adding labor to the production process because of the concepts of specialization and division of labor. At first, by having too few workers relative to total physical capital, the understaffing situation requires employees to multi-task and share duties. As more workers are added, employees can specialize, become more adept at their individual functions, and realize an increase in marginal productivity. But after a certain output level, the law of diminishing marginal returns becomes evident.

When more and more workers are added to a fixed capital base, the marginal return of the labor factor eventually decreases because the fixed input restricts the output potential of additional workers. As an illustration, consider automobile production. When an auto manufacturing plant is operating at full capacity, adding additional labor will not increase production because the physical plant is already 100% employed. More labor hours will merely add to costs without adding to output. Assuming all workers are of equal quality and motivation, the decline in marginal product occurs in the short run, where all other resources (typically, plant size, physical capital, and technology) are fixed.

Marginal returns are directly related to **input productivity**, a measure of the output per unit of input.

Productivity: The Relationship between Production and Cost

The cost of producing anything depends on the amount of *inputs*, or *factors of production* (these terms are synonymous), and the input prices. Examples of factors of production are employee hours, machine hours, raw materials, and so on. For simplicity, economists typically concentrate on only two inputs, labor and capital, although obviously there can be many inputs to a particular production process. The labor input is simply employee time, and it is measured as labor hours per time period, such as per week or per month. We denote labor hours as L. If a firm is using two laborers per week and each laborer works 35 hours per week, then L equals 70 labor hours per week. We denote hours of capital as K. If the firm is using three machines and each one is used for 12 hours per week, then K equals 36 machine hours per week. That is, the capital input is measured as machine hours used per time period. In this way, capital and labor are stated in similar terms. They represent flows of services—labor hours and machine hours—that are used to produce a flow of output per time period.

Accordingly, the respective input prices would be the wage rate per labor hour (we use w to denote wage rate) and the rental rate per machine hour (we use r to denote the rental rate per machine hour). It is helpful to think of a firm as renting the services of labor and of machines. Although the firm might own its own machines, it could in theory rent its machines out to another user, so it is forgoing the rate it could earn elsewhere when it is using its machines internally instead of renting them out. So, a firm is not using its own machines "for free." It is incurring the **opportunity cost** of not being able to rent those machines to another user.

The **total cost** of production (TC) is the number of hours of labor multiplied by the wage rate plus the number of machine hours multiplied by the rental rate of machines:

$$TC = (w)(L) + (r)(K)$$

This formula illustrates that the total cost is just the cost of all the firm's inputs. It is not a cost function, however, which is a relationship between the cost of production and the flow of output. The cost function $C = f(Q)$, where (Q) denotes the flow of output in units of production per time period, relates the production cost per time period to the number of units of output produced per time period.

Two things could cause the cost of producing any given level of output to fall: Either the price of one or both inputs could fall or the inputs themselves could become more productive and less of them would be needed (e.g., a worker is more productive when fewer hours of labor are needed to produce the same output). The reverse is true also: A rise in cost could result from either a rise in input prices or a fall in input productivity, or both.

Why is productivity important? Cost-minimization and profit-maximization behavior dictate that the firm strives to maximize productivity—for example, produce the most output per unit of input or produce any given level of output with the least amount of inputs. A firm that lags behind the industry in productivity is at a competitive disadvantage and is likely to face decreases in future earnings and shareholders' wealth. An increase in productivity lowers production costs, which leads to greater profitability and investment value. These productivity benefits can be fully or partially distributed to other stakeholders of the business, such as to consumers in the form of lower prices and to employees in the form of enhanced compensation. Transferring some or all of the productivity rewards to non-equity holders creates synergies that benefit shareholders over time.

The benefits from increased productivity are as follows:

- lower business costs, which translate into increased profitability;
- an increase in the market value of equity and shareholders' wealth resulting from an increase in profit; and
- an increase in worker rewards, which motivates further productivity increases from labor.

Undoubtedly, increases in productivity reinforce and strengthen the competitive position of the firm over the long run. A fundamental analysis of a company should examine the firm's commitment to productivity enhancements and the degree to which productivity is integrated into the competitive nature of the industry or market. In some cases, productivity is not only an important promoter of growth in firm value over the long term but is also the key factor for economic survival. A business that lags the market in terms of productivity often finds itself less competitive, while at the same time confronting profit erosion and deterioration in shareholders' wealth.

Total, Average, and Marginal Product of Labor

When measuring a firm's operating efficiency, it is easier and more practical to use a single resource factor as the input variable rather than a bundle of the different resources that the firm uses in producing units of output. As discussed in the previous section, labor is typically the input that is the most identifiable and calculable for measuring productivity. However, any input that is not difficult to quantify can be used. As an example, a business that manually assembles widgets has 50 workers, one production facility, and an assortment of equipment and hand tools. The firm would like to assess its productivity when using these three input factors to produce widgets. In this example, it is most appropriate to use labor as the input factor for determining productivity because the firm uses only one (fixed) plant building and a variety of other physical capital.

We will use labor as the input variable to illustrate the concepts of total product, average product, and marginal product. Exhibit 6 provides a summary of these three concepts.

Exhibit 6: Definitions and Calculations for Total, Marginal, and Average Product of Labor

Term	Calculation
Total product	Sum of the output from all inputs during a time period; usually illustrated as the total output (Q) using labor quantity (L)
Average product	Total product divided by the quantity of a given input; measured as total product divided by the number of worker hours used at that output level (Q/L)
Marginal product	The amount of additional output resulting from using one more unit of input assuming other inputs are fixed; measured by taking the difference in total product and dividing by the change in the quantity of labor ($\Delta Q/\Delta L$)

Total product (Q) is defined as the aggregate sum of production for a firm during a time period. As a measure of productivity, total product provides superficial information about how effective and efficient a firm is in terms of producing output. For instance, three firms—Company A, Company B, and Company C—that make up an entire industry have total output levels shown below.

Firm	Units	Market Share
A	100,000	20.8%
B	180,000	37.5%
C	200,000	41.7%
Total	480,000	100%

However, this information says little about how efficient each firm is in generating its total output level. Total product only provides insight into a firm's production volume relative to the industry; it does not show how efficient a firm is in producing its output.

Average product of labor (AP_L) measures the productivity of an input (in this case, labor) on average and is calculated by dividing total product by the total number of units for the given input that is used to generate that output. Average product is usually measured on the basis of the labor input. It is a representative or overall measure of labor's productivity: Some workers are more productive than average, and others are less productive than average.

Exhibit 7 compares the productivity of the three firms. Company A employs 100 worker hours and produces 100,000 widgets per hour. Company B employs 200 worker hours and produces 180,000 widgets per hour. Company C employs 250 worker hours and produces 200,000 widgets per hour.

Exhibit 7: Comparing Productivity

	Output (Q)	Number of Worker Hours (L)	Average Product of Labor (AP_L)
Company A	100,000	100	1,000
Company B	180,000	200	900
Company C	200,000	250	800

Using this metric, it is apparent that Company A, with AP_L equal to 1,000, is the most efficient firm, despite having the lowest market share. Company C has the largest market share, but it is the least efficient of the three, with AP_L equal to 800. Assuming that Company A can maintain its productivity advantage over the long run, it will be positioned to generate the greatest return on investment through lower costs and higher profit outcomes relative to the other firms in the market.

Marginal product of labor (MP_L), also known as *marginal return*, measures the productivity of each additional unit of input and is calculated by observing the difference in total product when adding another unit of input (assuming other resource quantities are held constant). It is a gauge of the productivity of the individual additional worker hour rather than an average across all workers.

Exhibit 8 provides a numerical illustration for total, average, and marginal products of labor.

Exhibit 8: Total, Average, and Marginal Product of Labor

Labor (L)	Total Product (Q_L)	Average Product (AP_L)	Marginal Product (MP_L)
0	0	—	—
1	100	100	100
2	210	105	110
3	300	100	90
4	360	90	60
5	400	80	40
6	420	70	20
7	350	50	−70

Total product increases as the firm adds each additional hour of labor—until the seventh labor hour, at which point total production declines by 70 units. Obviously, the firm would want to avoid negative worker productivity.

At an employment level of five labor hours, AP_L is 80 units (400/5) and MP_L is 40 units [(400 − 360)/(5 − 4)]. The average productivity for all five labor hours is 80 units, but the productivity of the fifth labor hour is only 40 units.

EXAMPLE 3

Calculation and Interpretation of Total, Average, and Marginal Product

Exhibit 9 illustrates the production relationship between the number of machine hours and total product.

Exhibit 9

Machine Hours (K)	Total Product (Q_K)	Average Product (AP_K)	Marginal Product (MP_K)
0	0	—	—
1	1,000	1,000	1,000
2	2,500	1,250	1,500
3	4,500	1,500	2,000
4	6,400	1,600	1,900
5	7,400	1,480	1,000

Machine Hours (K)	Total Product (Q_K)	Average Product (AP_K)	Marginal Product (MP_K)
6	7,500	1,250	100
7	7,000	1,000	−500

1. Interpret the results for total, average, and marginal product.

Solution to 1:

Total product increases up to six machine hours, where it tops out at 7,500. Because total product declines from Hour 6 to Hour 7, the marginal product for Machine Hour 7 is negative 500 units. Average product peaks at 1,600 units with four machine hours. Average product increases at a steady pace with the addition of Machine Hours 2 and 3. The addition of Machine Hour 4 continues to increase average product but at a decreasing rate. Beyond four machine hours, average product decreases—at an increasing rate. Marginal product peaks with Machine Hour 3 and decreases thereafter.

2. Indicate at what point increasing marginal returns change to diminishing marginal returns.

Solution to 2:

The marginal product, MP_K, of Machine Hour 3 is 2,000. The marginal product of each additional machine hour beyond Machine Hour 3 declines. Diminishing marginal returns are evident beyond Machine Hour 3.

A firm has a choice of using total product, average product, marginal product, or some combination of the three to measure productivity. Because total product is simply an indication of a firm's output volume and potential market share, average product and marginal product are better gauges of a firm's productivity. Both can reveal competitive advantage through production efficiency. However, individual worker productivity is not easily measurable when workers perform tasks collectively. In this case, average product is the preferred measure of productivity performance.

Referring to the total product column in Exhibit 8, output is more than twice as great (210 widgets) when two hours of labor are used as opposed to only one hour (100 widgets.) In this range of production, there is an increase in return when employee hours are added to the production process. This is the phenomenon of increasing marginal returns.

8. MARGINAL REVENUE, MARGINAL COST AND PROFIT MAXIMIZATION; SHORT-RUN COST CURVES: TOTAL, VARIABLE, FIXED, AND MARGINAL COSTS

☐ determine and interpret breakeven and shutdown points of production

It is assumed that any for-profit firm's management is tasked with achieving the goal of shareholder wealth maximization. Put most simply, that translates into the goal of economic profit maximization. Hereafter, when the word *profit* is used, it will be economic profit that we have in mind. Because profit is defined as TR minus TC, anything that increases revenue more than cost or decreases cost more than revenue will increase profit. Before we address profit maximization, we must introduce two important concepts: marginal revenue and marginal cost.

Marginal revenue (MR) is the additional revenue the firm realizes from the decision to increase output by one unit per time period. That is, MR = ΔTR/ΔQ. If the firm is operating in what economists call a perfectly competitive market, it is one of many sellers of identical products in an environment characterized by low or non-existent barriers to entry. Under perfect competition, the firm has no pricing power because there are many perfect substitutes for the product it sells. If it were to attempt to raise the price even by a very small amount, it would lose all of its sales to competitors. On the other hand, it can sell essentially any amount of product it wants without lowering the price below the market price.

Take the wheat market as an example of a perfectly competitive market. A seller of wheat would have no control over the market price of wheat; thus, because TR = (P)(Q), MR for this firm is simply price per unit of output. This firm is said to face a perfectly horizontal (zero-sloped), or infinitely elastic, demand curve for its product. For example, if the firm is selling 1,000 bushels of wheat per week at a price of £3 per bushel, TR is £3,000. If the firm were to increase its output by one unit, then TR would rise by exactly £3 because the firm would not have to lower its price to sell that added unit. So, for sellers in a market with perfect competition, MR = P.

In contrast, if a firm sells a product that is differentiated from other firms' products and that has a large market share, the firm is said to be operating in an environment of imperfect competition. In the extreme case of imperfect competition, there might be only one firm selling a product with no close substitutes. That firm holds a monopoly, and it is subject to the market demand curve for its product. Whether a monopoly or simply operating under imperfect competition, the firm faces a negatively sloped demand curve and must lower its price to sell another unit. Thus, MR will be lower than price.

To illustrate this concept, we will decompose MR. Recall from earlier in the reading that

TR = (P)(Q)

and

MR = ΔTR/ΔQ

Change in total revenue (ΔTR), the numerator of the ratio, can be written as $(P)(\Delta Q) + (Q)(\Delta P)$.

There are two competing forces affecting revenue: (1) Additional units are sold at the new price, and (2) all units must now be sold at the lower price. The firm is selling more units, but it is selling all units at a lower price than before.

To find MR, we divide the change in TR by the change in quantity:

$$\text{MR} = \frac{(P)(\Delta Q)}{\Delta Q} + \frac{(Q)(\Delta P)}{\Delta Q} = P + Q\frac{(\Delta P)}{\Delta Q}$$

In other words, MR is equal to price but with an "adjustment" equal to $(Q)(\Delta P/\Delta Q)$.

Taking this one step further, recall that earlier we said ($\Delta P/\Delta Q$) is the slope of the demand curve. From our expression just given, MR = $P + Q(\Delta P/\Delta Q)$; so, MR is equal to price with an adjustment equal to quantity times the slope of the demand curve.

A perfectly competitive firm faces a demand curve with a slope of zero. Substituting 0 for $\Delta P/\Delta Q$ into the expression given, it becomes clear that MR is equal to price for the perfectly competitive firm—it need not lower its price to sell an additional unit. For a firm in an imperfectly competitive market, however, the demand curve is negatively sloped ($\Delta P/\Delta Q < 0$). Substituting this negative number into the expression for MR, $P + Q(\Delta P/\Delta Q)$, it becomes clear that MR for an imperfectly competitive firm is less than price.

Marginal cost (MC) is the increase to total cost resulting from the firm's decision to increase output by one additional unit per time period: MC = $\Delta TC/\Delta Q$. Economists distinguish between short-run marginal cost (SMC) and long-run marginal cost (LMC). Labor is variable over the short run, but the quantity of capital cannot be changed in the short run because there is a lead time required to build or buy new plant equipment and put it in place. In the long run, all inputs are variable.

SMC is essentially the additional cost of the variable input, labor, that must be incurred to increase the level of output by one unit. LMC is the additional cost of all inputs necessary to increase the level of output, allowing the firm the flexibility of changing both labor and capital inputs in a way that maximizes efficiency.

Understanding MC is aided by recalling that cost is *directly* related to input prices and *inversely* related to productivity. For example, if the wage rate were to rise, cost would also rise. If labor were to become more productive, cost would fall. This relationship can be captured in an expression that relates SMC to wage rate (w) and MP_L: SMC = w/MP_L.

This relationship between cost and productivity also holds with average variable cost. **Variable costs** are all costs that fluctuate with the level of production and sales. **Average variable cost** (AVC) is the ratio of total variable cost to total output: AVC = TVC/Q. Again, if labor's wage rises, AVC also rises; but if labor were to become more productive, AVC falls. This relationship is captured by the expression AVC = w/AP_L.

Earlier, we noted that over some range of low output, the firm might benefit from increasing marginal productivity of its labor input as workers begin to specialize. As the MP_L increases, SMCs decline. Eventually, as more and more labor is added to a fixed amount of capital, the MP_L must fall, causing SMCs to rise.

We began this section by stating that the goal of management is to maximize profit. We now address the conditions necessary for reaching that goal. Consider a firm currently producing 1,000 widgets each week and whose management is contemplating increasing that output incrementally. Would that additional unit increase profit? Clearly, profit would be increased (or losses reduced) if the additional revenue from that next unit were greater than the additional cost. So, a profit-seeking firm should increase Q if MR > MC. Conversely, if the additional unit added more to cost than to revenue, the firm should reduce output because it would save more in cost than it would lose in revenue. Only if the additional cost were exactly equal to the additional revenue would the firm be maximizing its profit.

There is another condition (called a second-order condition) necessary for profit maximization: At the level of output at which MR = MC, MC cannot be falling. This condition is fairly intuitive. If MC is falling with additional output, MP_L would be rising. (Recall that SMC = w/MP_L). If one additional hour of labor input causes MC to fall, the firm would want to add that hour and continue adding labor until SMC becomes positively sloped. We can sum up the profit-maximization decision for an operating firm as follows: Produce the level of output such that (1) MR = MC and (2) MC is not falling.

Understanding the Interaction between Total, Variable, Fixed, and Marginal Cost and Output

Exhibit 10 shows the graphical relationships between total cost, total fixed cost, and total variable cost. TC is the summation of all costs, where costs are classified on the basis of whether they are fixed or variable. **Total fixed cost** (TFC) is the summation of all expenses that do not change as the level of production varies. **Total variable cost** (TVC) is the summation of all variable expenses; TVC rises with increased production and falls with decreased production. At zero production, TC is equal to TFC because TVC at this output level is zero. The curve for TC always lies parallel to and above the TVC curve by the amount of TFC.

Exhibit 10: Total Cost, Total Variable Cost, and Total Fixed Cost

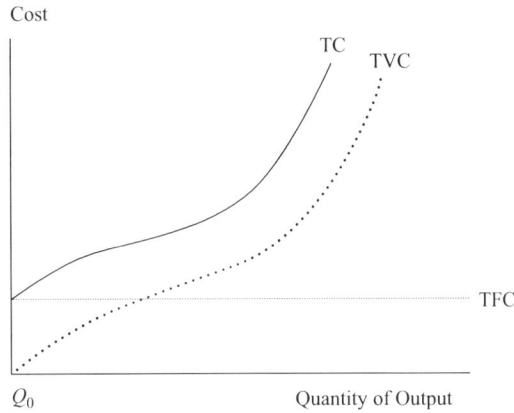

Exhibit 11 shows the relationships between the **average total cost** (ATC), average variable cost (AVC), **average fixed cost** (AFC), and marginal cost (MC) curves in the short run. As output quantity increases, AFC declines because TFCs are spread over a larger number of units. Both ATC and AVC take on a bowl-shaped pattern in which each curve initially declines, reaches a minimum average cost output level, and then increases after that point. The MC curve intersects both the ATC and the AVC at their minimum points—points S and T. When MC is less than AVC, AVC will be decreasing. When MC is greater than AVC, AVC will be increasing.

Exhibit 11: Average Total Cost, Average Variable Cost, Average Fixed Cost, and Marginal Cost

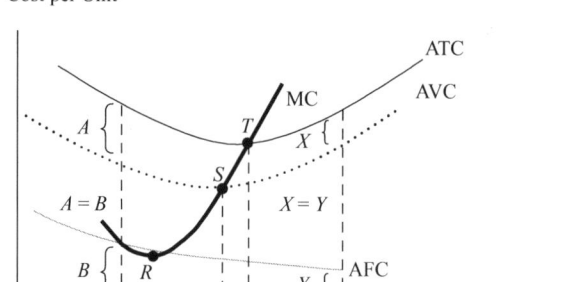

S, the lowest point on the AVC curve, is where MC equals AVC. Beyond quantity Q_{AVC}, MC is greater than AVC; thus, the AVC curve begins to rise. Note that it occurs at a quantity lower than the minimum point on the ATC curve.

T, the lowest point on the ATC curve, is where MC equals ATC. Beyond quantity Q_{ATC}, MC is greater than ATC; thus, the ATC curve is rising.

A, the difference between ATC and AVC at output quantity Q_1, is the amount of AFC.

R indicates the lowest point on the MC curve. Beyond this point of production, fixed input constraints reduce the productivity of labor.

X indicates the difference between ATC and AVC at quantity Q_2. It is less than A because AFC (Y) falls with output.

Exhibit 12 shows an example of how total, average, and marginal costs are derived. TC is calculated by summing TFC and TVC. MC is derived by observing the change in TC as the quantity variable changes. There is a relationship that always holds for average and marginal costs: If MC is less than average cost, average cost must fall, and if MC is greater than average cost, average cost must rise. For example, in Exhibit 12, AVC begins to increase as output rises from 2 to 3 units because MC (50) is greater than AVC (41.7). Also from Exhibit 12, ATC declines up to 3 units because MC is less than ATC. After 3 units, ATC increases because the MC of Unit 4 (85) exceeds the ATC of all prior units (75). Initially, the MC curve declines because of increasing marginal returns to labor, but at some point, it begins to increase because of the law of diminishing marginal returns.

Exhibit 12: Total, Average, Marginal, Fixed, and Variable Costs

Quantity (Q)	TFC[a]	AFC (TFC/Q)	TVC	AVC (TVC/Q)	TC	ATC (TC/Q)	MC
0	100	—	0	—	100	—	—
1	100	100.0	50	50.0	150	150.0	50
2	100	50.0	75	37.5	175	87.5	25
3	100	33.3	125	41.7	225	75.0	50
4	100	25.0	210	52.5	310	77.5	85
5	100	20.0	300	60.0	400	80.0	90
6	100	16.7	450	75.0	550	91.7	150
7	100	14.3	650	92.9	750	107.1	200

Quantity (Q)	TFC[a]	AFC (TFC/Q)	TVC	AVC (TVC/Q)	TC	ATC (TC/Q)	MC
8	100	12.5	900	112.5	1,000	125.0	250
9	100	11.1	1,200	133.3	1,300	144.4	300
10	100	10.0	1,550	155.0	1,650	165.0	350

[a] *Includes all opportunity costs.*

As stated earlier, TC increases as the firm expands output and decreases when production is cut. TC increases at a decreasing rate up to a certain output level. Thereafter, the rate of increase accelerates as the firm gets closer to full utilization of capacity. The rate of change in TC mirrors the rate of change in TVC. In Exhibit 12, TC at 5 units is 400—of which 300 is variable cost and 100 is fixed cost. At 10 units, TC is 1,650—of which 1,550 is variable cost and 100 is fixed cost.

Fixed costs typically are incurred whether the firm produces anything or not. Fixed costs may stay the same over a given range of production but can change to another constant level when production moves outside of that range. Examples of fixed costs are debt service, real estate lease agreements, and rental contracts. **Normal profit** is also considered to be a fixed cost because it is a return required by investors on their equity capital regardless of output level.

Other fixed costs evolve primarily from investments in such fixed assets as real estate, production facilities, and equipment. These fixed costs cannot be arbitrarily cut when production declines. When a firm downsizes, the last expense to be cut is usually fixed cost.

TVC has a direct relationship with quantity. When quantity increases, TVC increases; when quantity decreases, TVC declines. At zero production, TVC is always zero. Variable cost examples are payments for labor, raw materials, and supplies. The change in TVC declines up to a certain output point and then increases as production approaches capacity limits. In Exhibit 12, TVC increases with an increase in quantity. However, the change from 1 to 2 units is 25 (75 − 50), and the change from 9 to 10 units is 350.

Exhibit 13 illustrates the relationships between MC, ATC, AVC, and AFC for the data presented in Exhibit 12.

Exhibit 13: Average Total Cost, Average Variable Cost, Average Fixed Cost, and Marginal Cost for Exhibit 12 Data

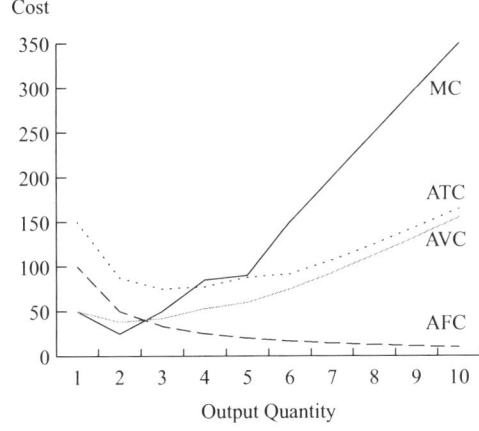

ATC is calculated by dividing TC by quantity (or by summing AFC and AVC). In Exhibit 12, at 3 units, ATC is 75 (TC of 225/3 units of production or AFC of 33.3 + AVC of 41.7). This is the least average cost point of production and the minimum point on the ATC curve. Although cost-minimizing behavior on the part of the firm would dictate operating at the minimum point on its ATC curve, the profit-maximizing quantity may not correspond to this minimum ATC point. Profit per unit, but not necessarily total profit, is maximized at this point.

EXAMPLE 4

Calculation and Interpretation of Total, Average, Marginal, Fixed, and Variable Costs

1. The first three columns of Exhibit 14 display data on quantity, TFC, and TVC, which are used to calculate TC, AFC, AVC, ATC, and MC. Examine the results for total, average, marginal, fixed, and variable costs. Identify the quantity levels at which the ATC, AVC, and MC values reach their minimum points. Explain the relationship between TFC and TC at a quantity of zero output.

Exhibit 14

Q	TFC[a]	TVC	AFC	AVC	TC	ATC	MC
0	5,000	0	—	—	5,000	—	—
1	5,000	2,000	5,000.0	2,000	7,000	7,000.0	2,000
2	5,000	3,800	2,500.0	1,900	8,800	4,400.0	1,800
3	5,000	5,400	1,666.7	1,800	10,400	3,466.7	1,600
4	5,000	8,000	1,250.0	2,000	13,000	3,250.0	2,600
5	5,000	11,000	1,000.0	2,200	16,000	3,200.0	3,000
6	5,000	15,000	833.3	2,500	20,000	3,333.3	4,000
7	5,000	21,000	714.3	3,000	26,000	3,714.3	6,000
8	5,000	28,800	625.0	3,600	33,800	4,225.0	7,800
9	5,000	38,700	555.6	4,300	43,700	4,855.6	9,900
10	5,000	51,000	500.0	5,100	56,000	5,600.0	12,300

[a] *Includes all opportunity costs*

Solution:

TFC remains unchanged at 5,000 throughout the entire production range, whereas AFC continuously declines from 5,000 at 1 unit to 500 at 10 units. Both AVC and MC initially decline and then reach their lowest level at 3 units, with costs of 1,800 and 1,600, respectively. Beyond 3 units, both AVC and MC increase, indicating that the cost of production rises with greater output. The least-cost point for ATC is 3,200 at 5 units. At zero output, TC is 5,000, which equals the amount of TFC (at zero output, the firm will need no variable inputs, but it is committed to its fixed plant and equipment in the short run).

SUMMARY

This reading addressed several important concepts that extend the basic market model of demand and supply to assist the analyst in assessing a firm's breakeven and shutdown points of production. Demand concepts covered include own-price elasticity of demand, cross-price elasticity of demand, and income elasticity of demand. Supply concepts covered include total, average, and marginal product of labor; total, variable, and marginal cost of labor; and total and marginal revenue. These concepts are used to calculate the breakeven and shutdown points of production.

- Elasticity of demand is a measure of how sensitive quantity demanded is to changes in various variables.
- Own-price elasticity of demand is the ratio of percentage change in quantity demanded to percentage change in a good or service's own price.
- If own-price elasticity of demand is greater than one in absolute terms, demand is elastic and a decline in price will result in higher total expenditure on that good.
  - If own-price elasticity of demand is less than one in absolute terms, demand is inelastic and a decline in price will result in a lower total expenditure on that good.
  - If own-price elasticity of demand is equal to negative one, demand is unit, or unitary, elastic and total expenditure on that good is independent of price.
  - Own-price elasticity of demand will almost always be negative.
- Income elasticity of demand is the ratio of the percentage change in quantity demanded to the percentage change in consumer income.
- Demand is negatively sloped because of either the substitution effect or the income effect.
  - The substitution effect is the phenomenon in which, as a good's price falls, more of this good is substituted for other, more expensive goods.
  - The income effect is the phenomenon in which, as a good's price falls, real income rises and, if this good is normal, more of it will be purchased.
  - If the good is inferior, the income effect will partially or fully offset the substitution effect.
- If income elasticity of demand is positive, the good is a normal good. If income elasticity of demand is negative, the good is an inferior good.
- Cross-price elasticity of demand is the ratio of the percentage change in quantity demanded of one good to the percentage change in the price of a related good.
- If cross-price elasticity between two goods is positive, they are substitutes, and if cross-price elasticity between two goods is negative, they are complements.
- The law of demand states that a decrease in price will cause an increase in quantity demanded.
- Total product of labor is a short-run concept that is the total quantity that is able to be produced for each level of labor input, holding all other inputs constant.

- Average product of labor (APL) is the total product of labor divided by number of labor hours.
- Marginal product of labor (MP_L) is the change in total product divided by the change in labor hours. MP_L might rise as more labor is added to a fixed amount of capital.
- The law of diminishing returns dictates that additional output must fall as more and more labor is added to a fixed amount of capital.
- Production costs increase as input prices rise and fall as inputs become more productive.
- Short-run total cost (STC) is the total expenditure on fixed capital plus the total expenditure on labor.
- Short-run marginal cost (SMC) equals the ratio of wage to marginal product of labor (MP_L).
- Average variable cost (AVC) is the ratio of wage to average product of labor (APL).
- Average total cost (ATC) is total cost (TC) divided by the number of units produced.
- Revenue is price times quantity sold.
- Marginal revenue (MR) is the ratio of change in revenue to change in output.
- Firms under conditions of perfect competition have no pricing power and, therefore, face a perfectly horizontal demand curve at the market price. For firms under conditions of perfect competition, price is identical to marginal revenue (MR).
- Firms under conditions of imperfect competition face a negatively sloped demand curve and have pricing power. For firms under conditions of imperfect competition, marginal revenue (MR) is less than price.
- Economic profit equals total revenue (TR) minus total economic cost, whereas accounting profit equals TR minus total accounting cost.
- Economic cost takes into account the total opportunity cost of all factors of production.
- Opportunity cost is the next best alternative forgone in making a decision.
- Maximum economic profit requires that (1) marginal revenue (MR) equals marginal cost (MC) and (2) MC not be falling with output.
- The breakeven point occurs when total revenue (TR) equals total cost (TC), otherwise stated as the output quantity at which average total cost (ATC) equals price.
- In the short run, it may be rational for a firm to continue to operate while earning negative economic profit if some unavoidable fixed costs are covered.
- Economies of scale are defined as decreasing long-run cost per unit as output increases. Diseconomies of scale are defined as increasing long-run cost per unit as output increases.
- Long-run average total cost is the cost of production per unit of output under conditions in which all inputs are variable.
- Specialization efficiencies and bargaining power in input price can lead to economies of scale.
- The minimum point on the long-run average total cost curve defines the minimum efficient scale for the firm.

PRACTICE PROBLEMS

1. If the price elasticity coefficient of the demand curve for paper clips is equal to −1, demand is:

   A. elastic.

   B. inelastic.

   C. unit elastic.

2. The demand for membership at a local health club is determined by the following equation:

   $Q^d_{hm} = 400 - 5P_{hm}$

   where Q^d_{hm} is the number of health club members and P_{hm} is the price of membership. If the price of health club membership is $35, the price elasticity of demand is *closest* to:

   A. −0.778.

   B. −0.500.

   C. −0.438.

The following information relates to questions 3-6

The market demand function for four-year private universities is given by the equation

$Q^d_{pr} = 84 - 3.1P_{pr} + 0.8I + 0.9P_{pu}$

where Q^d_{pr} is the number of applicants to private universities per year in thousands, P_{pr} is the average price of private universities (in thousands of USD), I is the household monthly income (in thousands of USD), and P_{pu} is the average price of public (government-supported) universities (in thousands of USD). Assume that P_{pr} is equal to 38, I is equal to 100, and P_{pu} is equal to 18.

3. The price elasticity of demand for private universities is *closest* to:

   A. −3.1.

   B. −1.9.

   C. 0.6.

4. The income elasticity of demand for private universities is *closest* to:

   A. 0.5.

   B. 0.8.

   C. 1.3.

5. The cross-price elasticity of demand for private universities with respect to the price of public universities is *closest* to:

   A. 0.3.

   B. 3.1.

   C. 3.9.

6. If the cross-price elasticity between two goods is negative, the two goods are classified as:

   A. normal.

   B. substitutes.

   C. complements.

---

7. Price elasticity of demand for a good will *most likely* be greater if:

   A. there are no substitutes for the good.

   B. consumers consider the good as discretionary.

   C. consumers spend a small portion of their budget on the good.

8. If the income elasticity of demand for a product is −0.6, a:

   A. 1% increase in income will result in a 0.6% increase in demand.

   B. 1% increase in income will result in a 0.6% decrease in demand.

   C. 0.6% increase in income will result in a 1% decrease in demand.

9. An individual's demand for onions is given by the following equation:

   $$Q_o^d = 3 - 0.05 P_o + 0.009 I - 0.16 P_t$$

   where Q_o^d is the number of onions demanded, P_o is the price per pound of onions, I is the household income, and P_t is the price per pound of tomatoes.

   If the price of onions is $1.25, household income is $2,500, and the price of tomatoes is $3.75, the cross-price elasticity of demand for onions with respect to the price of tomatoes is *closest* to:

   A. −1.0597.

   B. −0.0242.

   C. −0.0081.

10. Movement along the demand curve for good X occurs due to a change in:

    A. income.

    B. the price of good X.

    C. the price of a substitute for good X.

11. A wireless phone manufacturer introduced a next-generation phone that received a high level of positive publicity. Despite running several high-speed production assembly lines, the manufacturer is still falling short in meeting demand for the

phone nine months after introduction. Which of the following statements is the *most* plausible explanation for the demand/supply imbalance?

- A. The phone price is low relative to the equilibrium price.
- B. Competitors introduced next-generation phones at a similar price.
- C. Consumer incomes grew faster than the manufacturer anticipated.

12. In the case of a normal good with a decrease in own price, which of the following statements is *most likely* true?

    - A. Both the substitution and income effects lead to an increase in the quantity purchased.
    - B. The substitution effect leads to an increase in the quantity purchased, while the income effect has no impact.
    - C. The substitution effect leads to an increase in the quantity purchased, while the income effect leads to a decrease.

13. A company plans to hire additional factory employees. In the short run, marginal returns are most likely to decrease if:

    - A. the factory is operating at full capacity.
    - B. the factory is experiencing a labor shortage.
    - C. workers are required to multitask and share duties.

14. The production relationship between the number of machine hours and total product for a company is presented below.

Machine Hours	Total Product	Average Product
1	3	3.00
2	8	4.00
3	14	4.67
4	19	4.75
5	21	4.20

    Diminishing marginal returns first occur beyond machine hour:

    - A. 3.
    - B. 4.
    - C. 5.

SOLUTIONS

1. C is correct. When the price elasticity of demand coefficient is −1, demand is said to be unit elastic, or unitary elastic.

2. A is correct. Inserting the price of $35 into the demand function, quantity demanded is calculated as

   $Q_{hm}^d = 400 - 5(35) = 225$

   At a price of $35 per health club membership, the elasticity of demand is

   Price elasticity of demand = $(\Delta Q_{hm}^d / \Delta P_{hm}) \times (P_{hm} / Q_{hm}^d)$

   Price elasticity of demand = $-5 \times (35/225) = -0.778$

3. B is correct. From the demand function:
   Solve for Q_{pr}^d:

   $\Delta Q_{pr}^d / \Delta P_{pr} = -3.1$ (the coefficient in front of own price)

   $\begin{aligned} Q_{pr}^d &= 84 - 3.1 P_{pr} + 0.8 I + 0.9 P_{pu} \\ &= 84 - 3.1(38) + 0.8(100) + 0.9(18) \\ &= 62.4 \end{aligned}$

   At $P_{pr} = 38$,

   $\begin{aligned} \text{price elasticity of demand} &= (\Delta Q_{pr}^d / \Delta P_{pr})(P_{pr} / Q_{pr}^d) \\ &= (-3.1)(38/62.4) \\ &= -1.9 \end{aligned}$

4. C is correct. From the demand function:
   Solve for Q_{pr}^d:

   $\Delta Q_{pr}^d / \Delta I = 0.8$ (coefficient in front of the income variable)

   $\begin{aligned} Q_{pr}^d &= 84 - 3.1 P_{pr} + 0.8 I + 0.9 P_{pu} \\ &= 84 - 3.1(38) + 0.8(100) + 0.9(18) \\ &= 62.4 \end{aligned}$

   At $I = 100$,

   $\begin{aligned} \text{the income elasticity of demand} &= (\Delta Q_{pr}^d / \Delta I)(I / Q_{pr}^d) \\ &= (0.8)(100/62.4) \\ &= 1.3 \end{aligned}$

Solutions

5. A is correct. From the demand function:
   Solve for Q_{pr}^d:

   $\Delta Q_{pr}^d / \Delta P_{pu} = 0.9$ (the coefficient in front of P_{pu})

   $$Q_{pr}^d = 84 - 3.1 P_{pr} + 0.8I + 0.9 P_{pu}$$
   $$= 84 - 3.1(38) + 0.8(100) + 0.9(18)$$
   $$= 62.4$$

   At $P = 38$, and $P_{pu} = 18$,

   the cross-price elasticity of demand $= \left(\Delta Q_{pr}^d / \Delta P_{pu}\right)\left(P_{pu} / Q_{pr}^d\right)$
   $$= (0.9)(18/62.4)$$
   $$= 0.3$$

6. C is correct. With complements, consumption goes up or down together. With a negative cross-price elasticity, as the price of one good goes up, the demand for both falls.

7. B is correct. Price elasticity of demand is likely to be greater for items that are seen as optional or discretionary.

8. B is correct. Income elasticity is a measure of how sensitive quantity demanded is to a change in income. If the income elasticity of demand for the product is –0.6, whenever income increases by 1%, the quantity demanded of the product at each price decreases by 0.6%. Consequently, as income rises, consumers will purchase less of the product.

9. B is correct. The cross-price elasticity of demand measures the responsiveness of the demand for onions in response to a change in the price of tomatoes. From the demand function equation:

   $$Q_o^d = 3 - 0.05 P_o + 0.009I - 0.16 P_t$$
   $$Q_o^d = 3 - 0.05(1.25) + 0.009(2{,}500) - 0.16(3.75) = 24.8375$$

   At a price of onions of $1.25 and a price of tomatoes of $3.75, the cross-price elasticity of demand is calculated as follows:

   Cross-price elasticity of demand $= \left(\Delta Q_o^d / \Delta P_t\right) \times \left(P_t / Q_o^d\right)$

   Cross-price elasticity of demand $= -0.16 \times (3.75 / 24.8375) = -0.0242$

10. B is correct. The demand curve shows quantity demanded as a function of own price only.

11. A is correct. The situation described is one of excess demand because, in order for markets to clear at the given level of quantity supplied, the company would need to raise prices.

12. A is correct. In the case of normal goods, the income and substitution effects are reinforcing, leading to an increase in the amount purchased after a drop in price.

13. A is correct. The law of diminishing returns occurs in the short run when additional output falls as more and more labor is added to a fixed amount of capital. When a factory is operating at full capacity, adding additional employees will not

increase production because the physical plant is already 100% employed. More labor hours will add to costs without adding to output, thus resulting in diminishing marginal returns.

14. A is correct. Diminishing marginal returns occur when the marginal product of a resource decreases as additional units of that input are employed. Marginal product, which is the additional output resulting from using one more unit of input, is presented below.

Machine Hours	Total Product	Average Product	Marginal Product
1	3	3.00	3
2	8	4.00	5
3	14	4.67	6
4	19	4.75	5
5	21	4.20	2

The marginal product of the third machine hour is 6, and the marginal product declines thereafter. Consequently, diminishing marginal returns are first evident beyond three machine hours.

LEARNING MODULE 2

Introduction to the Firm and Market Organization

by Richard Fritz, PhD, and Michele Gambera, PhD, CFA.

Richard Fritz, PhD, is at the School of Economics at Georgia Institute of Technology (USA). Michele Gambera, PhD, CFA, is at UBS Asset Management and the University of Illinois at Urbana-Champaign (USA).

LEARNING OUTCOMES

Mastery	The candidate should be able to:
☐	describe characteristics of perfect competition, monopolistic competition, oligopoly, and pure monopoly
☐	explain relationships between price, marginal revenue, marginal cost, economic profit, and the elasticity of demand under each market structure
☐	describe a firm's supply function under each market structure
☐	describe and determine the optimal price and output for firms under each market structure
☐	describe pricing strategy under each market structure
☐	explain factors affecting long-run equilibrium under each market structure

1. ANALYSIS OF MARKET STRUCTURES

☐ describe characteristics of perfect competition, monopolistic competition, oligopoly, and pure monopoly

The purpose of this reading is to build an understanding of the importance of market structure. As different market structures result in different sets of choices facing a firm's decision makers, an understanding of market structure is a powerful tool in analyzing issues such as a firm's pricing of its products and, more broadly, its potential to increase profitability. In the long run, a firm's profitability will be determined by the forces associated with the market structure within which it operates. In a highly competitive market, long-run profits will be driven down by the forces of competition.

In less competitive markets, large profits are possible even in the long run; in the short run, any outcome is possible. Therefore, understanding the forces behind the market structure will aid the financial analyst in determining firms' short- and long-term prospects.

Analysis of Market Structures

Traditionally, economists classify a market into one of four structures: perfect competition, monopolistic competition, oligopoly, and monopoly.

Economists' Four Types of Structure

Economists define a market as a group of buyers and sellers that are aware of each other and can agree on a price for the exchange of goods and services. While the internet has extended a number of markets worldwide, certain markets are limited by geographic boundaries. For example, the internet search engine Google operates in a worldwide market. In contrast, the market for premixed cement is limited to the area within which a truck can deliver the mushy mix from the plant to a construction site before the compound becomes useless. Thomas L. Friedman's international best seller *The World Is Flat*[1] challenges the concept of the geographic limitations of the market. If the service being provided by the seller can be digitized, its market expands worldwide. For example, a technician can scan your injury in a clinic in Switzerland. That radiographic image can be digitized and sent to a radiologist in India to be read. As a customer (i.e., patient), you may never know that part of the medical service provided to you was the result of a worldwide market.

Some markets are highly concentrated, with the majority of total sales coming from a small number of firms. For example, in the market for internet search, three firms controlled 98.9 percent of the US market (Google 63.5 percent, Microsoft 24 percent, and Oath [formerly Yahoo] 11.4 percent) as of January 2018.[2] Other markets are very fragmented, such as automobile repairs, where small independent shops often dominate and large chains may or may not exist. New products can lead to market concentration: It is estimated that the Apple iPod had a world market share of over 70 percent among MP3 players in 2009.

Market structure can be broken down into four distinct categories: perfect competition, monopolistic competition, oligopoly, and monopoly.

Perfect Competition

- Profits under the conditions of perfect competition are driven to the required rate of return paid by the entrepreneur to borrow capital from investors (so-called normal profit or rental cost of capital).
- This does not mean that all perfectly competitive industries are doomed to extinction by a lack of profits.
- Many businesses earn their required return under the pressures of perfect competition.
- Perfect competition exists within several commodities markets—for example, in several commodities markets, where sellers and buyers have a strictly homogeneous product and no single producer is large enough to influence market prices.

---

1 Friedman (2006).
2 Source: www.statista.com/statistics/267161/market-share-of-search-engines-in-the-united-states/.

Analysis of Market Structures

Monopolistic Competition

- Highly competitive, but a form of imperfect competition.
- Strong elements of competition (large number of firms); monopoly-like conditions result from product differentiation.
- Seller has some pricing power by convincing consumer of product's unique characteristics.

Oligopoly

- Relatively small number of firms supplying the market.
- Each firm must consider what retaliatory strategies the other firms will pursue when prices and production levels change.
- Understanding the market structure of oligopoly markets can help in identifying a logical pattern of strategic price changes for the competing firms.

Monopoly

- In pure monopoly markets, no close substitute exists for the given product or service.
- Single seller which exercises considerable power over pricing and output decisions if allowed to operate without constraints. In most market-based economies, pure monopolies are regulated by a governmental authority.
- In most cases, the monopoly power provider is allowed to earn a normal return on its investment and prices are set by the regulatory authority to allow that return.

Factors That Determine Market Structure

Five factors determine market structure:

1. The number and relative size of firms supplying the product;
2. The degree of product differentiation;
3. The power of the seller over pricing decisions;
4. The relative strength of the barriers to market entry and exit; and
5. The degree of non-price competition.

Exhibit 1: Characteristics of Market Structure

Market Structure	Number of Sellers	Degree of Product Differentiation	Barriers to Entry	Pricing Power of Firm	Non-price Competition
Perfect competition	Many	Homogeneous/Standardized	Very Low	None	None
Monopolistic competition	Many	Differentiated	Low	Some	Advertising and Product Differentiation
Oligopoly	Few	Homogeneous/Standardized	High	Some or Considerable	Advertising and Product Differentiation
Monopoly	One	Unique Product	Very High	Considerable	Advertising

From the perspective of the owners of the firm, the most desirable market structure is that with the most control over price, because this control can lead to large profits. Monopoly and oligopoly markets offer the greatest potential control over price; monopolistic competition offers less control. Firms operating under perfectly competitive market conditions have no control over price. From the consumers' perspective, the most desirable market structure is that with the greatest degree of competition because prices are generally lower. Thus, consumers would prefer as many goods and services as possible to be offered in competitive markets.

As often happens in economics, there is a trade-off. While perfect competition gives the largest quantity of a good at the lowest price, other market forms may spur more innovation. Specifically, there may be high costs in researching a new product, and firms will incur such costs only if they expect to earn an attractive return on their research investment. This is the case often made for medical innovations, for example—the cost of clinical trials and experiments to create new medicines would bankrupt perfectly competitive firms but may be acceptable in an oligopoly market structure. Therefore, consumers can benefit from less-than-perfectly-competitive markets.

> **PORTER'S FIVE FORCES AND MARKET STRUCTURE**
>
> A financial analyst aiming to establish market conditions and consequent profitability of incumbent firms should start with the questions framed by Exhibit 1: How many sellers are there? Is the product differentiated? and so on. Moreover, in the case of monopolies and quasi monopolies, the analyst should evaluate the legislative and regulatory framework: Can the company set prices freely, or are there governmental controls? Finally, the analyst should consider the threat of competition from potential entrants.
>
> This analysis is often summarized by students of corporate strategy as "Porter's five forces," named after Harvard Business School professor Michael E. Porter. His book, *Competitive Strategy*, presented a systematic analysis of the practice of market strategy. Porter (2008) identified the five forces as:
>
> - Threat of entry;
> - Power of suppliers;
> - Power of buyers (customers);
> - Threat of substitutes; and
> - Rivalry among existing competitors.

2. PERFECT COMPETITION

☐ describe characteristics of perfect competition, monopolistic competition, oligopoly, and pure monopoly

☐ explain relationships between price, marginal revenue, marginal cost, economic profit, and the elasticity of demand under each market structure

Perfect competition is characterized by the five conditions presented in Exhibit 1, above:

1. There are a large number of potential buyers and sellers.
2. The products offered by the sellers are virtually identical.
3. There are few or easily surmountable barriers to entry and exit.

Perfect Competition

4. Sellers have no market-pricing power.
5. Non-price competition is absent.

While few markets achieve the distinction of being perfectly competitive, it is useful to establish the outcome associated with this market structure as a benchmark against which other market structures can be compared. The most typical example of perfect competition is found in certain aspects of the agriculture industry, such as the large number of farmers growing corn for animal feed. Corn is a primary source of food for pork, beef, and poultry production. A bushel of corn from Farmer Brown is virtually identical to a bushel of corn from Farmer Lopez. If a hog farmer needs corn to feed his hogs, it does not matter whether the corn comes from Farmer Brown or Farmer Lopez. Furthermore, the aggregate corn market is well defined, with active futures and spot markets. Information about the corn market is easy and inexpensive to access, and there is no way to differentiate the product, such as by advertising. Agribusiness is capital intensive, but where arable land is relatively abundant and water is available, the barriers to entry (e.g., capital and expertise) for corn production are relatively low.

Demand Analysis in Perfectly Competitive Markets

The price of a homogeneous product sold in a competitive market is determined by the demand and supply in that market.

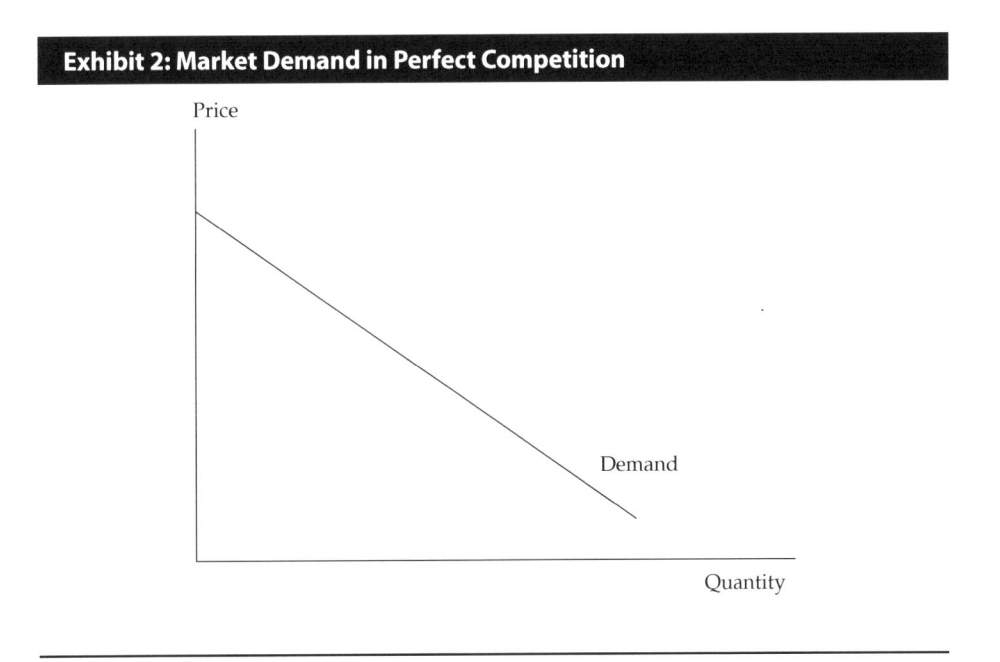

Exhibit 2: Market Demand in Perfect Competition

3. OTHER FACTORS AFFECTING DEMAND

☐ describe characteristics of perfect competition, monopolistic competition, oligopoly, and pure monopoly

☐ explain relationships between price, marginal revenue, marginal cost, economic profit, and the elasticity of demand under each market structure

There are two other important forces that influence shifts in consumer demand. One influential factor is consumer income and the other is the price of a related product. For normal goods, as consumer income increases, the demand increases. The degree to which consumers respond to higher incomes by increasing their demand for goods and services is referred to as income elasticity of demand. **Income elasticity of demand** measures the responsiveness of demand to changes in income. The calculation is similar to that of price elasticity, with the percentage change in income replacing the percentage change in price. Note the new calculation below:

$$\varepsilon_Y = (\% \text{ change in } Q_D) \div (\% \text{ change in } Y)$$

where ε_Y is income elasticity of demand, Q_D is the quantity demanded, and Y is consumer income. For normal goods, the measure ε_Y will be a positive value. That is, as consumers' income rises, more of the product is demanded. For products that are considered luxury items, the measure of income elasticity will be greater than one. There are other goods and services that are considered inferior products. For inferior products, as consumer income rises, less of the product is demanded. Inferior products will have negative values for income elasticity. For example, a person on a small income may watch television shows, but if this person had more income, she would prefer going to live concerts and theater performances; in this example, television shows would be the inferior good.

As a technical issue, the difference between price elasticity of demand and income elasticity of demand is that the demand adjustment for price elasticity represents a movement *along the demand schedule* because the demand schedule represents combinations of price and quantity. The demand adjustment for income elasticity represents a *shift in the demand curve* because with a higher income one can afford to purchase more of the good at any price. For a normal good, an increase in income would shift the demand schedule out to the right, away from the origin of the graph, and a decrease in income would shift the demand curve to the left, toward the origin.

The final factor influencing demand for a product is the change in price of a related product, such as a strong substitute or a complementary product. If a close competitor in the beverage market lowers its price, consumers will substitute that product for your product. Thus, your product's demand curve will shift to the left, toward the origin of the graph. **Cross-price elasticity of demand** is the responsiveness of the demand for product A that is associated with the change in price of product B:

$$\varepsilon_X = (\% \text{ change in } Q_{DA}) \div (\% \text{ change in } P_B)$$

where ε_X is cross-price elasticity of demand, Q_{DA} is the quantity demanded of product A, and P_B is the price of product B.

When the cross-price elasticity of demand between two products is *positive*, the two products are considered to be **substitutes**. For example, you may expect to have positive cross-price elasticity between honey and sugar. If the measure of cross-price elasticity is *negative*, the two products are referred to as **complements** of each other.

For example, if the price of DVDs goes up, you would expect consumers to buy fewer DVD players. In this case, the cross-price elasticity of demand would have a negative value.

Reviewing cross-price elasticity values provides a simple test for the degree of competition in the market. The more numerous and the closer the substitutes for a product, the lower the pricing power of firms selling in that market; the fewer the substitutes for a product, the greater the pricing power.

Because price elasticity of demand relates changes in price to changes in the quantity demanded, there must be a logical relationship between marginal revenue and price elasticity. Recall that marginal revenue equals the change in total revenue given a change in output or sales. An increase in total revenue results from a decrease in price that results in an increase in sales. In order for the increase in the quantity demanded to be sufficient to offset the decline in price, the percentage change in quantity demanded must be greater than the percentage decrease in price. The relationship between TR and price elasticity is as follows:

$\varepsilon_P > 1$ Demand is elastic $\uparrow P \rightarrow$ TR$\downarrow$ and $\downarrow P \rightarrow$ TR$\uparrow$

$\varepsilon_P = 1$ Demand is unitary elastic $\updownarrow P \rightarrow$ no change in TR

$0 < \varepsilon_P < 1$ Demand is inelastic $\uparrow P \rightarrow$ TR$\uparrow$ and $\downarrow P \rightarrow$ TR$\downarrow$

Total revenue is maximized when marginal revenue is zero. The logic is that as long as marginal revenue is positive (i.e., each additional unit sold contributes to additional total revenue), total revenue will continue to increase. Only when marginal revenue becomes negative will total revenue begin to decline. Therefore, the percentage decrease in price is greater than the percentage increase in quantity demanded. The relationship between marginal revenue (MR) and price elasticity can be expressed as

$$MR = P[1 - (1/\varepsilon_P)]$$

An understanding of price elasticity of demand is an important strategic tool. It would be very useful to know in advance what would happen to your firm's total revenue if you increased the product's price. If you are operating in the inelastic portion of the demand curve, increasing the price of the product will increase total revenue. On the other hand, if you are operating in the elastic portion of the product's demand curve, increasing the price will decrease total revenue.

How do business decision makers decide what level of output to bring to the market? To answer that question, the firm must understand its cost of resources, its production relations, and its supply function. Once the supply function is well defined and understood, it is combined with the demand analysis to determine the profit-maximizing levels of output.

CONSUMER SURPLUS: VALUE MINUS EXPENDITURE | 4

- ☐ describe characteristics of perfect competition, monopolistic competition, oligopoly, and pure monopoly
- ☐ explain relationships between price, marginal revenue, marginal cost, economic profit, and the elasticity of demand under each market structure

To this point, we have discussed the fundamentals of supply and demand curves and explained a simple model of how a market can be expected to arrive at an equilibrium combination of price and quantity. While it is certainly necessary for the analyst to understand the basic workings of the market model, it is also crucial to have a sense of why we might care about the nature of the equilibrium. In this section we review the concept of **consumer surplus**, which is helpful in understanding and evaluating business pricing strategies. Consumer surplus is defined as the difference between the value that a consumer places on the units purchased and the amount of money that was required to pay for them. It is a measure of the value gained by the buyer from the transaction.

To get an intuitive feel for the concept of consumer surplus, consider the last thing you purchased. Whatever it was, think of how much you paid for it. Now contrast that price with the maximum amount you *would have been willing to pay* rather than go without the item altogether. If those two numbers are different, we say you received some consumer surplus from your purchase. You got a "bargain" because you would have been willing to pay more than you had to pay.

Earlier, we referred to the law of demand, which says that as price falls, consumers are willing to buy more of the good. This observation translates into a negatively sloped demand curve. Alternatively, we could say that the highest price that consumers are willing to pay for an additional unit declines as they consume more and more of a good. In this way, we can interpret their *willingness to pay* as a measure of how much they *value* each additional unit of the good. This is a very important point: To purchase a unit of some good, consumers must give up something else they value. So, the price they are willing to pay for an additional unit of a good is a measure of how much they value that unit, in terms of the other goods they must sacrifice to consume it.

If demand curves are negatively sloped, it must be because the value of each additional unit of the good falls as more of the good is consumed. We shall explore this concept further below, but for now, it is enough to recognize that the demand curve can therefore be considered a **marginal value curve**, because it shows the highest price consumers would be willing to pay for each additional unit. In effect, the demand curve is the willingness of consumers to pay for each additional unit.

This interpretation of the demand curve allows us to measure the total value of consuming any given quantity of a good: It is the sum of all the marginal values of each unit consumed, up to and including the last unit. Graphically, this measure translates into the area under the consumer's demand curve, up to and including the last unit consumed, as shown in Exhibit 3, where the consumer is choosing to buy Q_1 units of the good at a price of P_1. The marginal value of the Q_1^{th} unit is clearly P_1 because that is the highest price the consumer is willing to pay for that unit. Importantly, however, the marginal value of each unit *up to* the Q_1^{th} is greater than P_1.

Exhibit 3: Consumer Surplus

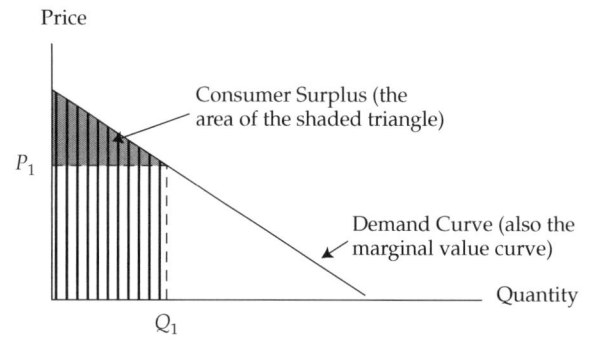

Note: Consumer surplus is the area beneath the demand curve and above the price paid.

Because the consumer would have been willing to pay more for each of those units than she paid (P_1), we can say she received more value than the cost to her of buying them. This extra value is the buyer's consumer surplus. The *total value* of quantity Q_1 to the buyer is the area of the shaded area in Exhibit 3. The *total expenditure* is only the area of the rectangle with height P_1 and base Q_1 (bottom section). The total consumer surplus received from buying Q_1 units at a level price of P_1 per unit is the difference between the area under the demand curve and the area of the rectangle $P_1 \times Q_1$. The resulting area is shown as the lightly shaded triangle (upper section).

EXAMPLE 1

Consumer Surplus

1. A market demand function is given by the equation $Q_D = 180 - 2P$. Find the value of consumer surplus if price is equal to 65.

Solution:

First, input 65 into the demand function to find the quantity demanded at that price: $Q_D = 180 - 2(65) = 50$. Then, to make drawing the demand curve easier, invert the demand function by solving for P in terms of Q_D: $P = 90 - 0.5Q_D$. Note that the price intercept is 90 and the quantity intercept is 180. Draw the demand curve:

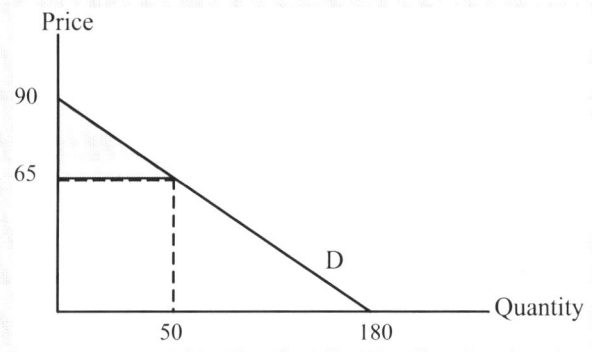

Find the area of the triangle above the price of 65 and below the demand curve, up to quantity 50: Area = ½ (Base)(Height) = ½ (50)(25) = 625.

SUPPLY ANALYSIS, OPTIMAL PRICE, AND OUTPUT IN PERFECTLY COMPETITIVE MARKETS

5

- ☐ explain relationships between price, marginal revenue, marginal cost, economic profit, and the elasticity of demand under each market structure
- ☐ describe a firm's supply function under each market structure
- ☐ describe and determine the optimal price and output for firms under each market structure
- ☐ describe pricing strategy under each market structure

Consider two corn farmers, Mr. Brown and Ms. Lopez. They both have land available to them to grow corn and can sell at one price, say USD3 per pound. They will try to produce as much corn as is profitable at that price. If the price is driven up to USD5 per pound by new consumers entering the market—say, ethanol producers—Mr. Brown and Ms. Lopez will try to produce more corn. To increase their output levels, they may have to use less productive land, increase irrigation, use more fertilizer, or all three. Their production costs will likely increase. They will both still try to produce as much corn as possible to profit at the new, higher price of USD5 per pound. Exhibit 4 illustrates this example. Note that the supply functions for the individual firms have positive slopes. Thus, as prices increase, the firms supply greater quantities of the product.

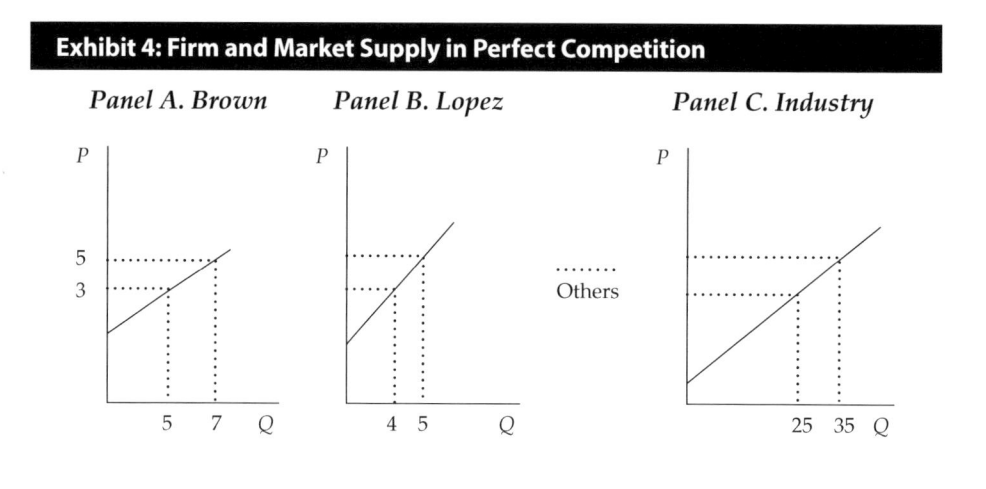

Exhibit 4: Firm and Market Supply in Perfect Competition

Panel A. Brown   *Panel B. Lopez*   *Panel C. Industry*

Notice that the market supply curve is the sum of the supply curves of the individual firms—Brown, Lopez, and others—that make up the market. Assume that the supply function for the market can be expressed as a linear relationship, as follows:

$Q_S = 10 + 5P$, or $P = -2 + 0.2Q_S$,

where Q_S is the quantity supplied and P is the price of the product.

Before we analyze the optimal supply level for the firm, we need to point out that economic costs and profits differ from accounting costs and profits in a significant way. **Economic costs** include all the remuneration needed to keep the productive resource in its current employment or to acquire the resource for productive use.

To evaluate the remuneration needed to keep the resource in its current use and attract new resources for productive use, economists refer to the resource's **opportunity cost**. Opportunity cost is measured by determining the resource's next best opportunity. If a corn farmer could be employed in an alternative position in the labor market with an income of USD50,000, then the opportunity cost of the farmer's labor is USD50,000. Similarly, the farmer's land and capital could be leased to another farmer or sold and reinvested in another type of business. The return forgone by not doing so is an opportunity cost. In economic terms, total cost includes the full normal market return on all the resources utilized in the business. **Economic profit** is the difference between TR and total cost (TC). Economic profit differs from accounting profit because accounting profit does not include opportunity cost. Accounting profit includes only explicit payments to outside providers of resources (e.g. workers, vendors, lenders) and depreciation based on the historic cost of physical capital.

Optimal Price and Output in Perfectly Competitive Markets

Carrying forward our examples from Sections 3.1 and 3.2, we can now combine the market supply and demand functions to solve for the equilibrium price and quantity, where Q^* represents the equilibrium level of both supply and demand.

$$P = 25 - 0.5Q_D = -2 + 0.2Q_S = P$$
$$25 - 0.5Q_D = -2 + 0.2Q_S$$
$$27 = 0.7Q^*$$
$$Q^* = 38.57$$

According to the market demand curve, the equilibrium price is

$$P = 25 - 0.5Q^* = 25 - 0.5(38.57) = 25 - 19.29 = 5.71.$$

With many firms in the market and total output in the market of almost 39 units of the product, the effective market price would be USD5.71. This result becomes the demand function for each perfectly competitive firm. Even if a few individual producers could expand production, there would not be a noticeable change in the market equilibrium price. In fact, if any one firm could change the equilibrium market price, the market would not be in perfect competition. Therefore, the demand curve that each perfectly competitive firm faces is a horizontal line at the equilibrium price, as shown in Exhibit 5, even though the demand curve for the whole market is downward sloping.

Exhibit 5: Individual Firm's Demand in Perfect Competition

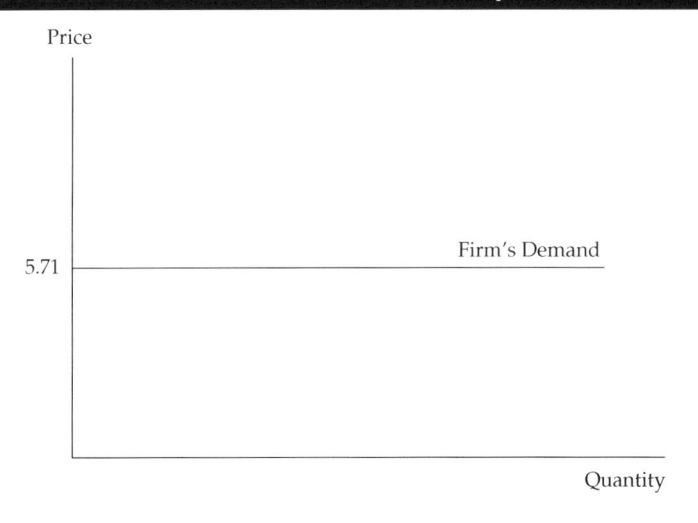

EXAMPLE 2

Demand Curves in Perfect Competition

1. Is it possible that the demand schedule faced by Firm A is horizontal while the demand schedule faced by the market as a whole is downward sloping?

    A. No, because Firm A can change its output based on demand changes.

    B. No, because a horizontal demand curve means that elasticity is infinite.

> **C.** Yes, because consumers can go to another firm if Firm A charges a higher price, and Firm A can sell all it produces at the market price.
>
> ## Solution:
> C is correct. Firm A cannot charge a higher price and has no incentive to sell at a price below the market price.

To analyze the firm's revenue position, recall that average revenue is equivalent to the firm's demand function. Therefore, the horizontal line that represents the firm's demand curve is the firm's AR schedule.

Marginal revenue is the incremental increase in total revenue associated with each additional unit sold. For every extra unit the firm sells, it receives USD5.71. Thus, the firm's MR schedule is also the horizontal line at USD5.71. TR is calculated by multiplying AR by the quantity of products sold. Total revenue is the area under the AR line at the point where the firm produces the output. In the case of perfect competition, the following conditions hold for the individual firm:

Price = Average revenue = Marginal revenue

The next step is to develop the firm's cost functions. The firm knows that it can sell the entire product it produces at the market's equilibrium price. How much should it produce? That decision is determined by analysis of the firm's costs and revenues. A corn farmer uses three primary resources: land, labor, and capital. In economics, capital is any man-made aid to production. For the corn farmer, his or her capital includes the irrigation system, tractors, harvesters, trucks, grain bins, fertilizer, and so forth. The labor includes the farmer, perhaps members of the farmer's family, and hired labor. In the initial stages of production, only the farmer and the farmer's family are cultivating the land, with a significant investment in capital. They have a tractor, fertilizer, irrigation equipment, grain bins, seed, and a harvester. The investment in land and capital is relatively high compared with the labor input. In this production phase, the average cost of producing a bushel of corn is high. As they begin to expand by adding labor to the collection of expensive land and capital, the average cost of producing corn begins to decline—for example, because one tractor can be used more intensively to plow a larger amount of land. When the combination of land, labor, and capital approaches an efficient range, the average cost of producing a bushel of corn declines.

Given a certain level of technology, there is a limit to the increase in productivity. Eventually something begins to cause declining marginal productivity. That is, each additional unit of input produces a progressively smaller increase in output. This force is called the **law of diminishing returns**. This "law" helps define the shape of the firm's cost functions. Average cost and marginal cost will be U-shaped. Over the initial stages of output, average and marginal costs will decline. At some level of output, the law of diminishing returns will overtake the efficiencies in production and average and marginal costs will increase.

Average cost (AC) is Total cost (TC) divided by Output (Q). Therefore,

AC = TC/Q

Note that we have defined average cost (AC) in terms of total costs. Many authors refer to this as "average total cost" to distinguish it from a related concept, "average variable cost," which omits fixed costs. In the remainder of this reading, *average cost should be understood to mean average total cost*.

Marginal cost (MC) is the change in TC associated with an incremental change in output:

MC = ΔTC/ΔQ

Supply Analysis, Optimal Price, and Output in Perfectly Competitive Markets

By definition, fixed costs do not vary with output, so marginal cost reflects only changes in variable costs.[3] MC declines initially because processes can be made more efficient and specialization makes workers more proficient at their tasks. However, at some higher level of output, MC begins to increase (e.g., must pay workers a higher wage to have them work overtime and, in agriculture, less fertile land must be brought into production). MC and AC will be equal at the level of output where AC is minimized. This is a mathematical necessity and intuitive. If you employ the least expensive labor in the initial phase of production, average and marginal cost will decline. Eventually, additional labor will be more costly. For example, if the labor market is at or near full employment, in order to attract additional workers, you must pay higher wages than they are currently earning elsewhere. Thus, the additional (marginal) labor is more costly, and the higher cost increases the overall average as soon as MC exceeds AC. Exhibit 6 illustrates the relationship between AC and MC.

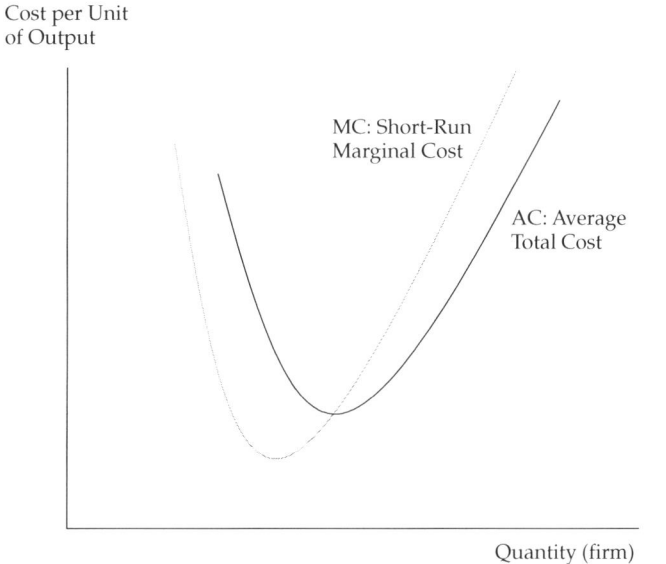

Exhibit 6: Individual Firm's Short-Run Cost Schedules

Now combine the revenue and cost functions from Exhibit 5 and Exhibit 6. In short-run equilibrium, the perfectly competitive firm can earn an economic profit (or an economic loss). In this example, the equilibrium price, USD5.71, is higher than the minimum AC. The firm will always maximize profit at an output level where MR = MC. Recall that in perfect competition, the horizontal demand curve is the marginal revenue and average revenue schedules. By setting output at point A in Exhibit 7, where MR = MC, the firm will maximize profits. Total revenue is equal to $P \times Q$—in this case, USD5.71 times Q_C. Total cost is equal to Q_C times the average cost of producing Q_C, at point B in Exhibit 7. The difference between the two areas is economic profit.

---

3 Readers who are familiar with calculus will recognize that MC is simply the derivative of total cost with respect to quantity produced.

Exhibit 7: Perfectly Competitive Firm's Short-Run Equilibrium

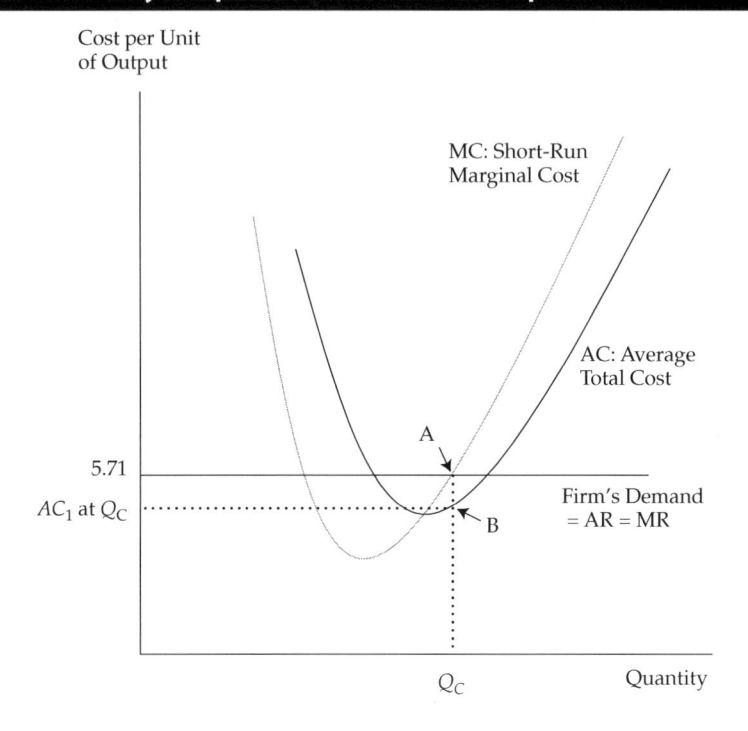

[Graph showing Cost per Unit of Output vs Quantity. MC: Short-Run Marginal Cost curve and AC: Average Total Cost curve intersect at point where horizontal line at 5.71 (Firm's Demand = AR = MR) is tangent. Points A and B marked near Q_C. AC_1 at Q_C shown on vertical axis.]

6

LONG-RUN EQUILIBRIUM IN PERFECTLY COMPETITIVE MARKETS

- ☐ explain factors affecting long-run equilibrium under each market structure
- ☐ describe pricing strategy under each market structure

In the long run, economic profit will attract other entrepreneurs to the market, resulting in the production of more output. The aggregate supply will increase, shifting the industry supply (S_1) curve to the right, away from the origin of the graph. For a given demand curve, this increase in supply at each price level will lower the equilibrium price, as shown in Exhibit 8.

Long-Run Equilibrium in Perfectly Competitive Markets

Exhibit 8: Perfectly Competitive Market with Increased Supply

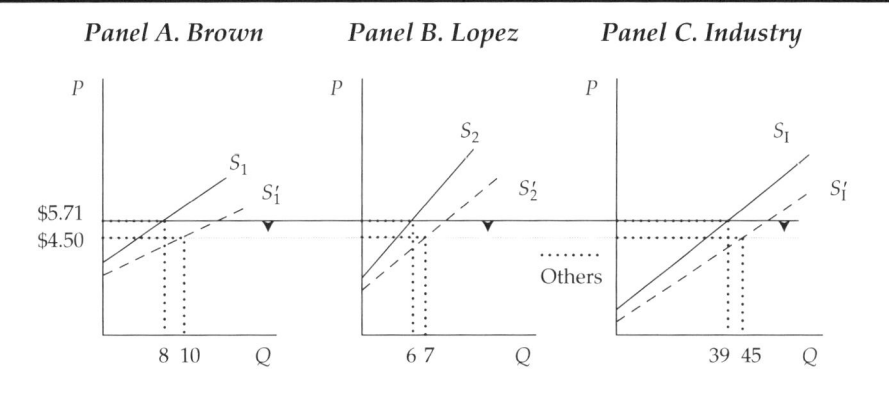

Panel A. Brown   *Panel B. Lopez*   *Panel C. Industry*

In the long run, the perfectly competitive firm will operate at the point where marginal cost equals the minimum of average cost, because at that point, entry is no longer profitable: In equilibrium, price equals not only marginal cost (firm equilibrium) but also minimum average cost, so that total revenues equal total costs. This result implies that the perfectly competitive firm operates with zero economic profit. That is, the firm receives its normal profit (rental cost of capital), which is included in its economic costs. Recall that economic profits occur when total revenue exceeds total cost (and therefore differ from accounting profits). With low entry cost and homogeneous products to sell, the perfectly competitive firm earns zero economic profit in the long run.

Exhibit 9 illustrates the long-run equilibrium position of the perfectly competitive firm. Note that total revenue equals price ($4.50) times quantity ($Q_E$) and total cost equals average cost ($4.50) times quantity ($Q_E$).

Exhibit 9: Perfectly Competitive Firm's Long-Run Equilibrium

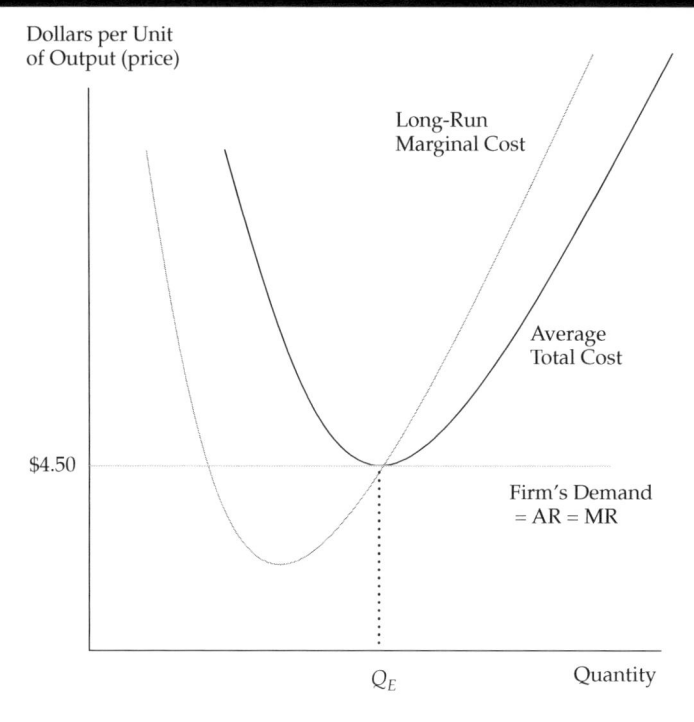

[Graph showing Dollars per Unit of Output (price) on y-axis and Quantity on x-axis. Long-Run Marginal Cost and Average Total Cost curves intersect at the minimum of ATC at price $4.50, which equals Firm's Demand = AR = MR, at quantity Q_E.]

The long-run marginal cost schedule is the perfectly competitive firm's supply curve. The firm's demand curve is dictated by the aggregate market's equilibrium price. The basic rule of profit maximization is that MR = MC, as is the case in long-run equilibrium. The firm's demand schedule is the same as the firm's marginal revenue and average revenue. Given its cost of operation, the only decision the perfectly competitive firm faces is how much to produce. The answer is the level of output that maximizes its return, and that level is where MR = MC. The demand curve is perfectly elastic. Of course, the firm constantly tries to find ways to lower its cost in the long run.

7. MONOPOLY MARKETS: DEMAND/SUPPLY AND OPTIMAL PRICE/OUTPUT

- [ ] describe characteristics of perfect competition, monopolistic competition, oligopoly, and pure monopoly
- [ ] explain relationships between price, marginal revenue, marginal cost, economic profit, and the elasticity of demand under each market structure
- [ ] describe a firm's supply function under each market structure

Monopoly Markets: Demand/Supply and Optimal Price/Output

- [ ] describe and determine the optimal price and output for firms under each market structure
- [ ] explain factors affecting long-run equilibrium under each market structure
- [ ] describe pricing strategy under each market structure

Monopoly market structure is at the opposite end of the spectrum from perfect competition. For various reasons, there are significant barriers to entry such that a single firm produces a highly specialized product and faces no threat of competition. There are no good substitutes for the product in the relevant market, and the market demand function is the same as the individual firm's demand schedule. *The distinguishing characteristics of monopoly are that a single firm represents the market and significant barriers to entry exist.* Exhibit 1 identified the characteristics of monopoly markets:

1. There is a single seller of a highly differentiated product.
2. The product offered by the seller has no close substitute.
3. Entry into the market is very difficult, with high costs and significant barriers to competition.
4. The firm has considerable pricing power.
5. The product is differentiated through non-price strategies such as advertising.

Monopoly markets are unusual. With a single seller dominating the market, power over price decisions is significant. For a single seller to achieve this power, there must be factors that allow the monopoly to exist. One obvious source of monopoly power would be a patent or copyright that prevents other firms from entering the market. Patent and copyright laws exist to reward intellectual capital and investment in research and development. In so doing, they provide significant barriers to entry.

Another possible source of market power is control over critical resources used for production. One example is De Beers Consolidated Mines Limited. De Beers owned or controlled all diamond mining operations in South Africa and established pricing agreements with other important diamond producers. In doing so, De Beers was able to control the prices for cut diamonds for decades. Technically, De Beers was a near-monopoly dominant firm rather than a pure monopoly, although its pricing procedure for cut diamonds resembled monopoly behavior.

Perhaps the most common form of monopolistic market power occurs as the result of government-controlled authorization. In most urban areas, a single source of water and sewer services is offered. In some cases, these services are offered by a government-controlled entity. In other cases, private companies provide the services under government regulation. Such "natural" monopolies require a large initial investment that benefits from economies of scale; therefore, government may authorize a single seller to provide a certain service because having multiple sellers would be too costly. For example, electricity in most markets is provided by a single seller. Economies of scale result when significant capital investment benefits from declining long-run average costs. In the case of electricity, a large gas-fueled power plant producing electricity for a large area is substantially more efficient than having a small diesel generator for every building. That is, the average cost of generating and delivering a kilowatt of electricity will be substantially lower with the single power station, but the initial fixed cost of building the power station and the lines delivering electricity to each home, factory, and office will be very high.

In the case of natural monopolies, limiting the market to a single seller is considered beneficial to society. One water and sewer system is deemed better for the community than dozens of competitors because building multiple infrastructures for running water and sewer service would be particularly expensive and complicated. One electrical power grid supplying electricity for a community can make large capital investments in generating plants and lower the long-run average cost, while multiple power grids would lead to a potentially dangerous maze of wires. Clearly, not all monopolies are in a position to make significant economic profits. Regulators, such as public utility commissions in the United States, attempt to determine what a normal return for the monopoly owners' investment should be, and they set prices accordingly. Nevertheless, monopolists attempt to maximize profits.

Not all monopolies originate from "natural" barriers. For some monopolists, barriers to entry do not derive from increasing returns to scale. We mentioned that marketing and brand loyalty are sources of product differentiation in monopolistic competition. In some highly successful cases, strong brand loyalty can become a formidable barrier to entry. For example, if the Swiss watchmaker Rolex is unusually successful in establishing brand loyalty, so that its customers think there is no close substitute for its product, then the company will have monopoly-like pricing power over its market.

The final potential source of market power is the increasing returns associated with network effects. Network effects result from synergies related to increasing market penetration. By achieving a critical level of adoption, Microsoft was able to extend its market power through the network effect—for example, because most computer users know how to use Microsoft Word. Therefore, for firms, Word is cheaper to adopt than other programs because almost every new hire will be proficient in using the software and will need no further training. At some level of market share, a network-based product or service reaches a point where each additional share point increases the probability that another user will adopt.[4] These network effects increase the value to other potential adopters.

Demand Analysis in Monopoly Markets

The monopolist's demand schedule is the aggregate demand for the product in the relevant market. Because of the income effect and the substitution effect, demand is negatively related to price, as usual. The slope of the demand curve is negative and therefore downward sloping. The general form of the demand relationship is

$$Q_D = a - bP \quad \text{or, rewritten,} \quad P = a/b - (1/b)Q_D$$

Therefore, total revenue $= TR = P \times Q = (a/b)Q_D - (1/b)Q_D^2$

Marginal revenue is the change in revenue given a change in the quantity demanded. Because an increase in quantity requires a lower price, the marginal revenue schedule is steeper than the demand schedule. If the demand schedule is linear, then the marginal revenue curve is twice as steep as the demand schedule.[5]

$$MR = \Delta TR/\Delta Q = (a/b) - (2/b)Q_D$$

The demand and marginal revenue relationship is expressed in Exhibit 10.

---

[4] When a network-based device reaches a 30 percent share, the next 50 percentage points are cheaper to promote, according to McGuigan, Moyer, and Harris (2016).

[5] Marginal revenue can be found using the technique shown in Section 3.1 or, for readers who are familiar with calculus, by taking the derivative of the total revenue function: $MR = \Delta TR/\Delta Q = (a/b) - (2/b)Q_D$.

Monopoly Markets: Demand/Supply and Optimal Price/Output

Exhibit 10: Monopolist's Demand and Marginal Revenue

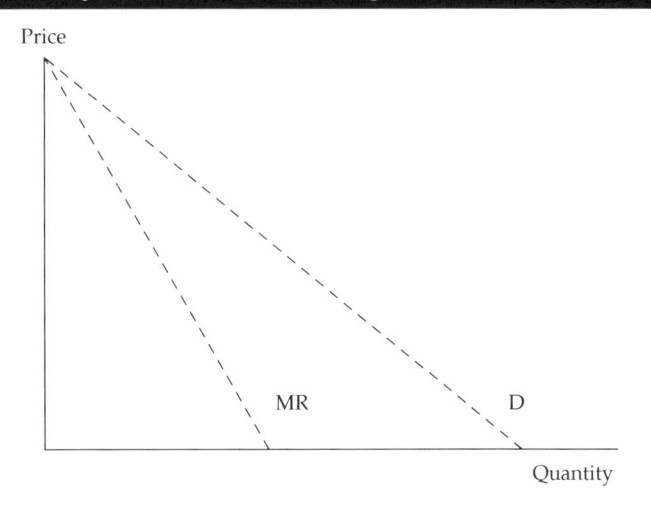

Suppose a company operating on a remote island is the single seller of natural gas. Demand for its product can be expressed as

$Q_D = 400 - 0.5P$, which can be rearranged as

$P = 800 - 2Q_D$

Total revenue is $P \times Q = \text{TR} = 800Q_D - 2Q_D^2$, and marginal revenue is MR = 800 − $4Q_D$.[6]

In Exhibit 10, the demand curve's intercept is 800 and the slope is −2. The marginal revenue curve in Exhibit 10 has an intercept of 800 and a slope of −4.

Average revenue is TR/Q_D; therefore, AR = $800 - 2Q_D$, which is the same as the demand function. In the monopoly market model, average revenue is the same as the market demand schedule.

Supply Analysis in Monopoly Markets

A monopolist's supply analysis is based on the firm's cost structure. As in the market structures of monopolistic competition and oligopoly, the monopolist does not have a well-defined supply function that determines the optimal output level and the price to charge. The optimal output is the profit-maximizing output level. The profit-maximizing level of output occurs where marginal revenue equals marginal cost, MR = MC.

Assume the natural gas company has determined that its total cost can be expressed as

$\text{TC} = 20{,}000 + 50Q + 3Q^2$

Marginal cost is $\Delta \text{TC}/\Delta Q = \text{MC} = 50 + 6Q$.[7]

Supply and demand can be combined to determine the profit-maximizing level of output. Exhibit 11 combines the monopolist's demand and cost functions.

---

6 MR = $\Delta \text{TR}/\Delta Q$ = 800 − 4Q.
7 The marginal cost equation can be found in this case by applying the technique used to find the marginal revenue equation in Section 3.1, or by taking the derivative of the total cost function.

Exhibit 11: Monopolist's Demand, Marginal Revenue, and Cost Structures

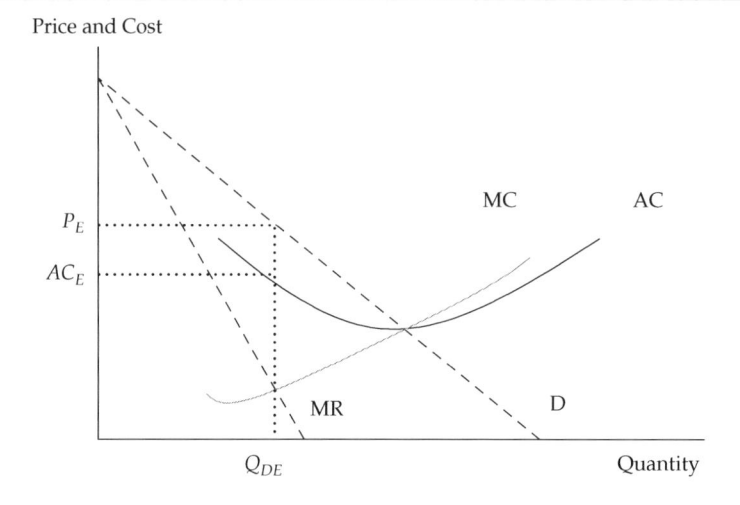

In Exhibit 11, the demand and marginal revenue functions are clearly defined by the aggregate market. However, the monopolist does not have a supply curve. The quantity that maximizes profit is determined by the intersection of MC and MR, Q_{DE}.

The price consumers are willing to pay for this level of output is P_E, as determined by the demand curve, P_E.

The profit-maximizing level of output is MR = MC: $800 - 4Q_D = 50 + 6Q_D$; therefore, $Q_D = 75$ when profit is maximized.

Total profit equals total revenue minus total cost:

$$\pi = 800Q - 2Q_D^2 - (20,000 + 50Q_D + 3Q_D^2) = -20,000 + 750Q_D - 5Q_D^2$$

Profit is represented by the difference between the area of the rectangle $Q_{DE} \times P_E$, representing total revenue, and the area of the rectangle $Q_{DE} \times AC_E$, representing total cost.

Optimal Price and Output in Monopoly Markets

Continuing the natural gas example from above, the total profit function can be solved using the quadratic formula.[8] Another method to solve the profit function is to evaluate $\Delta\pi/\Delta Q_D$ and set it equal to zero. This identifies the point at which profit is unaffected by changes in output.[9] Of course, this will give the same result as we found by equating marginal revenue with marginal cost. The monopoly will maximize profits when $Q^* = 75$ units of output and the price is set from the demand curve at 650.

$P^* = 800 - 2(75) = 650$ per unit

To find total maximum profits, substitute these values into the profit function above:

$$\pi = -20,000 + 750Q_D - 5Q_D^2 = -20,000 + 750(75) - 5(75^2) = 8,125$$

Note that the price and output combination that maximizes profit occurs in the elastic portion of the demand curve in Exhibit 11. This must be so because marginal revenue and marginal cost will always intersect where marginal revenue is positive.

---

[8] The quadratic formula, where $aQ^2 + bQ + c = 0$, is $Q = \left\{-b \pm \sqrt{(b^2 - 4ac)}\right\}/2a$.
[9] Maximum profit occurs where $\Delta\pi/\Delta Q_D = 0 = 750 - 10Q_D$. Therefore, profits are maximized at $Q_D = 75$.

Monopoly Markets: Demand/Supply and Optimal Price/Output

This fact implies that quantity demanded responds more than proportionately to price changes, i.e. demand is elastic, at the point at which MC = MR. As noted earlier, the relationship between marginal revenue and price elasticity, E_P, is:

$MR = P[1 - 1/E_P]$

In monopoly, MR = MC; therefore,

$P[1 - 1/E_P] = MC$

The firm can use this relationship to determine the profit-maximizing price if the firm knows its cost structure and the price elasticity of demand, E_P. For example, assume the firm knows that its marginal cost is constant at 75 and recent market analysis indicates that price elasticity is estimated to be 1.5. The optimal price is solved as

$P[1 - 1/1.5] = 75$ and

$P = 225$

Exhibit 11 indicated that the monopolist wants to produce at Q_E and charge the price of P_E. Suppose this is a natural monopoly that is operating as a government franchise under regulation. Natural monopolies are usually found where production is based on significant economies of scale and declining cost structure in the market. Examples include electric power generation, natural gas distribution, and the water and sewer industries. These are often called public utilities. Exhibit 12 illustrates such a market in long-run equilibrium.

Exhibit 12: Natural Monopoly in a Regulated Pricing Environment

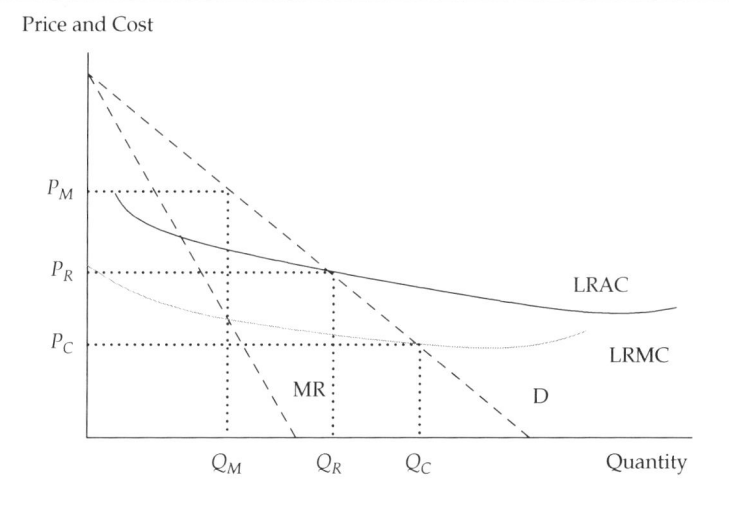

In Exhibit 12, three possible pricing and output solutions are presented. The first is what the monopolist would do without regulation: The monopolist would seek to maximize profits by producing Q_M units of the product, where long-run marginal cost equals marginal revenue, LRMC = MR. To maximize profits, the monopolist would raise the price to the level the demand curve will accept, P_M.

In perfect competition, the price and output equilibrium occurs where price is equal to the marginal cost of producing the incremental unit of the product. In a competitive market, the quantity produced would be higher, Q_C, and the price lower, P_C. For this regulated monopoly, the competitive solution would be unfair because at output Q_C, the price P_C would not cover the average cost of production. One possibility is to subsidize the difference between the long-run average cost, LRAC, and the competitive price, P_C, for each unit sold.

Another solution is for the regulator to set the price at the point where long-run average cost equals average revenue. Recall that the demand curve represents the average revenue the firm receives at each output level. The government regulator will attempt to determine the monopolistic firm's long-run average cost and set the output and price so that the firm receives a fair return on the owners' invested capital. The regulatory solution is output level Q_R, with the price set at P_R. Therefore, the regulatory solution is found between the unregulated monopoly equilibrium and the competitive equilibrium.

8. PRICE DISCRIMINATION AND CONSUMER SURPLUS

☐ describe pricing strategy under each market structure

Monopolists can be either more or less effective in taking advantage of their market structure. At one extreme, we have a monopolist that charges prices and supplies quantities that are the same as they would be in perfect competition; this scenario may be a result of regulation or threat of entry (if the monopolist charged more, another company could come in and price the former monopolist out of the market). At the opposite extreme, hated by all consumers and economists, is the monopolist that extracts the entire consumer surplus. This scenario is called **first-degree price discrimination**, where a monopolist can charge each customer the highest price the customer is willing to pay. This is called price discrimination because the monopolist charges a different price to each client. How can this be? For example, if the monopolist knows the exact demand schedule of the customer, then the monopolist can capture the entire consumer surplus. In practice, the monopolist can measure how often the product is used and charges the customer the highest price the consumer is willing to pay for that unit of good. Another possibility is that public price disclosure is non-existent, so that no customer knows what the other customers are paying. Interestingly, not every consumer is worse off in this case, because some consumers may be charged a price that is below that of monopoly, as long as the marginal revenue exceeds the marginal cost.

In **second-degree price discrimination** the monopolist offers a menu of quantity-based pricing options designed to induce customers to self-select based on how highly they value the product. Such mechanisms include volume discounts, volume surcharges, coupons, product bundling, and restrictions on use. In practice, producers can use not just the quantity but also the quality (e.g., "professional grade") to charge more to customers that value the product highly.

Third-degree price discrimination happens when customers are segregated by demographic or other traits. For example, some econometric software is licensed this way: A student version can handle only small datasets and is sold for a low price; a professional version can handle very large datasets and is sold at a much higher price because corporations need to compute the estimates for their business and are therefore willing to pay more for a license. Another example is that airlines know that passengers who want to fly somewhere and come back the same day are most likely business people; therefore, one-day roundtrip tickets are generally more expensive than tickets with a return flight at a later date or over a weekend.

Price discrimination has many practical applications when the seller has pricing power. The best way to understand how this concept works is to think of consumer surplus: As seen in this reading, a consumer may be willing to pay more for the first unit of a good, but to buy a second unit she will want to pay a lower price, thus getting a better deal on the first unit. In practice, sellers can sometimes use income and substitution effects to their advantage. Think of something you often buy, perhaps lunch at your favorite café. How much would you be willing to pay for a "lunch club membership card" that would allow you to purchase lunches at, say, half price? If the café could extract from you the maximum amount each month that you would be willing to pay for the half-price option, then it would successfully have removed the income effect from you in the form of a monthly fixed fee. Notice that a downward-sloping demand curve implies that you would end up buying more lunches each month than before you purchased the discount card, even though you would be no better or worse off than before. This is a way that sellers are sometimes able to extract consumer surplus by means of creative pricing schemes. It's a common practice among big-box retailers, sports clubs, and other users of what is called "two-part tariff pricing," as in the example below.

EXAMPLE 3

Price Discrimination

Nicole's monthly demand for visits to her health club is given by the following equation: $Q_D = 20 - 4P$, where Q_D is visits per month and P is euros per visit. The health club's marginal cost is fixed at €2 per visit.

1. Draw Nicole's demand curve for health club visits per month.

Solution to 1:

$Q_D = 20 - 4P$, so when $P = 0$, $Q_D = 20$. Inverting, $P = 5 - 0.25Q_D$, so when $Q = 0$, $P = 5$.

2. If the club charged a price per visit equal to its marginal cost, how many visits would Nicole make per month?

Solution to 2:

$Q_D = 20 - 4(2) = 12$. Nicole would make 12 visits per month at a price of €2 per visit.

3. How much consumer surplus would Nicole enjoy at that price?

Solution to 3:

Nicole's consumer surplus can be measured as the area under her demand curve and above the price she pays for a total of 12 visits, or $(0.5)(12)(3) = 18$. Nicole would enjoy a consumer surplus of €18 per month.

4. How much could the club charge Nicole each month for a membership fee?

Solution to 4:

The club could extract all of Nicole's consumer surplus by charging her a monthly membership fee of €18 plus a per-visit price of €2. This pricing method is called a two-part tariff because it assesses one price per unit of

> the item purchased plus a per-month fee (sometimes called an "entry fee") equal to the buyer's consumer surplus evaluated at the per-unit price.

9. MONOPOLY MARKETS: LONG-RUN EQUILIBRIUM

☐ explain factors affecting long-run equilibrium under each market structure

The unregulated monopoly market structure can produce economic profits in the long run. In the long run, all factors of production are variable, while in the short run, some factors of production are fixed. Generally, the short-run factor that is fixed is the capital investment, such as the factory, machinery, production technology, available arable land, and so forth. The long-run solution allows for all inputs, including technology, to change. In order to maintain a monopoly market position in the long run, the firm must be protected by substantial and ongoing barriers to entry. If the monopoly position is the result of a patent, then new patents must be continuously added to prevent the entry of other firms into the market.

For regulated monopolies, such as natural monopolies, there are a variety of long-run solutions. One solution is to set the price equal to marginal cost, $P = MC$. However, that price will not likely be high enough to cover the average cost of production, as Exhibit 19 illustrated. The answer is to provide a subsidy sufficient to compensate the firm. The national rail system in the United States, Amtrak, is an example of a regulated monopoly operating with a government subsidy.

National ownership of the monopoly is another solution. Nationalization of the natural monopoly has been a popular solution in Europe and other parts of the world. The United States has generally avoided this potential solution. One problem with this arrangement is that once a price is established, consumers are unwilling to accept price increases, even as factor costs increase. Politically, raising prices on products from government-owned enterprises is highly unpopular.

Establishing a governmental entity that regulates an authorized monopoly is another popular solution. Exhibit 19 illustrated the appropriate decision rule. The regulator sets price equal to long-run average cost, $P_R = LRAC$. This solution assures that investors will receive a normal return for the risk they are taking in the market. Given that no other competitors are allowed, the risk is lower than in a highly competitive market environment. The challenge facing the regulator is determining the authentic risk-related return and the monopolist's realistic long-run average cost.

The final solution is to franchise the monopolistic firm through a bidding war. Again, the public goal is to select the winning firm based on price equaling long-run average cost. Retail outlets at rail stations and airports and concession outlets at stadiums are examples of government franchises. The long-run success of the monopoly franchise depends on its ability to meet the goal of pricing its products at the level of its long-run average cost.

Monopoly Markets: Long-Run Equilibrium

EXAMPLE 4

Monopolies and Efficiency

1. Are monopolies *always* inefficient?
   - **A.** No, because if they charge more than average cost they are nationalized.
   - **B.** Yes, because they charge all consumers more than perfectly competitive markets would.
   - **C.** No, because economies of scale and regulation (or threat of entry) may give a better outcome for buyers than perfect competition.

Solution:

C is correct. Economies of scale and regulation may make monopolies more efficient than perfect competition.

SUMMARY

In this reading, we have surveyed how economists classify market structures. We have analyzed the distinctions between the different structures that are important for understanding demand and supply relations, optimal price and output, and the factors affecting long-run profitability. We also provided guidelines for identifying market structure in practice. Among our conclusions are the following:

- Economic market structures can be grouped into four categories: perfect competition, monopolistic competition, oligopoly, and monopoly.
- The categories differ because of the following characteristics: The number of producers is many in perfect and monopolistic competition, few in oligopoly, and one in monopoly. The degree of product differentiation, the pricing power of the producer, the barriers to entry of new producers, and the level of non-price competition (e.g., advertising) are all low in perfect competition, moderate in monopolistic competition, high in oligopoly, and generally highest in monopoly.
- A financial analyst must understand the characteristics of market structures in order to better forecast a firm's future profit stream.
- The optimal marginal revenue equals marginal cost. However, only in perfect competition does the marginal revenue equal price. In the remaining structures, price generally exceeds marginal revenue because a firm can sell more units only by reducing the per unit price.
- The quantity sold is highest in perfect competition. The price in perfect competition is usually lowest, but this depends on factors such as demand elasticity and increasing returns to scale (which may reduce the producer's marginal cost). Monopolists, oligopolists, and producers in monopolistic competition attempt to differentiate their products so that they can charge higher prices.
- Typically, monopolists sell a smaller quantity at a higher price. Investors may benefit from being shareholders of monopolistic firms that have large margins and substantial positive cash flows.

- Competitive firms do not earn economic profit. There will be a market compensation for the rental of capital and of management services, but the lack of pricing power implies that there will be no extra margins.
- While in the short run firms in any market structure can have economic profits, the more competitive a market is and the lower the barriers to entry, the faster the extra profits will fade. In the long run, new entrants shrink margins and push the least efficient firms out of the market.
- Oligopoly is characterized by the importance of strategic behavior. Firms can change the price, quantity, quality, and advertisement of the product to gain an advantage over their competitors.
- Measuring market power is complicated. Ideally, econometric estimates of the elasticity of demand and supply should be computed. However, because of the lack of reliable data and the fact that elasticity changes over time (so that past data may not apply to the current situation), regulators and economists often use simpler measures.

REFERENCES

Friedman, Thomas L. 2006. The World Is Flat: A Brief History of the Twenty-first Century. New York: Farrar, Straus and Giroux.

McGuigan, James R., R. Charles Moyer, Frederick H. Harris. 2016. Managerial Economics: Applications, Strategy and Tactics. 14th ed. Mason, OH: Thomson South-Western.

PRACTICE PROBLEMS

1. A market structure characterized by many sellers with each having some pricing power and product differentiation is *best* described as:

   A. oligopoly.

   B. perfect competition.

   C. monopolistic competition.

2. A market structure with relatively few sellers of a homogeneous or standardized product is *best* described as:

   A. oligopoly.

   B. monopoly.

   C. perfect competition.

3. The demand schedule in a perfectly competitive market is given by P = 93 − 1.5Q (for Q ≤ 62) and the long-run cost structure of each company is:

   Total cost: $256 + 2Q + 4Q^2$

   Average cost: $256/Q + 2 + 4Q$

   Marginal cost: $2 + 8Q$

   New companies will enter the market at any price greater than:

   A. 8.

   B. 66.

   C. 81.

4. If companies earn economic profits in a perfectly competitive market, over the long run the supply curve will *most likely*:

   A. shift to the left.

   B. shift to the right.

   C. remain unchanged.

5. Market competitors are *least likely* to use advertising as a tool of differentiation in an industry structure identified as:

   A. monopoly.

   B. perfect competition.

   C. monopolistic competition.

6. Upsilon Natural Gas, Inc. is a monopoly enjoying very high barriers to entry. Its marginal cost is $40 and its average cost is $70. A recent market study has determined the price elasticity of demand is 1.5. The company will *most likely* set

its price at:

- A. $40.
- B. $70.
- C. $120.

7. A government entity that regulates an authorized monopoly will *most likely* base regulated prices on:

   A. marginal cost.

   B. long run average cost.

   C. first degree price discrimination.

SOLUTIONS

1. C is correct. Monopolistic competition is characterized by many sellers, differentiated products, and some pricing power.

2. A is correct. Few sellers of a homogeneous or standardized product characterizes an oligopoly.

3. B is correct. The long-run competitive equilibrium occurs where MC = AC = P for each company. Equating MC and AC implies $2 + 8Q = 256/Q + 2 + 4Q$. Solving for Q gives $Q = 8$. Equating MC with price gives $P = 2 + 8Q = 66$. Any price above 66 yields an economic profit because P = MC > AC, so new companies will enter the market.

4. B is correct. The economic profit will attract new entrants to the market and encourage existing companies to expand capacity.

5. B is correct. The product produced in a perfectly competitive market cannot be differentiated by advertising or any other means.

6. C is correct. Profits are maximized when MR = MC. For a monopoly, MR = $P[1 - 1/E_p]$. Setting this equal to MC and solving for P:

   $\$40 = P[1 - (1/1.5)] = P \times 0.333$

   $P = \$120$

7. B is correct. This allows the investors to receive a normal return for the risk they are taking in the market.

LEARNING MODULE 3

Aggregate Output, Prices, and Economic Growth

by Paul R. Kutasovic, PhD, CFA, and Richard Fritz, PhD.

Paul R. Kutasovic, PhD, CFA, is at New York Institute of Technology (USA). Richard Fritz, PhD, is at the School of Economics at Georgia Institute of Technology (USA).

LEARNING OUTCOMES

Mastery	The candidate should be able to:
☐	calculate and explain gross domestic product (GDP) using expenditure and income approaches
☐	compare the sum-of-value-added and value-of-final-output methods of calculating GDP
☐	compare nominal and real GDP and calculate and interpret the GDP deflator
☐	compare GDP, national income, personal income, and personal disposable income
☐	explain the fundamental relationship among saving, investment, the fiscal balance, and the trade balance
☐	explain how the aggregate demand curve is generated
☐	explain the aggregate supply curve in the short run and long run
☐	explain causes of movements along and shifts in aggregate demand and supply curves
☐	describe how fluctuations in aggregate demand and aggregate supply cause short-run changes in the economy and the business cycle
☐	distinguish among the following types of macroeconomic equilibria: long-run full employment, short-run recessionary gap, short-run inflationary gap, and short-run stagflation
☐	explain how a short-run macroeconomic equilibrium may occur at a level above or below full employment
☐	analyze the effect of combined changes in aggregate supply and demand on the economy

LEARNING OUTCOMES

Mastery	The candidate should be able to:
☐	describe sources, measurement, and sustainability of economic growth
☐	describe the production function approach to analyzing the sources of economic growth
☐	define and contrast input growth and growth of total factor productivity as components of economic growth

1 INTRODUCTION

Macroeconomic analysis examines a nation's aggregate output and income, its competitive and comparative advantages, the productivity of its labor force, its price level and inflation rate, and the actions of its national government and central bank. The objective of macroeconomic analysis is to address such fundamental questions as the following:

- What is an economy's aggregate output, and how is aggregate income measured?
- What factors determine the level of aggregate output/income for an economy?
- What are the levels of aggregate demand and aggregate supply of goods and services within the country?
- Is the level of output increasing or decreasing, and at what rate?
- Is the general price level stable, rising, or falling?
- Is unemployment rising or falling?
- Are households spending or saving more?
- Are workers able to produce more output for a given level of inputs?
- Are businesses investing in and expanding their productive capacity?
- Are exports (imports) rising or falling?

From an investment perspective, investors must be able to evaluate a country's current economic environment and to forecast its future economic environment in order to identify asset classes and securities that will benefit from economic trends occurring within that country. Macroeconomic variables—such as the level of inflation, unemployment, consumption, government spending, and investment—have different effects on the growth and profitability of industries within a country, the companies within those industries, and the returns of the securities issued by those companies.

The following section describes gross domestic product and related measures of domestic output and income. Short-run and long-run aggregate demand and supply curves are discussed next, followed by the causes of shifts and movements along those curves, as well as factors that affect equilibrium levels of output, prices, and interest rates. The last section discusses sources, sustainability, and measures of economic growth.

AGGREGATE OUTPUT AND INCOME

☐ calculate and explain gross domestic product (GDP) using expenditure and income approaches

☐ compare the sum-of-value-added and value-of-final-output methods of calculating GDP

☐ compare nominal and real GDP and calculate and interpret the GDP deflator

☐ compare GDP, national income, personal income, and personal disposable income

☐ explain the fundamental relationship among saving, investment, the fiscal balance, and the trade balance

The **aggregate output** of an economy is the value of all the goods and services produced during a specified period. The **aggregate income** of an economy is the value of all the payments earned by the suppliers of factors used in the production of goods and services. Because the value of the output produced must accrue to the factors of production, aggregate output and aggregate income within an economy must be equal.

There are four broad forms of payments (i.e., income): compensation of employees, rent, interest, and profits. Compensation of employees includes wages and benefits (primarily employer contributions to private pension plans and health insurance) that individuals receive in exchange for providing labor. **Rent** is payment for the use of property. **Interest** is payment for lending funds. **Profit** is the return that owners of a company receive for the use of their capital and the assumption of financial risk when making their investments. We can think of the sum of rent, interest, and profit as the *operating surplus* of a company. It represents the return on all capital used by the business.

Although businesses are the direct owners of much of the property and physical capital in the economy, by virtue of owning the businesses, households are the ultimate owners of these assets and hence the ultimate recipients of the profits. In reality, of course, a portion of profits are usually retained within businesses to help finance maintenance and expansion of capacity. Similarly, because the government is viewed as operating on a non-profit basis, any revenue it receives from ownership of companies and/or property may be viewed as being passed back to households in the form of lower taxes. Therefore, for simplicity, it is standard in macroeconomics to attribute all income to the household sector unless the analysis depends on a more precise accounting.

Aggregate *expenditure*, the total amount spent on the goods and services produced in the (domestic) economy during the period, must also be equal to aggregate output and aggregate income. Some of this expenditure, however, may come from other countries in the form of net exports. Thus, aggregate output, aggregate income, and aggregate expenditure all refer to different ways of decomposing the same quantity.

Exhibit 1 illustrates the flow of inputs, output, income, and expenditures in a very simple economy. Households supply the factors of production (labor and capital) to businesses in exchange for wages and profit (aggregate income) totaling £100. These flows are shown by the top two arrows. Companies use the inputs to produce goods and services (aggregate output) that they sell to households (aggregate expenditure) for £100. The output and expenditure flows are shown by the bottom two arrows. Aggregate output, income, and expenditure are all equal to £100.

In this simplified example, households spend all of their income on domestically produced goods and services. They do not buy non-domestic goods, save for the future, or pay taxes. Similarly, businesses do not sell internationally or to the government, and they do not invest to increase their productive capacity. These important components of the economy will be added in a later section. But first we need to discuss how output and income are measured.

Exhibit 1: Output, Income, and Expenditure in a Simple Economy: The Circular Flow

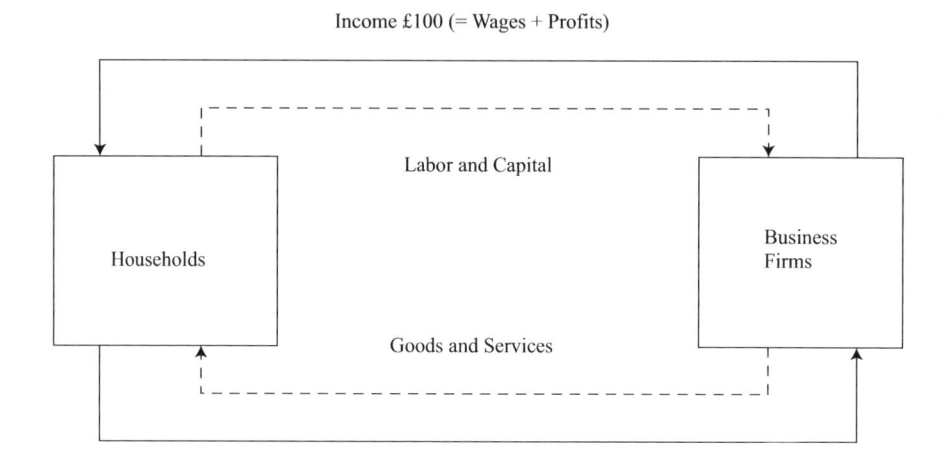

Income £100 (= Wages + Profits)

Labor and Capital

Households

Business Firms

Goods and Services

Consumption Expenditure £100

Gross Domestic Product

Gross domestic product (GDP) measures

- the market value of all final goods and services produced within the economy during a given period (output definition) or, equivalently,
- the aggregate income earned by all households, all companies, and the government within the economy during a given period (income definition).

Intuitively, GDP measures the flow of output and income in the economy. GDP represents the broadest measure of the value of economic activity occurring within a country during a given period.

Therefore, GDP can be determined in two different ways. In the income approach, GDP is calculated as the total amount earned by households and companies in the economy. In the expenditure approach, GDP is calculated as the total amount spent on the goods and services produced within the economy during a given period. For the economy as a whole, total income must equal total expenditures, so the two approaches yield the same result.

Many developed countries use a standardized methodology for measuring GDP. This methodology is described in the official handbook of the Organisation for Economic Co-Operation and Development (Paris: OECD Publishing). The OECD reports the national accounts for many developed nations. In the United States, the National Income and Product Accounts (also called NIPA, or national accounts, for short) is the official US government accounting of all the income and expenditure flows in the US economy. The national accounts are the responsibility of the US Department of

Commerce and are published in its *Survey of Current Business*. In Canada, similar data are available from Statistics Canada, whereas in China, the National Bureau of Statistics of China provides GDP data.

To ensure that GDP is measured consistently over time and across countries, the following three broad criteria are used:

- All goods and services included in the calculation of GDP *must be produced during the measurement period.* Therefore, items produced in previous periods—such as houses, cars, machinery, or equipment—are excluded. In addition, transfer payments from the government sector to individuals, such as unemployment compensation or welfare benefits, are excluded. Capital gains that accrue to individuals when their assets appreciate in value are also excluded.

- The only goods and services included in the calculation of GDP are those whose value *can be determined by being sold in the market.* This criterion enables the price of goods or services to be objectively determined. For example, a liter of extra virgin olive oil is more valuable than a liter of spring water because extra virgin olive oil has a higher market price than spring water does. The value of labor used in activities that are not sold on the market, such as commuting or gardening, is also excluded from GDP. Byproducts of production processes are also excluded if they have no explicit market value, such as air pollution, water pollution, and acid rain.

- Only the market value of final goods and services is included in GDP. Final goods and services are those that are not resold. *Intermediate goods* are goods that are resold or used to produce another good. Note that "intermediate goods" should not be confused with inventories and "final goods" should not be confused with so-called final sales. The value of intermediate goods is excluded from GDP because additional value is added during the production process, and all the value added during the entire production process is reflected in the final sale price of the finished good. An alternative approach to measuring GDP is summing all the value added during the production and distribution processes. The most direct approach, however, is to sum the market value of all the final goods and services produced within the economy during a given period.

Two distinct, but closely related, measurement methods can be used to calculate GDP based on expenditures: value of final output and sum of value added. Exhibit 2 illustrates these two methods. In this example, a farmer sells wheat to a miller. The miller grinds the wheat into flour and sells it to a baker, who makes bread and sells it to a retailer. Finally, the bread is sold to retail customers. The wheat and flour are both intermediate goods in this example because they are used as inputs to produce another good. Thus, they are not counted (directly) in GDP. For the purposes of GDP, the value of the final product is €1.00, which includes the value added by the bread retailer as a distributor of the bread. If, in contrast, the baker sold directly to the public, the value counted in GDP would be the price at which the baker sold the bread, €0.78. The left column of the exhibit shows the total revenue received at each stage of the process, whereas the right column shows the value added at each stage. Note that the market value of the final product (€1.00) is equal to the sum of the value added at each of the stages. Thus, the contribution to GDP can be measured as either the final sale price or the sum of the value added at each stage.

Exhibit 2: Value of Final Product Equals Income Created

	Receipts at Each Stage (€)	Value Added (= Income Created) at Each Stage (€)	
Receipts of farmer from miller	0.15	0.15	Value added by farmer
Receipts of miller from baker	0.46	0.31	Value added by miller
Receipts of baker from retailer	0.78	0.32	Value added by baker
Receipts of retailer from final customer	1.00	0.22	Value added by retailer
	1.00	1.00	
	Value of final output	Total value added = Total income created	

EXAMPLE 1

Contribution of Automobile Production to GDP

1. Exhibit 3 provides simplified information on the cost of producing an automobile in the United States at various stages of the production process. The example assumes the automobile is produced and sold domestically and assumes no imported material is used. Calculate the contribution of automobile production to GDP using the value-added method, and show that it is equivalent to the expenditure method. What effect would the use of imported steel or plastics have on GDP?

Exhibit 3: Cost of Producing Automobiles

Stage of Production	Sales Value ($)
1. Production of basic materials	
Steel	1,000
Plastics	3,000
Semiconductors	1,000
2. Assembly of automobile (manufacturer price)	15,000
3. Wholesale price for automobile dealer	16,000
4. Retail price	18,000

Solution:

GDP includes only the value of final goods and ignores intermediate goods in order to avoid double counting. Thus, the final sale price of $18,000 and not the total sales value of $54,000 (summing sales at all the levels of production) would be included in GDP. Alternatively, we can avoid double counting by calculating and summing the value added at each stage. At each stage of production, the difference between what a company pays for its inputs and what it receives for the product is its contribution to GDP. The value added for each stage of production is computed as follows:

Stage of Production	Sales Value ($)	Value Added ($)	
1. Production of basic materials			
Steel	1,000	1,000	
Plastics	3,000	3,000	
Semiconductors	1,000	1,000	
Total inputs		5,000	(sum of three inputs)
2. Assembly of car (manufacturer price)	15,000	10,000	= (15,000 − 5,000)
3. Wholesale price for car dealer	16,000	1,000	= (16,000 − 15,000)
4. Retail price	18,000	2,000	= (18,000 − 16,000)
Total expenditures	18,000		
Total value added		18,000	

Thus, the sum of the value added by each stage of production is equal to $18,000, which is equal to the final selling price of the automobile. If some of the inputs (steel, plastics, or semiconductors) are imported, the value added would be reduced by the amount paid for the imports.

Goods and Services Included at Imputed Values

As a general rule, only the value of goods and services whose *value can be determined by being sold in the market* are included in the measurement of GDP. Owner-occupied housing and government services, however, are two examples of services that are not sold in the marketplace but are still included in the measurement of GDP.

When a household (individual) rents a place to live, she is buying housing services. The household pays the owner of the property rent in exchange for shelter. The income that a property owner receives is included in the calculation of GDP. When a household purchases a home, however, it is implicitly paying itself in exchange for the shelter. As a result, the government must estimate (impute) a value for this owner-occupied rent, which is then added to GDP.

The value of government services provided by police officers, firemen, judges, and other government officials is a key factor that affects the level of economic activity. Valuing these services is difficult, however, because they are not sold in a market like other services; individual customers cannot decide how much to consume or how much they are willing to pay. Therefore, these services are simply included in GDP at their cost (e.g., wages paid) with no value added attributed to the production process.

For simplicity and global comparability, the number of goods and services with imputed values that are included in the measurement of GDP are limited. In general, non-market activity is excluded from GDP. Thus, activities performed for one's own benefit, such as cooking, cleaning, and home repair, are excluded. Activities in the so-called underground economy are also excluded. The underground economy reflects economic activity that people hide from the government either because it is illegal or because they are attempting to evade taxation. Undocumented laborers who are paid "off the books" are one example. The illegal drug trade is another. Similarly, barter transactions, such as neighbors exchanging services with each other (e.g., helping your neighbor repair his fence in exchange for him plowing your garden), are excluded from GDP.

Exhibit 4 shows a historical study on the estimated size of the underground economy in various countries as a percentage of nominal GDP. The estimates range from 8% in the United States to 60% in Peru. Based on these estimates, the US national income accounts fail to account for roughly 7.4% (= 8/108) of economic activity, whereas in Peru, the national accounts miss roughly 37.5% (= 60/160) of the economy. For most of the countries shown, the national accounts miss 12%–20% of the economy.

Exhibit 4: Underground Economy as a Percentage of Nominal GDP (2006)

Country	Underground Economy as a Percentage of Nominal GDP (%)
Peru	60.0
Mexico	32.1
South Korea	27.5
Costa Rica	26.8
Greece	26.0
India	24.4
Italy	23.1
Spain	20.2
Sweden	16.3
Germany	15.4
Canada	14.1
China	14.0
France	13.2
Japan	8.9
United States	8.0

Source: Friedrich Schneider and Andreas Buehm, Linz University, 2009.

It should be clear from these estimates of the underground economy that the reliability of official GDP data varies considerably across countries. Failure to capture a significant portion of activity is one problem. Poor data collection practices and unreliable statistical methods within the official accounts are also potential problems.

Nominal and Real GDP

To evaluate an economy's health, it is often useful to remove the effect of changes in the general price level on GDP because higher (lower) income driven solely by changes in the price level is not indicative of a higher (lower) level of economic activity. To account for these effects, economists use **real GDP**, which indicates what would have been the total expenditures on the output of goods and services if prices were unchanged. **Per capita real GDP** (real GDP divided by the size of the population) has often been used as a measure of the average standard of living in a country.

Suppose we are interested in measuring the GDP of an economy. For the sake of simplicity, suppose that the economy consists of a single automobile maker and that in 2019, 300,000 vehicles are produced with an average market price of €18,750. GDP in 2019 would be €5,625,000,000. Economists define the value of goods and services measured at current prices as **nominal GDP**. Suppose that in 2020, 300,000 vehicles are again produced but that the average market price for a vehicle increases by 7% to €20,062.50. GDP in 2020 would be €6,018,750,000. Even though no more cars were produced in 2020 than in 2019, it appears that the economy grew by (€6,018,750,000/€5,625,000,000) − 1 = 7% between 2019 and 2020, although it actually did not grow at all.

Aggregate Output and Income

Nominal and real GDP can be expressed as

Nominal GDP$_t$ = $P_t \times Q_t$

where

P_t = prices in year t

Q_t = quantity produced in year t

Real GDP$_t$ = $P_B \times Q_t$

where

P_B = prices in the base year

Taking the base year to be 2019 and putting in the 2019 and 2020 numbers gives the following:

Nominal GDP$_{2019}$ = (€18,750 × 300,000) = €5,625,000,000

Real GDP$_{2019}$ = (€18,750 × 300,000) = €5,625,000,000

Nominal GDP$_{2020}$ = (€20,062.50 × 300,000) = €6,018,750,000

Real GDP$_{2020}$ = (€18,750 × 300,000) = €5,625,000,000

In this example, real GDP did not change between 2019 and 2020 because the total output remained the same: 300,000 vehicles. The difference between nominal GDP in 2020 and real GDP in 2020 was the 7% inflation rate.

Now suppose that the auto manufacturer produced 3% more vehicles in 2020 than in 2019 (i.e., production in 2020 was 309,000 vehicles). Real GDP would increase by 3% from 2019 to 2020. With a 7% increase in prices, nominal GDP for 2020 would now be as follows:

Nominal GDP$_{2020}$ = (1.03 × 300,000) × (1.07 × €18,750)

= (309,000 × €20,062.50)

= €6,199,312,500

The **implicit price deflator for GDP**, or simply the **GDP deflator**, is defined as follows:

GDP deflator = $\dfrac{\text{Value of current year output at current year prices}}{\text{Value of current year output at base year prices}} \times 100$

Thus, in the example, the GDP deflator for 2020 is [(309,000 × €20,062.50)/(309,000 × €18,750)](100) = (1.07)(100) = 107. The GDP deflator broadly measures the aggregate changes in prices across the overall economy, and hence changes in the deflator provide a useful gauge of inflation within the economy.

Real GDP is equal to nominal GDP divided by the GDP deflator scaled by 100:

Real GDP = Nominal GDP/(GDP deflator/100)

This relation gives the GDP deflator its name. That is, the measure of GDP in terms of current prices, nominal GDP, is adjusted for inflation by dividing it by the deflator. The expression also shows that the GDP deflator is the ratio of nominal GDP to real GDP scaled by 100:

GDP deflator = (Nominal GDP/Real GDP) × 100

Thus, real GDP for 2020 would be

Real GDP$_{2020}$ = Nominal GDP/(GDP deflator/100)

= €6,199,312,500/(107/100)

= €5,793,750,000

Note that €5,793,750,000 represents 3% real growth over 2019 GDP and 3% higher real GDP for 2020 than under the assumption of no growth in unit car sales in 2020.

What would be the increase in *nominal* GDP for 2020 compared with 2019 with the 3% greater automobile production and 7% inflation?

(Nominal GDP$_{2020}$/Nominal GDP$_{2019}$) − 1

= (€6,199,312,500/€5,625,000,000) − 1

= 0.102

So, nominal GDP would increase by 10.2%, which equals (1.07 × 1.03) − 1, or approximately 7% + 3% = 10%. Which number is more informative about growth in economic activity: 3% real growth or 10.2% nominal growth? The real growth rate is more informative because it exactly captures increases in output. Nominal growth, by blending price changes with output changes, is less directly informative about output changes. In summary, real economic growth is measured by the percentage change in real GDP. When measuring real economic activity or when comparing one nation's economy with another, real GDP and real GDP growth should be used because they more closely reflect the quantity of output available for consumption and investment.

EXAMPLE 2

Calculating the GDP Deflator

1. John Lambert is an equity analyst with Equitytrust, an investment management firm that primarily invests in domestic stocks and bonds in a hypothetical country. Equitytrust's investment policy committee is concerned about the possibility of inflation. The implicit GDP deflator is an important measure of the overall price level in the economy, and changes in the deflator provide an important gauge of inflation within the economy. Released GDP data are shown in Exhibit 5. The committee asks Lambert to use the GDP data to calculate the implicit GDP price deflator from 2016 to 2020 and the inflation rate for 2020.

Exhibit 5: Real and Nominal GDP

Seasonally adjusted at annual rates (SAAR)

	2016	2017	2018	2019	2020
GDP at market prices	1,822,808	1,897,531	1,990,183	1,994,911	2,035,506
Real GDP	1,659,195	1,698,153	1,747,478	1,762,561	1,786,677

Solution:

The implicit GDP price deflator measures inflation across all sectors of the economy, including the consumer, business, government, exports, and imports. It is calculated as the ratio of nominal to real GDP and reported as an index number with the base year deflator equal to 100. The implicit GDP price deflator for the economy for 2020 is calculated as (2,035,506/1,786,677) × 100 = 113.9. The results for the other years are shown in the following table:

	2016	2017	2018	2019	2020
GDP at market prices ($ millions)	1,822,808	1,897,531	1,990,183	1,994,911	2,035,506
Real GDP (2007 $ millions)	1,659,195	1,698,153	1,747,478	1,762,561	1,786,677
Implicit GDP price deflator	113.9	111.7	113.9	113.2	113.9

For 2016, the annual inflation rate is equal to [(113.9/113.2) − 1] or 0.62 percent. This shows that Canada experienced a very low rate of inflation in 2016.

The Components of GDP

Having defined GDP and discussed how it is measured, we can now consider the major components of GDP, the flows among the four major sectors of the economy—the household sector, the business sector, the government sector, and the foreign or external sector (consisting of transactions with the "rest of the world")—and the markets through which they interact. An expression for GDP, based on the expenditure approach, is

$$\text{GDP} = C + I + G + (X − M) = (C + G^C) + (I + G^I) + (X − M) \qquad (1)$$

where

C = consumer spending on final goods and services

I = gross private domestic investment, which includes business investment in capital goods (e.g., fixed capital such as plant and equipment) and changes in inventory (**inventory investment**)

G = government spending on final goods and services for both current consumption and investment in capital goods = $G^C + G^I$

X = exports

M = imports

Exhibit 6 shows the flow of expenditures, income, and financing among the four sectors of the economy and the three principal markets. In the exhibit, solid arrows point in the direction of expenditure on final goods and services. For simplicity, corresponding flows of output are not shown separately. The flow of factors of production is also shown with a solid arrow. Financial flows, including income and net taxes, are shown with dashed arrows pointing to the recipient of funds.

Exhibit 6: Output, Income, and Expenditure Flows

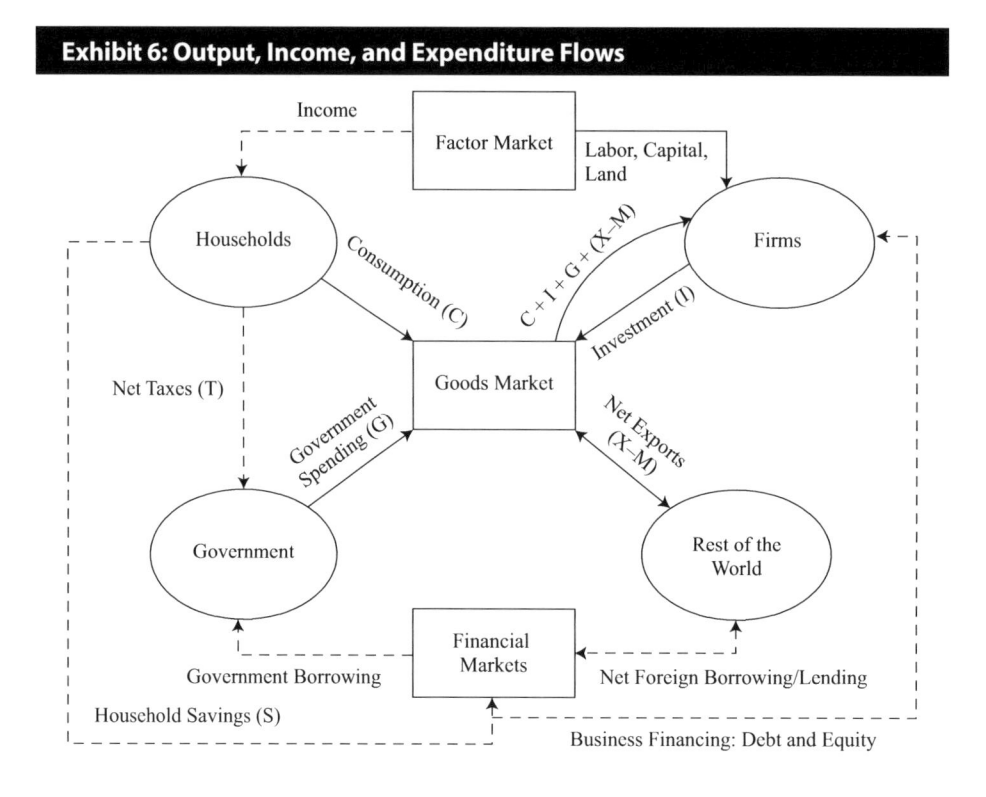

[Diagram showing circular flow of output, income, and expenditure among Households, Firms, Government, Rest of the World, Factor Market, Goods Market, and Financial Markets. Flows include Income, Labor/Capital/Land, Consumption (C), Investment (I), Government Spending (G), Net Exports (X−M), Net Taxes (T), Household Savings (S), Government Borrowing, Net Foreign Borrowing/Lending, Business Financing: Debt and Equity, and C+I+G+(X−M).]

The Household and Business Sectors

The very top portion of Exhibit 6 shows the services of labor, land, and capital flowing through the *factor market* to business firms and the flow of income back from firms to households. Households spend part of their income on consumption (C) and save (S) part of their income for future consumption. Current consumption expenditure flows through the *goods market* to the business sector. Household saving flows into the *financial markets*, where it provides funding for businesses that need to borrow or raise equity capital. Firms borrow or raise equity primarily to finance investment (I) in inventory, property, plant, and equipment. Investment (I) is shown flowing from firms through the goods market and back to firms because the business sector both demands and produces the goods needed to build productive capacity (*capital goods*).

In most developed economies, such as Italy and the United States, expenditures on capital goods represent a significant portion of GDP. As we will examine in greater detail later, investment spending is an important determinant of an economy's long-term growth rate. At the same time, investment spending is the most volatile component of the economy, and changes in capital spending—especially spending on inventories—are one of the main factors causing short-run economic fluctuations.

The Government Sector

The government sector collects taxes from households and businesses. For simplicity, only the taxes collected from the household sector are shown in Exhibit 6. In turn, the government sector purchases goods and services (G) for both consumption and investment from the business sector. For example, the government sector hires construction companies to build roads, schools, and other infrastructure goods. Government expenditure (G) also reflects spending on the military, police and fire protection, the postal service, and other government services. To keep Exhibit 6 simple, however, we combine consumption and investment expenditures into government expenditure, G.

Aggregate Output and Income

Governments also make transfer payments to households. In general, such payments are designed to address social objectives such as maintaining minimum living standards, providing health care, and assisting the unemployed with retraining and temporary support. In Exhibit 6, transfer payments are subtracted from taxes and reflected in net taxes (T).

Transfer payments are not included in government expenditures on goods and services (G) because they represent a monetary transfer by the government of tax revenue back to individuals, with no corresponding receipt of goods or services. The household spending facilitated by the transfer payments is, of course, included in consumption (C) and, hence, GDP. It is worth noting that transfers do not always take the form of direct payments to beneficiaries. Instead, the government may pay for or even directly provide goods or services to individuals. For example, universal health care programs often work in this way.

If, as is usually the case, government expenditure (G) exceeds net taxes (T), then the government has a *fiscal deficit* and must borrow in the financial markets. Thus, the government may compete with businesses in the financial markets for the funds generated by household saving. The only other potential source of funds in an economy is capital flows from the rest of the world, discussed in the next section.

The External Sector

Trade and capital flows involving the rest of the world are shown in the bottom right quadrant of Exhibit 6. Net exports ($X - M$) reflect the difference between the value of goods and services sold internationally—exports (X)—and the portion of domestic consumption (C), investment (I), and government expenditure (G) that represents purchases of goods and services from the rest of the world—imports (M).

A **balance of trade deficit** means that the domestic economy is spending more on international goods and services than other nations' economies are spending on domestic goods and services. It also means that the country is spending more than it produces because domestic saving is insufficient to finance domestic investment plus the government's fiscal balance. A trade deficit must be funded by borrowing from the rest of the world through the financial markets. The rest of the world is able to provide this financing because, by definition, it must be running a corresponding trade surplus and is spending less than it produces.

It bears emphasizing that trade and capital flows between an economy and the rest of the world must balance. One area's deficit is another's surplus, and vice versa. This dynamic is an accounting identity that must hold. In effect, having allowed a country to run a trade deficit, other nations must, in aggregate, finance it. The financing terms, however, may or may not be attractive.

Relationship among Saving, Investment, the Fiscal Balance and the Trade Balance

Total expenditure on domestically produced output comes from four sources: household consumption (C), investments (I), government spending (G), and net exports ($X - M$). This can be expressed as follows:

$$\text{Expenditure} = C + I + G + (X - M)$$

Personal disposable income is equal to GDP (Y) plus transfer payments (F) minus retained earnings and depreciation (= business saving, S_B) minus direct and indirect taxes (R). Households allocate disposable income between consumption of goods and services (C) and household saving (S_H). Therefore,

$$Y + F - S_B - R = C + S_H$$

Rearranging this equation, we get

$$Y = C + S + T$$

where $T = (R - F)$ denotes net taxes and $S = (S_B + S_H)$ denotes total private sector saving.

Because total expenditures must be identical to aggregate income (Y), we have the following relationship:

$$C + S + T = C + I + G + (X - M)$$

By rearranging this equation, we get the following fundamental relationship among domestic saving, investment, the fiscal balance, and the trade balance:

$$S = I + (G - T) + (X - M) \tag{2}$$

This equation shows that domestic private saving is used or absorbed in one of three ways: investment spending (I), financing government deficits ($G - T$), and building up financial claims against overseas economies [positive trade balance, $(X - M) > 0$]. If there is a trade deficit [$(X - M) < 0$], then domestic private saving is being supplemented by inflows of foreign saving and other countries' economies are building up financial claims against the domestic economy.

By rearranging the identity, we can examine the implications of government deficits and surpluses:

$$G - T = (S - I) - (X - M)$$

A fiscal deficit [$(G - T) > 0$] implies that the private sector must save more than it invests [$(S - I) > 0$] or the country must run a trade deficit [$(X - M) < 0$] with corresponding inflow of foreign saving—or both.

Equation 2 is the key relationship that must hold in order for aggregate income and aggregate expenditure to be equal. Up to this point, we have treated it as simply an accounting identity. We now need to think of it as the outcome of explicit decisions on the part of households, businesses, government, and people in other countries. When we do so, we face the question of what underlies these decisions and how the requisite balance is established.

Economists have found that the dominant determinant of consumption spending is disposable income ($Y - S_B - T$). This relationship can be expressed formally by indicating that consumption is a function $C(\cdot)$ of disposable income,

$$C = C(Y - S_B - T)$$

or, dropping the technically correct but practically insignificant adjustment for retained earnings and depreciation (S_B), a function of GDP minus net taxes:

$$C = C(Y - T)$$

When households receive an additional unit of income, some proportion of this additional income is spent and the remainder is saved. The **marginal propensity to consume** (MPC) represents the proportion of an additional unit of disposable income that is consumed or spent. Because the amount that is not spent is saved, the **marginal propensity to save** (MPS) is MPS = 1 − MPC.

According to the consumption function, either an increase in real income or a decrease in taxes will increase aggregate consumption. Somewhat more sophisticated models of consumption recognize that consumption depends not only on current disposable income but also on wealth. Except for the very rich, individuals tend to spend a higher fraction of their current income as their wealth increases because with higher current wealth, there is less need to save to provide for future consumption.

Exhibit 7 shows household consumption expenditures as a percentage of GDP for selected countries.

Exhibit 7: Household Final Consumption Expenditures as a Percentage of GDP, 2018

United States	68.0%
Mexico	64.8
Italy	60.3
Japan	55.6
Canada	57.9
France	53.9
Germany	52.1

Source: The World Bank, https://data.worldbank.org/indicator/NE.CON.PRVT.ZS

These figures reflect the *average propensity to consume* (APC)—that is, the ratio C/Y—rather than a measure of how the next unit of income would be divided between spending and saving, the MPC. However, they are reasonable proxies for the MPC in each country. Comparing Germany's 55.0% APC with Mexico's 67.8%, the implication is that the Mexican economy is more sensitive to changes in disposable household income than is the German economy. All else being equal, macroeconomic policies that increase disposable household income, such as lowering government taxes, would have a larger effect on the economies of Mexico (67.8%) and the United States (68.3%) than similar policies would have in Germany (55.0%) or France (55.4%).

Companies are the primary source of investment spending (I). They make investment decisions in order to expand their stock of physical capital, such as building new factories or adding new equipment to existing facilities. A definition of physical capital is *any manmade aid to production*. Companies also buy investment goods, such as manufacturing plants and equipment to replace existing facilities and equipment that wear out. Total investment, including replacement of worn-out capital, is called *gross investment*, as opposed to *net investment*, which reflects only the addition of new capacity. GDP includes gross investment—hence the name *gross* domestic product. Total investment spending in such developed countries as Italy, Germany, the United Kingdom, and the United States ranged between 12% and 16% of GDP in 2015 (OECD. Stat Extracts: Country Statistical Profiles 2017, stats.oecd.org).

Investment decisions depend primarily on two factors: the level of interest rates and aggregate output/income. The level of interest rates reflects the cost of financing investment. The level of aggregate output serves as a proxy for the expected profitability of new investments. When an economy is underutilizing its resources, interest rates are typically very low, and yet investment spending often remains dormant because the expected return on new investments is also low. Conversely, when output is high and companies have little spare capacity, the expected return on new investments is high. Thus, investment decisions may be modeled as a decreasing function $I(\cdot,\cdot)$ of the **real interest rate** (nominal interest rate minus the expected rate of inflation) and an increasing function of the level of aggregate output. Formally,

$$I = I(r, Y)$$

where I is investment spending, r is the real interest rate, and Y is, as usual, aggregate income. This investment function leaves out some important drivers of investment decisions, such as the availability of new and better **technology**. Nonetheless, it reflects the two most important considerations: the cost of funding (represented by the real interest rate) and the expected profitability of the new capital (proxied by the level of aggregate output).

Many government spending decisions are insensitive to the current level of economic activity, the level of interest rates, the currency exchange rate, and other economic factors. Thus, economists often treat the level of government spending on goods and services (*G*) as an *exogenous* policy variable determined outside the macroeconomic model. In essence, this means that the adjustments required to maintain the balance among aggregate spending, income, and output must occur primarily within the private sector.

Tax policy may also be viewed as an exogenous policy tool. The actual amount of net taxes (*T*) collected, however, is closely tied to the level of economic activity. Most countries impose income taxes or value-added taxes (VAT) or both that increase with the level of income or expenditure. Similarly, at least some transfer payments to the household sector are usually based on economic need and are hence inversely related to aggregate income. Each of these factors makes net taxes (*T*) rise and fall with aggregate income, *Y*. The government's fiscal balance can be represented as

$$G - T = \overline{G} - t(Y)$$

where $\overline{G}$ is the exogenous level of government expenditure and $t(Y)$ indicates that net taxes are an (increasing) function of aggregate income, *Y*. The fiscal balance decreases (smaller deficit or larger surplus) as aggregate income (*Y*) increases and increases as income declines. This effect is called an *automatic stabilizer* because it tends to mitigate changes in aggregate output.

Net exports (*X* − *M*) are primarily a function of income in the domestic country and in the rest of the world and of the relative prices of domestic and non-domestic goods and services. As domestic income rises, some of the additional demand that is induced will be for imported goods. Thus, net exports will decline. An increase in income in the rest of the world will lead to an increase in demand for the domestic country's products and hence an increase net exports. A decrease in the relative price of domestically produced goods and services, perhaps because of a depreciation in the domestic currency, will shift demand toward these products and hence increase net exports.

3. AGGREGATE DEMAND AND AGGREGATE SUPPLY

☐ explain how the aggregate demand curve is generated

☐ explain the aggregate supply curve in the short run and long run

☐ explain causes of movements along and shifts in aggregate demand and supply curves

☐ describe how fluctuations in aggregate demand and aggregate supply cause short-run changes in the economy and the business cycle

☐ distinguish among the following types of macroeconomic equilibria: long-run full employment, short-run recessionary gap, short-run inflationary gap, and short-run stagflation

☐ explain how a short-run macroeconomic equilibrium may occur at a level above or below full employment

☐ analyze the effect of combined changes in aggregate supply and demand on the economy

Short-term fluctuations in an economy's output arise for a number of reasons. The fluctuations of output and price level can have a significant effect on issuers of securities and therefore come under close scrutiny by practitioners and policymakers.

We will build a model of aggregate demand and aggregate supply and use it to discuss how aggregate output and the level of prices are determined in the economy. **Aggregate demand** (AD) represents the quantity of goods and services that households, businesses, government, and international customers want to buy at any given level of prices. **Aggregate supply** (AS) represents the quantity of goods and services that producers are willing to supply at any given level of prices. It also reflects the amount of labor and capital that households are willing to offer into the marketplace at given real wage rates and cost of capital.

Aggregate Demand

As we will see, the **aggregate demand curve** looks like the ordinary demand curves that we encounter in microeconomics: quantity demanded increases as the price level declines. But our intuitive understanding of that relationship—lower price allows us to buy more of a good *with a given level of income*—does not apply here because income is not fixed. Instead, aggregate income/expenditure (GDP) is to be determined within the model along with the price level. Thus, we need to explain the relationship between price and quantity demanded somewhat differently.

The aggregate demand curve represents the combinations of aggregate income and the price level at which two conditions are satisfied. First, aggregate expenditure equals aggregate income. As indicated in our discussion of GDP accounting, this relation must always be true after the fact. Second, the available real money supply is willingly held by households and businesses. Recall that GDP is defined as

$GDP = C + I + G + (X - M)$,

where

C = consumer spending on final goods and services

I = gross private domestic investment

G = government spending on final goods and services

X = exports

M = imports

We assume that government spending (G) is exogenous, set by government policy. To explain why the aggregate demand curve slopes downward, we analyze how the price level in the economy affects the consumption (C), investment (I), and net export ($X - M$) components of GDP. The downward slope of the aggregate demand curve results from three effects: the **wealth effect**, the **interest rate effect**, and the **real exchange rate effect**. We assume that the nominal money supply is held constant.

Wealth Effect

The **wealth effect** is based on the concept of purchasing power of nominal wealth, including nominal value of the money held by consumers, physically or in a bank account. Nominal wealth does not change: One British pound is always worth one British pound. Similarly, one euro is worth one euro, and one yen is worth one yen. The real value, however—the value of money in terms of goods and services—is *not* fixed. It fluctuates with the prices of goods and services. Assume that our favorite loaf of bread costs one pound (£1 = one loaf of bread). If we have £10 in a pocket, then we have money that is equivalent to 10 loaves of bread. The real money holdings are therefore 10 loaves of bread.

$$\frac{£10}{\left(\frac{£1}{\text{loaf}}\right)} = 10 \text{ loaves}$$

If the price of a loaf of bread increases to £2 (£2 = one loaf of bread), the same £10 is now worth only five loaves of bread. Our real money holdings, and therefore our real wealth, have decreased. Conversely, if the price of a loaf of bread decreases to one-half pound (£0.50 = one loaf of bread), the same £10 is now worth 20 loaves of bread. Our real money holdings, and therefore our real wealth, have increased.

The effect of the change in the price level and the resulting change in the real value of money holdings give the wealth effect its name, because as the real value of our money holdings changes, so does our real wealth.

The wealth effect is one reason that the aggregate demand curve is downward sloping. An increase in the price level decreases the quantity of goods and services that can be purchased with the fixed quantity of nominal wealth—consumers are less wealthy (in real terms) and therefore demand fewer goods and services. Exhibit 8 illustrates this dynamic as the movement from Point A to Point B. An increase in the price level from P_1 to P_2 reduces income from Y_1 to Y_2. Conversely, a decrease in the price level increases the quantity of goods and services that can be purchased with the fixed quantity of money available—consumers are wealthier (in real terms) and therefore demand more goods and services.

Exhibit 8: The Aggregate Demand Curve

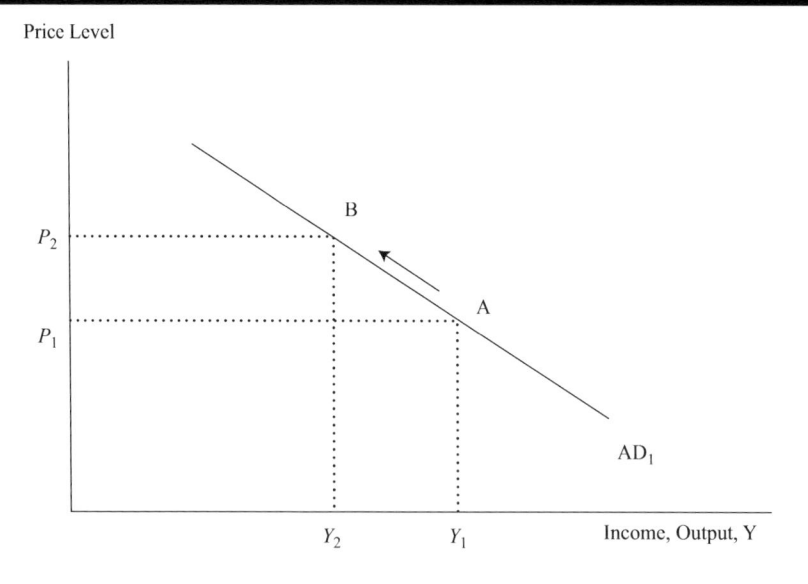

The Interest Rate Effect

When the price level changes, the demand for money also changes. For example, if the price for your lunch today is 10 euros (€10 = lunch), then we need to have 10 euros in our pocket to eat lunch. Now, assume that the price of lunch doubles to 20 euros (€20 = lunch). If we want to eat lunch, we need to get more money—our demand for money increases. With a fixed supply of money, the price of money increases. Because the price of money is the interest rate, then as the price level increases, the interest rate increases.

The converse is also true. If the price of lunch decreases to five euros (€5 = lunch), we don't need to carry around as much money as before – our demand for money decreases. With a fixed supply of money, the price of money decreases. Therefore, as the price level decreases, the interest rate decreases.

Why not just keep extra "lunches" (money) in our pocket? Because holding extra money in such liquid form means that we are giving up the interest that we could be earning by lending the money out to others (*e.g.* through purchasing a government or corporate bond or just leaving the money in a bank account and letting the bank do the lending for us). The interest we would earn is the opportunity cost of keeping money in our pocket. So, when the price level decreases, we will want to keep more of our money in interest-bearing assets and our demand for money decreases.

Changes in the interest rate affect the quantity of goods and services demanded. If interest rates increase, businesses invest less because their borrowing costs increase. This shift leads to fewer profitable projects to invest in and also negatively affects the demand for commercial real estate. In addition, higher interest rates lead to lower consumption—especially for large purchases such as automobiles or residential real estate, which are usually purchased with loans. If interest rates decrease, then businesses have more profitable projects to invest in, and consumers would be expected to spend more.

This leads us to the **interest rate effect**. A higher price level creates greater demand for money, which raises the interest rate. The higher interest rate decreases demand for investment and consumption expenditures, which leads to less demand for goods and services. Conversely, a lower price level leads to a lower demand for money, which leads to a lower interest rate. The lower interest rate increases demand for investment and consumption expenditures, which leads to more demand for goods and services.

The Real Exchange Rate Effect

An increase in the domestic price level causes appreciation of the real exchange rate. Real exchange rates will be explained later, but for the purpose of this discussion, it is important to understand that the real exchange rate is the observed, quoted nominal exchange rate adjusted for price level. So a higher price level affects the real exchange rate and makes domestic goods more expensive in other countries, reducing exports. It also makes non-domestic goods less expensive domestically, increasing imports. The result is lower demand for domestic goods and services. Conversely, a decrease in the domestic price level (assuming the price level abroad remains unchanged) leads to a depreciation of the real exchange rate. This decrease in the real exchange rate makes domestic goods less expensive in other countries, increasing exports, and non-domestic goods more expensive domestically, decreasing imports. The result is higher demand for domestic goods and services. This dynamic gives us the **real exchange rate effect**.

An additional channel affecting exchange rates involves the interest rate effect. When interest rates increase (because of a higher price level), non-domestic investors increase their demand for the domestic currency in the foreign exchange market because they want to earn the higher return on their savings. This increased demand causes the domestic currency to appreciate, which in turn increases the real exchange rate.

When interest rates decrease (because of a lower price level), a similar but opposite effect occurs. Domestic savers seek higher returns in non-domestic markets. This increased supply of the domestic currency in the foreign exchange market causes the domestic currency to depreciate, which in turn decreases the real exchange rate.

The interest rate effect just described is an additional channel through which a higher price level leads to a higher real exchange rate. The two effects are complementary, operate in the same direction and magnify the impact of the change in price level on aggregate demand. Exhibit 9 provides a summary.

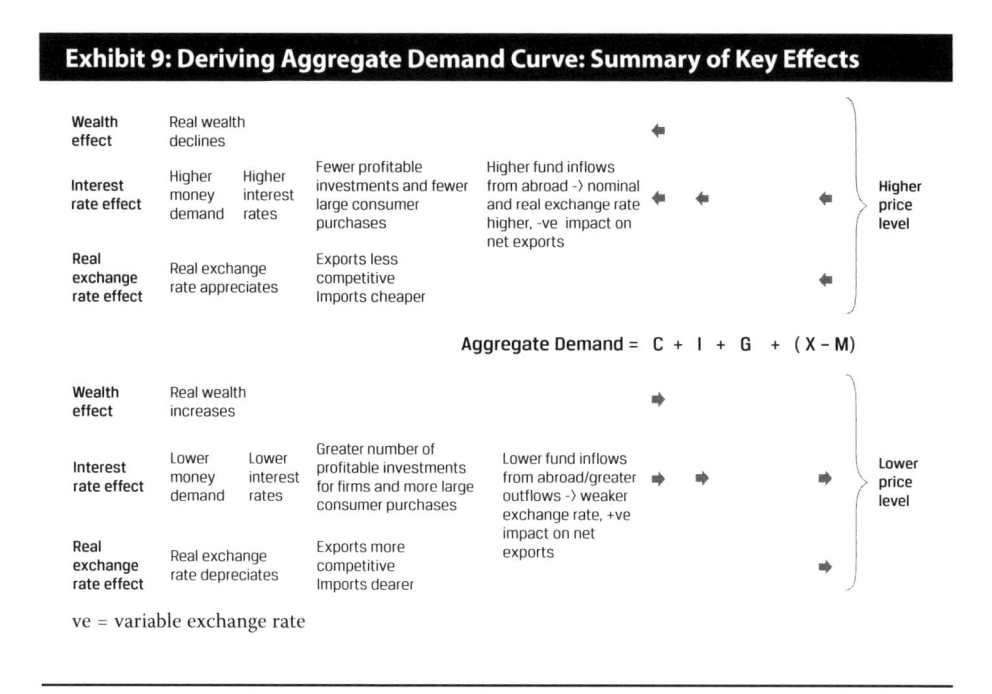

Exhibit 9: Deriving Aggregate Demand Curve: Summary of Key Effects

Wealth effect	Real wealth declines				Higher price level
Interest rate effect	Higher money demand	Higher interest rates	Fewer profitable investments and fewer large consumer purchases	Higher fund inflows from abroad -> nominal and real exchange rate higher, -ve impact on net exports	
Real exchange rate effect	Real exchange rate appreciates		Exports less competitive Imports cheaper		

Aggregate Demand = C + I + G + (X − M)

Wealth effect	Real wealth increases				Lower price level
Interest rate effect	Lower money demand	Lower interest rates	Greater number of profitable investments for firms and more large consumer purchases	Lower fund inflows from abroad/greater outflows -> weaker exchange rate, +ve impact on net exports	
Real exchange rate effect	Real exchange rate depreciates		Exports more competitive Imports dearer		

ve = variable exchange rate

EXAMPLE 3

Slope of the Aggregate Demand Curve

1. Considering the movement along the aggregate demand curve, which of the following statements best explains the interest rate effect when the price level decreases?

    A. Decrease in money demand, with a fixed money supply, leads to lower interest rates. Lower interest rates induce businesses to invest more because there is now a greater number of profitable projects. Consumers also spend more when interest rates are lower. Lower interest rates also weaken the exchange rate, boosting net exports. These effects cause output to be higher at a lower price level.

    B. Decrease in money demand, with a fixed money supply, leads to lower interest rates. Lower interest rates induce businesses to invest less because there are now fewer profitable projects. Lower interest rates also weaken the exchange rate, boosting net exports.

    C. Decrease in money demand, with a fixed money supply, leads to higher interest rates, which induce businesses to invest less and consumers to save more. Higher interest rates cause the exchange rate to appreciate, boosting net exports.

> **Solution:**
>
> A is correct. B is incorrect because the statement suggests that lower interest rates lead to less business investment. C is incorrect because the statement suggests that a lower price level leads to higher interest rates.

Aggregate Supply

Aggregate demand tells us only the relationship between the price level and the amount of output demanded at those prices. To understand what price and output level will prevail in the economy, we need to add aggregate supply, the amount of output producers are willing to provide at various prices. The **aggregate supply curve** (AS curve) represents the level of domestic output that companies will produce at each price level. Unlike the demand side, we must distinguish between the short- and long-run AS curves, which differ with respect to how wages and other input prices respond to changes in final output prices. "Long run" and "short run" are relative terms and are necessarily imprecise with respect to calendar time. The "long run" is long enough that wages, prices, and expectations can adjust but not long enough that physical capital is a variable input. Capital and the available technology to use that capital remain fixed. This condition implies a period of at least a few years and perhaps a decade. The truly long run, in which even the capital stock is variable, may be thought of as covering multiple decades. Consideration of the very long run is postponed to our subsequent discussion of economic growth.

In the very short run, perhaps a few months or quarters, companies will increase or decrease output to some degree without changing prices. Exhibit 10 illustrates this dynamic with the horizontal line labeled VSRAS. If demand is somewhat stronger than expected, companies earn higher profit by increasing output as long as they can cover their variable costs. So they will run their plant and equipment more intensively, demand more effort from their salaried employees, and increase the hours of employees who are paid on the basis of hours worked. If demand is somewhat weaker than projected, companies can run their plants less intensively, cut labor hours, and use staff to perform maintenance and carry out efficiency-enhancing projects that are often postponed during busier periods.

Exhibit 10: Aggregate Supply Curve

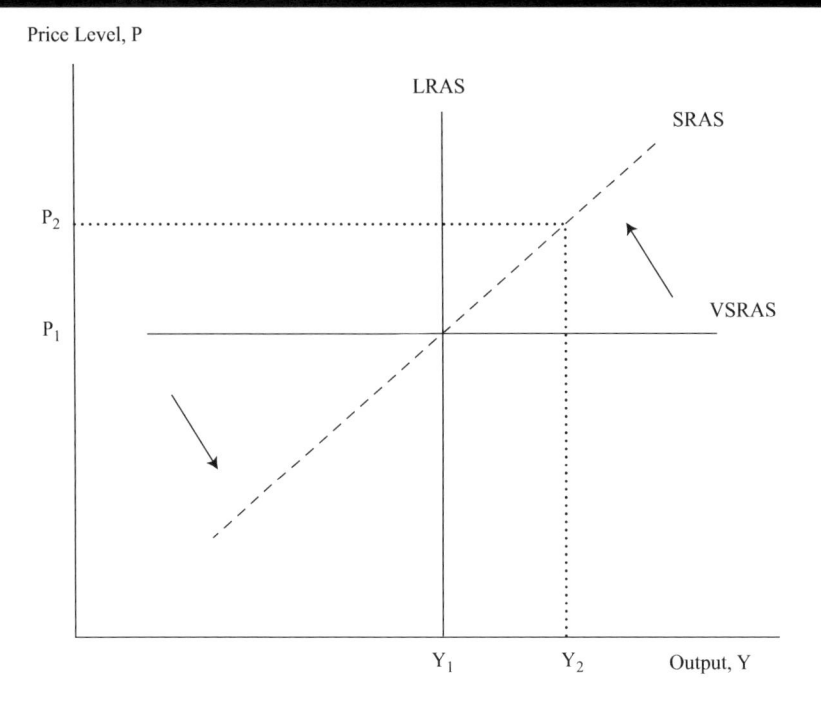

Over somewhat longer periods, the AS curve is upward sloping because more costs become variable. This dynamic is represented by the short-run aggregate supply (SRAS) curve in Exhibit 10. In most businesses, wages are adjusted once a year, but for companies with union contracts, several years may pass before the contracts expire. The prices for raw materials and other inputs may also be established under long-term contracts. Hence, wages and other input costs are relatively inflexible in the short run and do not fully adjust to changes in output prices. As the price level rises, most companies enjoy higher profit margins and hence expand production. In Exhibit 10, when prices move from P_1 to P_2, the quantity of aggregate output supplied increases from Y_1 to Y_2. Conversely, a reduction in the price level squeezes profit margins and causes companies to reduce production.

Over time, however, wages and other input prices tend to "catch up" with the prices of final goods and services. In other words, wages and prices that are inflexible or slow to adjust in the short run adjust to changes in the price level over the long run. Thus, over the long run, when the aggregate price level changes, wages and other input prices change proportionately so that the higher aggregate price level has no effect on aggregate supply. This dynamic is illustrated by the vertical long-run aggregate supply (LRAS) curve in Exhibit 10. As prices move from P_1 to P_2, the quantity of output supplied remains at Y_1 in the long run. The only change that occurs is that prices shift to a higher level (from P_1 to P_2).

The position of the LRAS curve is determined by the potential output of the economy. The amount of output produced depends on the fixed amount of capital and labor and the available technology. This classical model of aggregate supply can be expressed as

$$Y = F(\overline{K}, \overline{L}) = \overline{Y},$$

where $\overline{K}$ is the fixed amount of capital and $\overline{L}$ is the available labor supply. The stock of capital is assumed to incorporate the existing technological base. Note that investment (I) reflects replacement of worn-out capital plus the change in capital,

Aggregate Demand and Aggregate Supply

ΔK. Over short periods, net investment is assumed to have a negligible effect on aggregate supply. The available labor supply is also held constant, and workers are assumed to have a given set of skills. The long-run equilibrium level of output, Y_1 in Exhibit 10, is referred to as the *full employment*, or *natural*, level of output. At this level of output, the economy's resources are deemed to be fully employed, and (labor) *unemployment is at its natural rate*. This concept of a natural rate of unemployment assumes the macroeconomy is currently operating at an efficient and unconstrained level of production. Companies have enough spare capacity to avoid bottlenecks, and there is a modest, stable pool of unemployed workers (job seekers equal job vacancies) looking for and transitioning into new jobs.

Shifts in the Aggregate Demand Curve

In the next two sections, the aggregate demand (AD) and aggregate supply (AS) models are used to address three critical macroeconomic questions:

1. What causes an economy to expand or contract?
2. What causes inflation and changes in the level of unemployment?
3. What determines an economy's rate of sustainable growth, and how can it be measured?

Before addressing these questions, we need to distinguish between 1) the long-run growth rate of real GDP and 2) short-run fluctuations in real GDP around this long-run trend.

The business cycle is a direct result of short-term fluctuations of real GDP. It consists of periods of economic expansion and contraction. In an expansion, real GDP is increasing, the unemployment rate is declining, and capacity utilization is rising. In a contraction, real GDP is decreasing, the unemployment rate is rising, and capacity utilization is declining. Shifts in the AD and AS curves determine the short-run changes in the economy associated with the business cycle. In addition, the AD–AS model provides a framework for estimating the sustainable growth rate of an economy, which is addressed in Section 4.

From an asset allocation perspective, it is important to determine the current phase of the business cycle as well as how fast the economy is growing relative to its sustainable growth rate. The expected rate of return on equities and fixed-income securities, for example, depends on estimates of the growth rate of GDP and inflation. For equities, GDP growth is the primary determinant of aggregate corporate profits. For fixed-income securities, the expected rate of inflation determines the spread between real and nominal rates of return. In order to use the AD and AS model to analyze the economy and to make investment decisions, we need to first understand what factors cause the curves to shift.

Shifts in Aggregate Demand

In addition to price, factors that influence the level of spending by households, companies, governments, and people in other countries (i.e., the aggregate level of expenditures) will cause the AD curve to shift. A shift to the right represents an increase in aggregate demand at any price level. Exhibit 11 shows this dynamic as a shift from AD_1 to AD_2. A shift to the left represents a decrease in aggregate demand at any price level. This dynamic is indicated by a move from AD_1 to AD_3. Key factors that directly or indirectly influence the level of aggregate expenditures and cause the aggregate demand curve to shift include changes in the following:

- household wealth,
- consumer and business expectations,

- capacity utilization,
- monetary policy,
- the exchange rate,
- growth in the global economy, and
- fiscal policy (government spending and taxes).

Exhibit 11: Shifts in the Aggregate Demand Curve

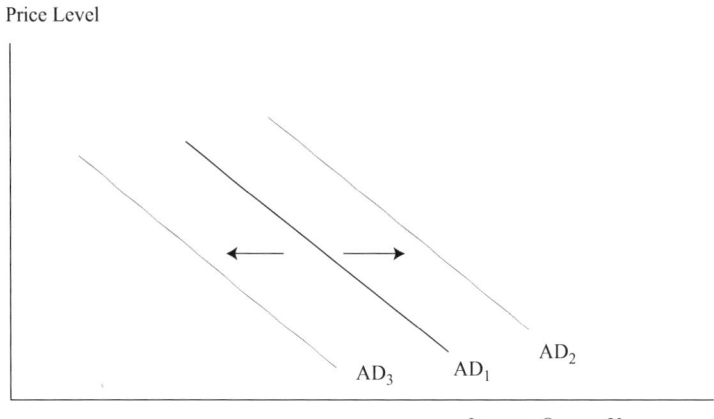

Household Wealth

Household wealth includes the value of both financial assets (e.g., cash, savings accounts, investment securities, and pensions) and real assets (e.g., real estate). The primary reason households save a portion of their current income is to accumulate wealth for consumption in the future. The proportion of disposable income that households save depends partly on the value of the financial and real assets that they have already accumulated. If these assets increase in value, households will tend to save less and spend a greater proportion of their income because they will still be able to meet their wealth accumulation goals. As a result, an increase in household wealth increases consumer spending and shifts the aggregate demand curve to the right. In contrast, a decline in wealth will reduce consumer spending and shift the AD curve to the left. This dynamic, often referred to as the **wealth effect**, provides one explanation for how changes in equity prices affect economic activity. Higher equity prices increase household wealth, which increases consumer spending and reduces the amount saved out of current income. Economic studies estimate that an increase or decrease in wealth in developed countries increases or decreases annual consumer spending by 3%–7% of the change in wealth (Case, Quigley, and Shiller 2005). A smaller but still statistically significant wealth effect has been found in a number of emerging markets (developing countries) (Funke 2004).

Aggregate Demand and Aggregate Supply

Exhibit 12: Housing Prices and the Savings Rate in the United Kingdom, 2000–2019

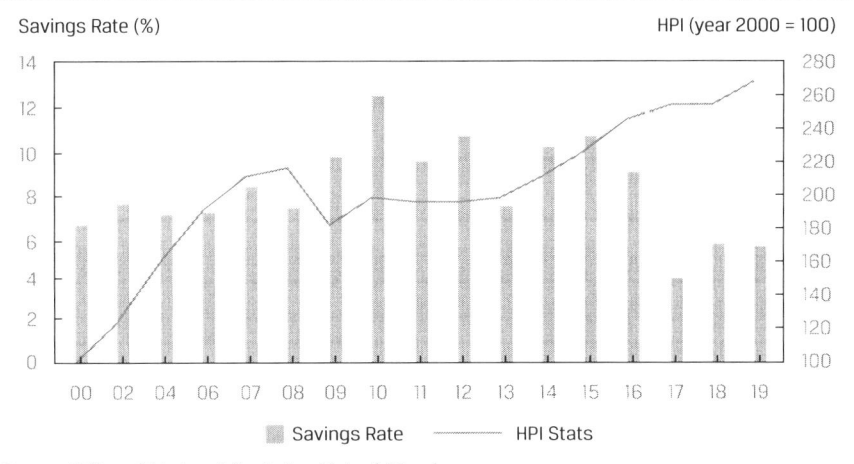

Source: Office of National Statistics, United Kingdom.

Note: HPI = Housing Price Index.

EXAMPLE 4

The Wealth Effect on Saving and Consumption

1. The importance of the wealth effect on consumption, and its relationship to housing prices, was evident in the sharp global economic downturn. A major factor associated with the economic downturn was the sharp fall in housing prices, especially in countries that experienced a housing boom earlier in the decade, such as the United States, the United Kingdom, Spain, and Ireland. In each of these countries, consumers reduced spending sharply and raised the level of saving in response to the decline in wealth. Do the data in Exhibit 12 provide support for the wealth effect?

Solution:

Housing prices in the United Kingdom rose by nearly 111% [(211.1 − 100)/100] between 2000 and 2007. During this period, the saving rate averaged 7.2% of income up until 2008. As predicted, when housing prices fell by 11% between 2008 and 2009, the saving rate rose dramatically from 7.2% in 2008 to 12.4% in 2010. Of course, the decline in housing prices was not the only factor contributing to the increase in the saving rate. Stock prices also declined during this period, further reducing wealth in the United Kingdom, and the slowdown raised uncertainty over future jobs and income. Then, as the economy recovered, house prices rose again from 2013, which led to a (lagged) decline in the saving rate.

Consumer and Business Expectations

Psychology has an important impact on consumer and business spending. When consumers are confident about their future income and the stability/safety of their jobs, they tend to spend a higher portion of their disposable income. This dynamic shifts the AD curve to the right. Consumer spending declines and the AD curve shifts to the left when consumers become less confident. Similarly, when businesses are optimistic about their future growth and profitability, they spend (invest) more on capital projects, which also shifts the AD curve to the right.

Capacity Utilization

Capacity utilization is a measure of how fully an economy's production capacity is being used. Companies with excess capacity have little incentive to invest in new property, plant, and equipment. In contrast, when companies are operating at or near full capacity, they will need to increase investment spending in order to expand production. Data from the OECD and the US Federal Reserve indicate that when aggregate capacity utilization reaches 82%–85%, production blockages arise, prompting companies to increase their level of investment spending. This dynamic shifts the AD curve to the right.

Fiscal Policy

Fiscal policy is the use of taxes and government spending to affect the level of aggregate expenditures. An increase in government spending, one of the direct components of AD, shifts the AD curve to the right, whereas a decrease in government spending shifts the AD curve to the left. Taxes affect GDP indirectly through their effect on consumer spending and business investment. Lower taxes will increase the proportion of personal income and corporate pre-tax profits that consumers and businesses have available to spend and will shift the AD curve to the right. In contrast, higher taxes will shift the AD curve to the left.

Monetary Policy

Money is generally defined as currency in circulation plus deposits at commercial banks. **Monetary policy** refers to action taken by a nation's central bank to affect aggregate output and prices through changes in bank reserves, reserve requirements, or its target interest rate.

Most countries have fractional reserve banking systems in which each bank must hold reserves (vault cash plus deposits at the central bank) at least equal to the required reserve ratio times its customer deposits. Banks with excess reserves can lend them to banks that need reserves to meet their reserve requirements. The central bank can increase the money supply by 1) buying securities from banks, 2) lowering the required reserve ratio if such a tool is available, and/or 3) reducing its target for the interest rate at which banks borrow and lend reserves among themselves. In each case, the opposite action would decrease the money supply.

When the central bank buys securities from banks in an open-market operation, it pays for them with a corresponding increase in bank reserves. This dynamic increases the amount of deposits banks can accept from their customers—that is, the money supply. Similarly, cutting the required reserve ratio increases the level of deposits (i.e., money) consistent with a given level of reserves in the system. If the central bank chooses to target an interbank lending rate, as the Federal Reserve targets the federal funds rate in the United States, then it must add or drain reserves via open-market operations to maintain the target interest rate. If it raises (lowers) its target interest rate, it will have to drain (add) reserves in order to make reserves more (less) expensive in the interbank market. Thus, open-market operations and interest rate targeting are very closely related. The main distinction is whether the central bank chooses to target a level of reserves and let the market determine the interest rate or chooses to target the interest rate and let the market (i.e., banks) determine the level of reserves they desire to hold at that rate.

An increase in the money supply shifts the AD curve to the right so that each price level corresponds to a higher level of income and expenditure. There are various channels through which the additional expenditures may be induced. For example, the interest rate reduction required to induce investors to hold the additional money

Aggregate Demand and Aggregate Supply

balances will encourage companies to invest more and households to borrow to purchase durable goods, such as cars. In addition, banks may facilitate greater expenditure by raising credit limits and loosening credit standards. Conversely, a reduction in the money supply shifts the AD curve to the left.

Exhibit 13 illustrates the short-run and long-run effect of expansionary monetary policy. Suppose the central bank expands the money supply in an attempt to stimulate demand when the economy is already in long-run equilibrium. The expansionary policy will shift the AD curve to the right, from AD_1 to AD_2. In the very short run, output will expand from Y_1 to Y_2 without an increase in the price level. After operating at higher-than-normal production rates for a few months or quarters, companies will begin to push for price increases and input prices will begin to rise as well. The aggregate supply curve will steepen, and prices will increase to P_3 while output declines to Y_3. As input prices become more flexible, the AS curve will steepen until, in the long run, it is vertical and output has returned to the long-run natural level, Y_1, with prices rising to P_4. Thus, expanding the money supply increases output in the short run, but in the long run it affects only the price level.

Exhibit 13: Short-Run and Long-Run Effects of Monetary Expansion

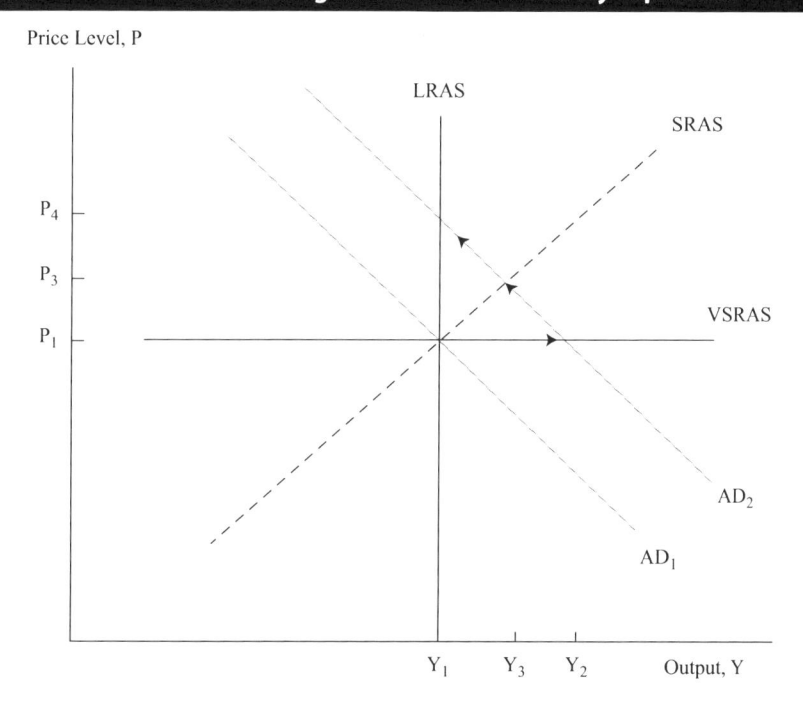

Exchange Rate

Changes in the exchange rate affect the price of exports and imports and thus aggregate demand. For example, a lower euro relative to other currencies makes European exports cheaper in world markets and non-European products sold in Europe (European imports) more expensive. Therefore, a lower euro should cause European exports to increase and imports to decline, leading the AD curve to shift to the right. Conversely, a stronger euro reduces exports and raises imports, and the AD curve shifts to the left.

Growth in the Global Economy

International trade is what links countries together and creates a global economy. Faster economic growth in non-domestic markets encourages people in other countries to buy more products from domestic producers and increases exports. For example, rapid GDP growth in ASEAN member countries has increased their demand for products from other nations. Japan has benefited from this rapid growth because it has exported more products to ASEAN countries. In terms of the AD and AS model, the AD curve for Japan has shifted to the right because of increased demand for Japanese products in ASEAN countries, resulting in higher exports. A decline in the growth rates of ASEAN members' economies would have a negative effect on the Japanese economy because exports would be lower. This change would cause the Japanese AD curve to shift to the left.

What happens to interest rates when the AD curve shifts? In the case of an increase in the money supply, the interest rate declines at each price level because the increase in income (Y) increases saving, and rates must decline to induce a corresponding increase in investment spending (I). In each of the other cases considered above, a rightward shift in the AD curve will increase the interest rate at each price level. With the real money supply held constant, the interest rate must rise as income increases. The increase in the interest rate reduces the demand for money at each level of expenditure/income and, therefore, allows expenditure/income to increase without an increase in the money supply. In terms of the quantity theory of money equation, this shift corresponds to a higher velocity of money, V.

Exhibit 14 summarizes the main factors that shift the AD curve. In each case, the impact of the factor is considered in isolation. In practice, however, various factors may be at work simultaneously and there may be interaction among them. This is especially true with regard to expectational factors—consumer and business confidence—which are likely to be influenced by other developments.

Exhibit 14: Impact of Factors Shifting Aggregate Demand

An Increase in the Following Factors	Shifts the AD Curve	Reason
Stock prices	Rightward: Increase in AD	Higher consumption
Housing prices	Rightward: Increase in AD	Higher consumption
Consumer confidence	Rightward: Increase in AD	Higher consumption
Business confidence	Rightward: Increase in AD	Higher investment
Capacity utilization	Rightward: Increase in AD	Higher investment
Government spending	Rightward: Increase in AD	Government spending a component of AD
Taxes	Leftward: Decrease in AD	Lower consumption and investment
Bank reserves	Rightward: Increase in AD	Lower interest rate, higher investment and possibly higher consumption
Exchange rate (foreign currency per unit domestic currency)	Leftward: Decrease in AD	Lower exports and higher imports
Global growth	Rightward: Increase in AD	Higher exports

Aggregate Demand and Aggregate Supply

EXAMPLE 5

Shifts in Aggregate Demand

Francois Ubert is a portfolio manager with EuroWorld, a French investment management firm. Ubert is considering increasing his clients' portfolio exposure to Brazilian equities. Before doing so, he asks you to prepare a report on the following recent economic events in Brazil and to summarize the effect of each event on the Brazilian economy and on Brazilian equity and fixed-income securities.

1. The Brazilian central bank reduced bank reserves, resulting in a lower money supply.

Solution to 1:

This monetary policy action is designed to reduce consumption and business investment spending. The reduction in real money balances will increase interest rates and discourage lending within the banking system. Higher interest rates and tighter credit will reduce both investment and consumption expenditures and shift the AD curve to the left. The prices of fixed-income securities will fall because of the rise in interest rates. The reduction in aggregate output should lower corporate profits, and it is likely that equity prices will also fall.

2. The capacity utilization rate in Brazil is currently estimated to be 86.4%, a 2.7% increase from the previous year.

Solution to 2:

Capacity utilization is a key factor determining the level of investment spending. A current utilization rate of more than 86% and an increase from the previous year indicate a growing lack of spare capacity in the Brazilian economy. As a result, businesses will probably increase their level of capital spending. This change will increase AD and shift the AD curve to the right. Higher economic activity (income/output) will cause upward pressure on interest rates and may have a negative effect on fixed-income securities. Higher income/output should increase corporate profits and is likely to have a positive effect on equity securities.

3. Corporate profits reported by Brazilian companies increased by 30% over last year's levels, and corporations have revised their forecasts of future profitability upward.

Solution to 3:

Expected corporate profits are an important determinant of the level of investment spending. The large increase in expected profits will raise the level of investment spending and increase aggregate demand. This change will shift the AD curve to the right. The increase in corporate profits and the resulting increase in economic output should have a positive effect on equities. The increase in output will put upward pressure on interest rates and downward pressure on the prices of fixed-income securities.

4. The government recently announced that it plans to start construction on a number of hydroelectric projects to increase renewable energy sources.

Solution to 4:

Fiscal policy uses government spending to influence the level and growth rate of economic activity. The announcement indicates an increase in government spending, which is a direct component of AD. Therefore, higher spending on the projects will increase AD and shift the AD curve to the right. The increase in output and expenditure should be positive for equities. But it will be negative for existing fixed-income investments because higher interest rates will be required to induce investors to buy and hold the government debt issued to fund the new projects.

5. Forecasts by private sector economists project that the European economy will enter a sharp slowdown and decline in the next year.

Solution to 5:

A sharp slowdown in Europe will decrease the demand for Brazilian exports by European households and businesses and shift the AD curve to the left. The resulting decline in income and downward pressure on prices will be positive for fixed-income securities but negative for equities.

Shifts in the Short-Run Aggregate Supply Curve

Factors that change the cost of production or expected profit margins will cause the SRAS curve to shift. These factors include changes in

- nominal wages,
- input prices, including the price of natural resources,
- expectations about future output prices and the overall price level,
- business taxes and subsidies, and
- the exchange rate.

In addition, factors that shift the long-run AS curve (discussed elsewhere) will also shift the SRAS curve by a corresponding amount because the SRAS and LRAS reflect the same underlying resources and technology. As the economy's resources and technology change, the full employment (or natural) level of output changes, and both the LRAS and SRAS shift accordingly.

Change in Nominal Wages

Changes in nominal wages shift the short-run AS curve because wages are often the largest component of a company's costs. An increase in nominal wages raises production costs, resulting in a decrease in AS and a leftward shift in the SRAS curve. Lower wages shift the AS curve to the right. It is important to note that changes in nominal wages have no effect on the LRAS curve.

A better way to measure the impact of labor costs on the AS curve is to measure the change in unit labor cost. We define the change in unit labor cost as

$$\% \text{ Change in unit labor cost} = \% \text{ Change in nominal wages} - \% \text{ Change in productivity}$$

Aggregate Demand and Aggregate Supply

EXAMPLE 6

Unit Labor Cost and Short-Run Aggregate Supply

1. Suppose Finnish workers are paid €20 an hour and are able to produce 100 cell phones in an hour. The labor cost per cell phone is €0.20 (€20 divided by 100 units). If the wages per hour for Finnish workers rise by 10% from €20 to €22 and they are able to raise their productivity by 10%, what is the impact on unit labor cost and the short-run aggregate supply curve?

Solution:

The workers can now produce 110 cell phones per hour, and unit labor cost will not change (22/110 = 0.20). In this case, the SRAS curve will remain in its original position. If wages had increased by 20% instead of 10%, then unit labor cost would have increased and the SRAS would shift to the left. Conversely, if the wage increase were only 5%, then unit labor cost would have decreased and the SRAS would shift to the right.

Change in Input Prices

The price of raw materials is an important component of cost for many businesses. Lower input prices reduce the cost of production, which, in turn, makes companies willing to produce more at any output price. This dynamic is reflected in a rightward shift of the SRAS curve. Conversely, higher input prices increase production costs, which, in turn, causes companies to reduce production at any output price. This dynamic shifts the SRAS curve to the left. During the 1970s, high oil prices caused the SRAS curve in most countries to shift to the left. In contrast, in the mid-1980s, declining oil prices lowered the cost of production and shifted the SRAS curve in most countries to the right. Oil prices currently have a smaller effect on the global economy than in the 1970s and 1980s because most countries have reduced their reliance on oil and improved their energy efficiency so that they now use less energy per unit of GDP.

Change in Expectations about Future Prices

The impact of expected future prices on current output decisions is not as straightforward as it might seem. First, each company is primarily concerned about the price of its own output rather than the general price level. The latter may be more reflective of its costs. If it expects its own output price to rise (fall) relative to the general price level, then it may increase (decrease) production in response to the perceived change in its profit margin. As more and more companies become optimistic (pessimistic) about their ability to raise the relative price of their product, the SRAS will shift to the right (left). In the aggregate, of course, companies can neither raise nor lower their prices relative to the general price level. Hence, shifts in the SRAS driven by such price expectations are likely to be modest and temporary. Second, considering future prices introduces a temporal aspect into decision making. If the future price level is expected to be higher, companies may decide to produce more today in order to expand inventory available for future sale. But they will only do so if the cost of carrying inventory (financing, storage, and spoilage) is less than they expect to save on production costs by producing more today and less in the future. Conversely, they may cut current production and sell out of existing inventory if they expect future prices (and costs) to be lower.

The upshot is that expectations of higher (lower) future prices are likely to shift the SRAS curve to the right (left), but the effect may be modest and/or temporary.

Change in Business Taxes and Subsidies

Higher business taxes increase production costs per unit and shift the short-run AS curve to the left. Business subsidies are a payment from the government to the producer. Subsidies for businesses lower their production costs and shift the SRAS curve to the right.

Change in the Exchange Rate

Many countries import raw materials, including energy and intermediate goods. As a result, changes in the exchange rate can affect the cost of production and, therefore, aggregate supply. A higher yen relative to the euro, for instance, would lower the cost of raw materials and intermediate goods imported to Japan from Europe. This, in turn, will lower the production costs of Japanese producers and shift the AS curve in Japan to the right. A lower yen would have the opposite effect.

Shifts in the Long-Run Aggregate Supply Curve

As discussed, the position of the LRAS curve is determined by the potential output of the economy. **Potential GDP** measures the productive capacity of the economy and is the level of real GDP that can be produced at full employment. Potential GDP is not a static concept but can increase each year at a steady rate as the economy's resource capacity grows. Therefore, any factor increasing the resource base of an economy causes the LRAS curve to shift as shown in Exhibit 15.

Exhibit 15: Shift in the Long-Run Aggregate Supply (LRAS) Curve

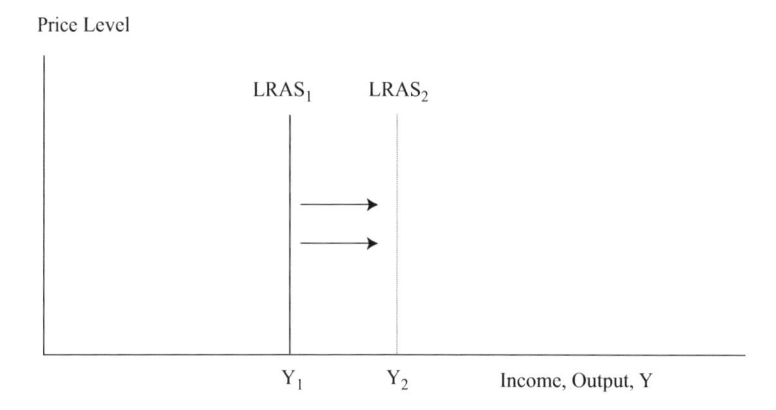

These factors include changes in

- supply of labor and quality of labor forces (human capital),
- supply of natural resources,
- supply of physical capital, and
- productivity and technology.

Supply of Labor

The larger the supply of labor, the more output the economy can produce. The labor supply depends on growth in the population, the labor force participation rate (the percentage of the population working or looking for work), and net immigration. The determinants of the labor supply are discussed in more detail later in our coverage. Increases in the labor supply shift the LRAS curve to the right. Decreases shift the curve to the left.

Aggregate Demand and Aggregate Supply

Supply of Natural Resources
Natural resources are essential inputs to the production process and include everything from available land to oil to water. Increased availability of natural resources shifts the LRAS curve to the right.

Supply of Physical Capital
Investment in new property, plant, equipment, and software is an essential ingredient for growth. An increase in the stock of physical capital will increase the capacity of the economy to produce goods and services. Simply put, if workers are provided with more and better equipment to use, they should be able to produce more output than they could with the older equipment. Thus, strong growth in business investment, which increases the supply of physical capital, shifts the LRAS curve to the right.

Supply of Human Capital
Another way to raise the productive capacity of a country is to increase human capital—the quality of the labor force—through training, skills development, and education. Improvement in the quality of the labor force shifts the LRAS curve to the right.

Labor Productivity and Technology
Another important factor affecting the productive capacity of an economy is how efficient labor is in transforming inputs into final goods and services. **Productivity** measures the efficiency of labor and is the amount of output produced by workers during a given period—for example, output per hour worked. An increase in productivity decreases labor cost, improves profitability, and results in higher output. Two of the main drivers of labor productivity—physical capital per worker and the quality of the workforce—have been discussed already. The third key determinant of productivity is technology. Advances in technology shift the LRAS curve to the right.

EXAMPLE 7

Unit Labor Cost and Long-Run Aggregate Supply

1. Finnish workers are paid €20 per hour and are able to produce 100 cell phones in an hour. If workers develop a new technique for assembly and are able to produce 200 cell phones per hour, what is the effect on the long-run aggregate supply curve?

Solution:

Labor cost per unit will decline to €0.10 (20/200 = €0.10 per cell phone). As a result, profit per unit will rise and companies will have an incentive to increase production. Thus, the LRAS curve will shift to the right.

Exhibit 16 summarizes the factors shifting the AS curve. Rightward shifts in the SRAS or LRAS curves are defined as an increase in supply, while leftward shifts represent a decrease in supply.

Exhibit 16: Impact of Factors Shifting Aggregate Supply

An Increase in	Shifts SRAS	Shifts LRAS	Reason
Supply of labor	Rightward	Rightward	Increases resource base
Supply of natural resources	Rightward	Rightward	Increases resource base
Supply of human capital	Rightward	Rightward	Increases resource base

An Increase in	Shifts SRAS	Shifts LRAS	Reason
Supply of physical capital	Rightward	Rightward	Increases resource base
Productivity and technology	Rightward	Rightward	Improves efficiency of inputs
Nominal wages	Leftward	No effect	Increases labor cost
Input prices (e.g., energy)	Leftward	No effect	Increases cost of production
Expectation of future prices	Rightward	No effect	Anticipation of higher costs and/or perception of improved pricing power
Business taxes	Leftward	No effect	Increases cost of production
Subsidy	Rightward	No effect	Lowers cost of production
Exchange rate	Rightward	No effect	Lowers cost of production

As with our summary of factors that shift the AD curve, Exhibit 16 considers each of the factors affecting aggregate supply in isolation. In practice, various factors will be at work simultaneously, and there may be interaction among them. This is especially important with respect to interaction between factors listed as affecting only SRAS and those that also affect LRAS.

For example, consider an increase in the cost of natural resource inputs (e.g., energy). This change shifts the SRAS curve to the left, but according to Exhibit 16, it has no effect on LRAS. This presumes that the relative prices of the factors of production have not changed permanently. If a permanent change has occurred, companies will be forced to conserve on the now more expensive input and will be unable to produce as efficiently. The LRAS curve would, therefore, shift to the left, just as it would if the available supply of natural resources had declined relative to the supply of other inputs. Indeed, that is the most likely cause of a permanent change in relative input prices.

EXAMPLE 8

Shifts in Aggregate Supply

In this hypothetical scenario, John Donovan is a portfolio manager for a global mutual fund. Currently, his fund has 10% of its assets invested in Chinese equities. He is considering increasing the fund's allocation to the Chinese equity market. His decision will be based on an analysis of the following economic developments and their effect on the Chinese economy and equity market. What is the effect on SRAS and LRAS from the following factors?

1. Global oil prices, currently near their longer-run trend at US$75 a barrel, have increased from US$35 a barrel over the last three years because of strong demand from emerging markets.

Solution to 1:

Higher energy prices cause a decrease in short-run AS and shift the SRAS curve to the left. Because oil prices are back to their longer-run trend, the leftward shift in SRAS essentially reverses a previous shift that occurred when oil prices fell to US$35 a barrel, and it is likely that there will be no effect on the LRAS curve. Lower output and profit are likely to have a negative effect on Chinese equity prices.

2. The number of students studying engineering has dramatically increased at Chinese universities during the last decade.

Solution to 2:

More students studying engineering indicates an improvement in the quality of the labor force—an increase in human capital. As a result, AS increases and the AS curve shifts to the right. Both short-run and long-run curves are affected. Higher output and profits may be expected to have a positive effect on Chinese equity prices.

3. Wages for China's workers are rising, leading some multinational companies to consider shifting their investments to Vietnam or Cambodia.

Solution to 3:

The increase in wages increases labor costs for businesses, causes short-run aggregate supply to decline, and shifts the SRAS curve to the left. Lower output and profit should have a negative effect on Chinese equity prices.

4. Data show that business investment as a share of GDP is more than 40% in China.

Solution to 4:

The high level of business investment indicates that the capital stock in China is growing at a fast rate. This growth means that workers have more capital to use, which increases their productivity. Thus, AS increases and the AS curve shifts to the right. Both short-run AS and long-run AS are affected. Higher output should have a positive effect on Chinese equity prices.

5. The People's Bank of China is likely to permit the yuan to appreciate by 10% during the next year.

Solution to 5:

The probable appreciation of the yuan means that the cost of imported raw materials, such as iron ore, coal, and oil, will be lower for Chinese companies. As a result, short-run AS increases and the SRAS curve shifts to the right. The LRAS curve may also shift to the right if the appreciation of the yuan is permanent and global commodity prices do not fully adjust. Higher output and profit should have a positive effect on Chinese equity prices. Note that the stronger yuan will also reduce export demand and shift the AD curve to the left. The combined effect of the AD and AS shifts on output, profit, and equity prices is ambiguous.

The implications of the aforementioned factors for equity investment in China are ambiguous. If the long-run effects dominate, however, then the net effect should be positive. The positive factors—the high level of investment and the growing pool of engineering students—have a lasting effect on output and profit. The negative factors—higher wages and oil prices—should be temporary, because wages will realign with the price level and the increase in oil prices appears to offset a previous temporary decline. The reduction in raw material prices resulting from the stronger currency is positive for output, profit, and equities in the short run and perhaps in the long run as well.

Equilibrium GDP and Prices

Now that we have discussed the components of the AD and AS model, we can combine them to determine the real level of GDP and the price level. Equilibrium occurs where the AD and AS curves intersect. At this point, the quantity of aggregate output demanded (or the level of aggregate expenditures) is equal to the quantity of aggregate output supplied. In Exhibit 17, equilibrium price and GDP occur at P_1 and Y_1. If the price level is above P_1, then the quantity of output supplied exceeds the amount demanded. This situation would result in unsold inventories and would require a reduction in production and in prices. If the price level is below P_1, then the quantity of aggregate output demanded exceeds the quantity of aggregate output supplied. This situation would result in a shortage of goods that would put upward pressure on prices.

It is important to understand that short-run macroeconomic equilibrium may occur at a level above or below full employment. We consider four possible types of macroeconomic equilibrium:

1. Long-run full employment
2. Short-run recessionary gap
3. Short-run inflationary gap
4. Short-run stagflation

From an investment perspective, the performance of asset classes and financial markets will differ in each case as the economy makes the adjustment toward the macroeconomic equilibrium. We look at these differences later in the reading.

Long-Run Equilibrium

Exhibit 17 shows the long-run full employment equilibrium for an economy. In this case, equilibrium occurs where the AD curve intersects the SRAS curve at a point on the LRAS curve. Because equilibrium occurs at a point on the LRAS curve, the economy is at potential real GDP. Both labor and capital are fully employed, and everyone who wants a job has one. *In the long run, equilibrium GDP is equal to potential GDP.*

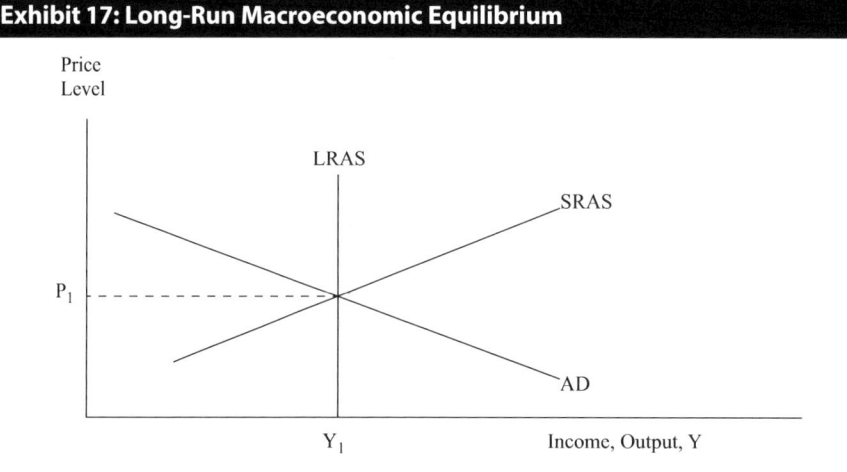

Exhibit 17: Long-Run Macroeconomic Equilibrium

In practice, the level of potential GDP is difficult to measure with precision. Because of fluctuations arising from shifts in the AD and SRAS curves, the economy rarely operates at potential GDP. Thus, potential GDP is not observable from the data on actual GDP. In addition, potential GDP is determined by factors that are themselves difficult to measure. Thus, "bottom-up" estimates of the *level* of potential output are also quite imprecise. As we will cover subsequently, however, economists have confidence that the long-run *growth rate* of potential GDP can be estimated well enough to provide meaningful guidance for analysts and policymakers. Hence, in the short run, economists generally focus on factors that cause actual GDP to grow faster or slower than their estimate of the long-run growth rate of potential output. In addition, they focus on measures that indicate, albeit imprecisely, the extent to which the economy is operating above or below its productive capacity, such as unemployment and capacity utilization.

Recessionary Gap

Cyclical fluctuations in real GDP and prices are caused by shifts in both the AD and SRAS curves. A decline in AD or a leftward shift in the AD curve results in lower GDP and lower prices. Such declines in AD lead to economic contractions, and if such declines drive demand below the economy's potential GDP, the economy goes into a **recession** (defined as a period during which real GDP decreases for at least two consecutive quarters). In Exhibit 18, when aggregate demand falls, the equilibrium shifts from Point A to Point B. Real GDP contracts from Y_1 to Y_2, and the aggregate price level falls from P_1 to P_2. Because of the decline in demand, companies reduce their workforce and the unemployment rate rises. The economy is in recession, and the recessionary gap is measured as the difference between Y_2 and Y_1 or the amount by which equilibrium output is below potential GDP. Thus, a recessionary gap occurs when the AD curve intersects the short-run AS curve at a short-run equilibrium level of GDP below potential GDP. *Most importantly, in contrast to full employment, equilibrium GDP is below potential GDP.*

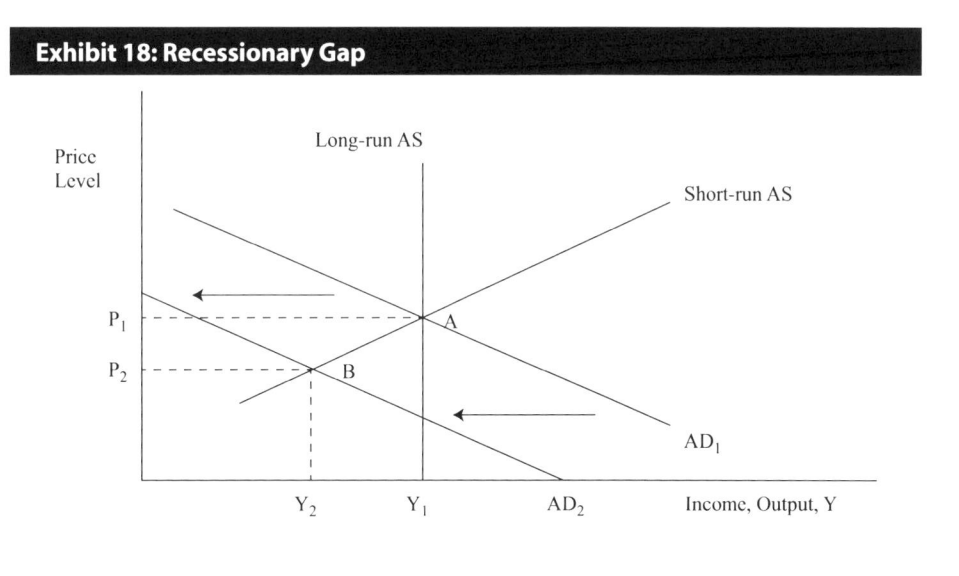

Exhibit 18: Recessionary Gap

Any of the factors discussed earlier could cause the shift in the AD curve. Tightening of monetary policy, higher taxes, more pessimistic consumers and businesses, and lower equity and housing prices all reduce AD and are all possible causes of a recession.

The question is, how does the economy return to full employment? There is considerable debate among economists about the answer to this question. Some economists argue that an automatic, self-correcting mechanism will push the economy back to its potential, without the need for government action. The idea is that because of the decline in prices and higher unemployment, workers will be willing to accept lower nominal wages. Workers will do this because each currency unit of wages now buys more goods and services because of their lower price. As a result, lower wages and input prices will shift the SRAS curve to the right (see Exhibit 16) and push the economy back to full employment and potential GDP.

The problem is that this price mechanism can take several years to work. As an alternative, government can use the tools of fiscal and monetary policy to shift the AD curve to the right (from Point B to Point A in Exhibit 18) and move the economy back to full employment. On the fiscal side, policymakers can reduce taxes or increase government spending. On the monetary side, the central bank can lower interest rates or increase the money supply. The problem, however, is that variable lags in the effectiveness of these policy measures imply that policy adjustments may end up reinforcing rather than counteracting underlying shifts in the economy.

Investment Implications of a Decrease in AD

Aggregate demand and aggregate supply are theoretical measures that are hard to measure directly. Most governments, however, publish statistics that provide an indication of the direction that aggregate demand and supply are moving over time. For example, statistics on consumer sentiment, factory orders for durable and nondurable goods, the value of unfilled orders, the number of new housing starts, the number of hours worked, and changes in inventories provide an indication of the direction of aggregate demand. If these statistics suggest that a recession is caused by a decline in AD, the following conditions are likely to occur:

- Corporate profits will decline.
- Commodity prices will decline.
- Interest rates will decline.
- Demand for credit will decline.

This situation suggests the following investment strategy:

- Reduce investments in **cyclical companies**, companies with sales and profits that regularly expand and contract with the business cycle or state of economy, because their earnings are likely to decline the most in an economic slowdown.
- Reduce investments in commodities and/or commodity-oriented companies because the decline in commodity prices will slow revenue growth and reduce profit margins.
- Increase investments in **defensive companies**, companies with sales and profits that have little sensitivity to the business cycle or state of the economy, because they are likely to experience only modest earnings declines in an economic slowdown.
- Increase investments in investment-grade or government-issued fixed-income securities. The prices of these securities should increase as interest rates decline.
- Increase investments in long-maturity fixed-income securities because their prices will be more responsive to the decline in interest rates than the prices of shorter-maturity securities.
- Reduce investments in speculative equity securities and in fixed-income securities with low credit quality ratings.

As with most investment strategies, this strategy will be most successful if it is implemented before other market participants recognize the opportunities and asset prices adjust.

EXAMPLE 9

Using AD and AS: A Historical Example: 2007–2009

Many Asian economies were more adversely affected than the United States by the global recession that began in late 2007. In the first quarter of 2009, real GDP fell at an annualized rate of 16% in Japan and 11% in Singapore, compared with a 6% annualized decline in the United States. Using the data on exports as a share of GDP shown in Exhibit 19, explain how the following economic factors contributed to the recession in the Asian economies:

Exhibit 19: Exports as a Share of GDP, 2007 and 2016

	2007		2016	
Economy	Exports as a Percentage of GDP	Percentage of Exports Going to United States	Exports as a Percentage of GDP	Percentage of Exports Going to United States
Hong Kong SAR	186	11.2	192	8.3
Singapore	166	11.5	175	6.5
Thailand	62	11.6	69	11.2
Germany	53	10.9	47	9
South Korea	47	7.1	44	12
Mexico	37	26.4	37	81.2
Canada	28	80.2	31	76.2
Chinese mainland	27	19	21	19
India	17	20.1	20	16
Japan	14	17	17	20.2
Kenya	12	—	16	6.7
United States	12	—	12	—
Ethiopia	11	6.7	9	9.9

Sources: World Bank, World Development Indicators, NE.EXP.GNFS.ZS; atlas.media.mit.edu/en/profile/country.

1. Collapse of house prices and home construction in the United States.

Solution to 1:

The collapse in housing prices caused housing construction spending, a component of business investment, to decline in the United States. The decline in housing prices also caused a sharp fall in household wealth. As a result, consumption spending in the United States declined because of the wealth effect. The decline in both consumption and housing construction shifted the AD curve for the United States to the left, resulting in a US recession. The link to the Asian economies was through global trade because exports represented such a large share of the Asian economies' GDP (Exhibit 20). In turn, these economies exported a significant amount of goods and services to the United States. Thus, the recession in the United States and especially the decline in US consumption spending caused a sharp fall in exports among Asian economies. This decrease lowered their AD and shifted the AD curve to the left, resulting in a recessionary gap in these economies.

2. Oil prices rising from around US$30 a barrel in 2004 to nearly US$150 a barrel in 2008. (Note that most Asian economies rely on imports for almost all of their oil and energy needs. In contrast, the United States has a large domestic energy industry and imports only about half of its oil.)

Solution to 2:

The rise in oil prices increased input cost and shifted the short-run AS curve to the left. Because the eastern Asian economies depend heavily on imported oil, their economies were more adversely affected than that of the United States.

3. The dramatic reduction in credit availability following the collapse or near collapse of major financial institutions in 2008.

Solution to 3:

The decline in housing prices caused financial institutions in the United States to suffer large losses on housing-related loans and securities. Several large lenders collapsed, and the US Treasury and the Federal Reserve had to intervene to prevent a wave of bankruptcies among large financial institutions. As a result of the crisis, it became difficult for households and businesses to obtain credit to finance their spending. This dynamic caused AD to fall and increased the severity of the recession in the United States, resulting in a significant decline in US imports and thus exports from the Asian economies. In addition, the financial crisis made it more difficult to obtain trade finance, further reducing exports from Asia.

In summary, global investors need to be aware of the growing linkages among economies and the extent that one economy's growth depends on demand from within as well as from outside of that economy. Data on exports as a percentage of an economy's GDP provide an indication of this dependence. Although Japan is often viewed as an export-driven economy, Exhibit 20 shows that in 2018, exports were only 18% of its GDP. Similarly, the economy of India depends largely on domestic spending for growth because in 2018, exports accounted for only 20% of GDP.

Inflationary Gap

Increases in AD lead to economic expansions as real GDP and employment increase. If the expansion drives the economy beyond its production capacity, however, **inflation** will occur. The inflation rate is defined as the increase in the general price level from one period to the next. As summarized in Exhibit 14, higher government spending, lower taxes, a more optimistic outlook among consumers and businesses, a weaker domestic currency, rising equity and housing prices, and an increase in the money supply would each stimulate aggregate demand and shift the AD curve to the right. If aggregate supply does not increase to match the increase in AD, a rise in the overall level of prices will result.

As shown in Exhibit 20, an increase in AD will shift the equilibrium level of GDP from Point A to Point B. Real output increases from Y_1 to Y_2, and the aggregate price level rises from P_1 to P_2. As a result of the increase in aggregate demand, companies increase their production and hire more workers. The unemployment rate declines. Once an economy reaches its potential GDP, however, companies must pay higher wages and other input prices to further increase production. The economy now faces

Aggregate Demand and Aggregate Supply

an inflationary gap, measured by the difference between Y_2 and Y_1 in Exhibit 20. *An inflationary gap occurs when the economy's short-run level of equilibrium GDP is above potential GDP, resulting in upward pressure on prices.*

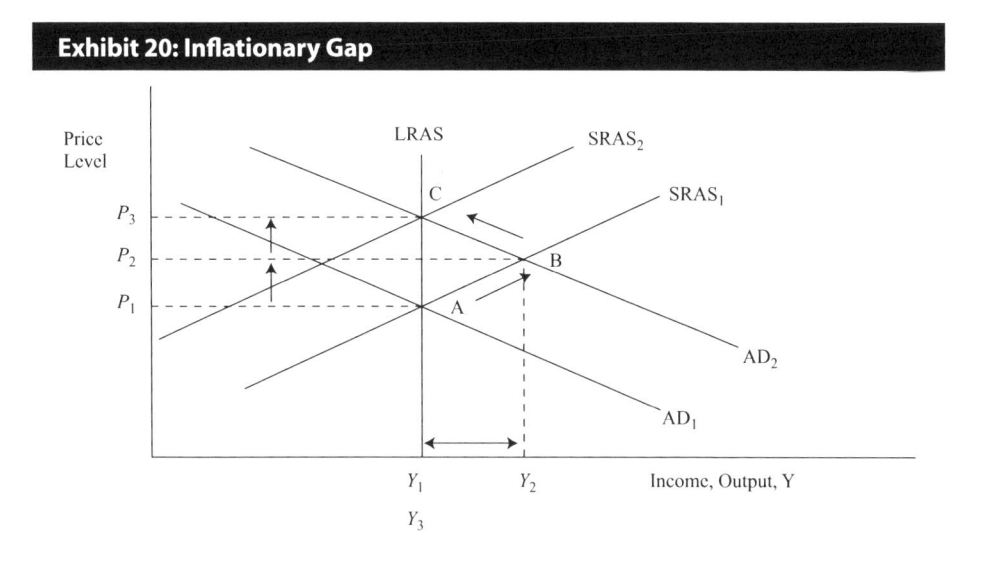

Exhibit 20: Inflationary Gap

GDP cannot remain at Y_2 for long because the economy is overutilizing its resources—that is, extra shifts of workers are hired and plant and equipment are operating at their maximum capacity. Eventually, workers become tired and plants and equipment wear out. The increase in the general price level and input prices will set in motion the process of returning the economy back to potential GDP. Higher wages and input prices shift the SRAS curve to the left (from $SRAS_1$ to $SRAS_2$), moving the economy to Point C in Exhibit 20. Again, this self-correcting mechanism may work slowly.

A nation's government and/or its central bank can attempt to use the tools of fiscal and monetary policy to control inflation by shifting the AD curve to the left (AD_2 to AD_1 in Exhibit 20) so that the return to full employment occurs without the price increase. From a fiscal perspective, policymakers can raise taxes or cut government spending. From a monetary perspective, the central bank can reduce bank reserves, resulting in a decrease in the growth of the money supply and higher interest rates.

Investment Implications of an Increase in AD Resulting in an Inflationary Gap

If economic statistics (consumer sentiment, factory orders for durable and nondurable goods, etc.) suggest that there is an expansion caused by an increase in AD, the following conditions are likely to occur:

- Corporate profits will rise.
- Commodity prices will increase.
- Interest rates will rise.
- Inflationary pressures will build.

This situation suggests the following investment strategy:

- Increase investment in cyclical companies because they are expected to have the largest increase in earnings.
- Reduce investments in defensive companies because they are expected to have only a modest increase in earnings.

- Increase investments in commodities and commodity-oriented equities because they will benefit from higher production and output.
- Reduce investments in fixed-income securities, especially longer-maturity securities, because they will decline in price as interest rates rise. Raise exposure to speculative fixed-income securities (junk bonds) because default risks decrease in an economic expansion.

Stagflation: Both High Inflation and High Unemployment

Structural fluctuations in real GDP are caused by fluctuations in SRAS. Declines in aggregate supply bring about **stagflation**—high unemployment and increased inflation. Increases in aggregate supply conversely give rise to high economic growth and low inflation.

Exhibit 21 shows the case of a decline in aggregate supply, perhaps caused by an unexpected increase in basic material and oil prices. The equilibrium level of GDP shifts from Point A to B. The economy experiences a recession as GDP falls from Y_1 to Y_2, but the price level, instead of falling, rises from P_1 to P_2. Over time, the reduction in output and employment should put downward pressure on wages and input prices and shift the SRAS curve back to the right, re-establishing full employment equilibrium at Point A. However, this mechanism may be painfully slow. Policymakers may use fiscal and monetary policy to shift the AD curve to the right, as previously discussed, but at the cost of a permanently higher price level at Point C.

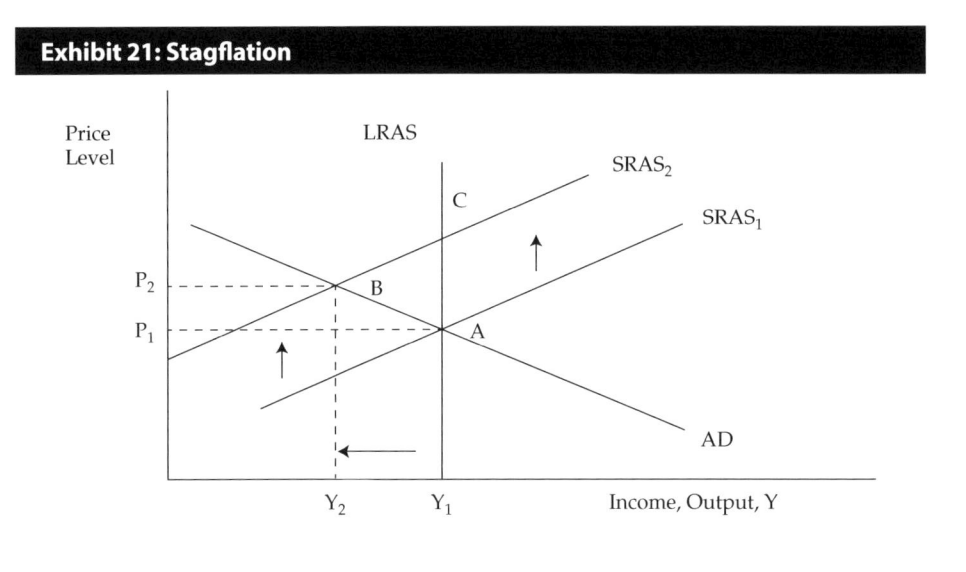

Exhibit 21: Stagflation

The global economy experienced stagflation in the mid-1970s and early 1980s. Both unemployment and inflation soared. The problem was caused by a sharp decline in aggregate supply fueled by higher input prices, especially the price of oil. In 1973, the price of oil quadrupled. A steep global recession began in late 1973 and lasted through early 1975. The recession was unusual because prices rose rather than declined as would be expected in a typical demand-caused downturn. In 1979–1980, the price of oil doubled. Higher energy prices shifted the SRAS curve to the left, as shown in Exhibit 21, leading to a global recession in 1980–1982. In the United States, the contraction in output was reinforced by the Federal Reserve's decision to tighten monetary policy to fight the supply-induced inflation.

Investment Implications of a Shift in AS

Labor and raw material costs, including energy prices, determine the direction of shifts in short-run aggregate supply: Higher costs for labor, raw materials, and energy lead to a decrease in aggregate supply, resulting in lower economic growth and higher prices. Conversely, lower labor costs, raw material prices, and energy prices lead to an increase in aggregate supply, resulting in higher economic growth and a lower aggregate price level. Productivity is also an important factor. Higher rates of productivity growth shift the AS to the right, resulting in higher output and lower unit input prices. Lower rates of productivity growth do the opposite and shift the AS curve to the left.

From an investment perspective, a decline in AS (leftward shift of the SRAS curve) suggests:

- reducing investment in fixed income because rising output prices (i.e., inflation) put upward pressure on nominal interest rates,
- reducing investment in most equity securities because profit margins are squeezed and output declines, and
- increasing investment in commodities or commodity-based companies because prices and profits are likely to rise.

On the other hand, an increase in AS (rightward shift of the SRAS curve) resulting from higher productivity growth or lower labor, raw material, and energy costs is favorable for most asset classes other than commodities.

Conclusions on AD and AS

The business cycle and the resulting fluctuations in real GDP are caused by shifts in the AD and AS curves. The effects of these shifts can be summarized as follows:

- An increase in AD raises real GDP, lowers the unemployment rate, and increases the aggregate level of prices.
- A decrease in AD lowers real GDP, increases the unemployment rate, and decreases the aggregate level of prices.
- An increase in AS raises real GDP, lowers the unemployment rate, and lowers the aggregate level of prices.
- A decrease in AS lowers real GDP, raises the unemployment rate, and raises the aggregate level of prices.

Whether the growth of the economy is demand- or supply-driven has an effect on asset prices. Demand-driven expansions are normally associated with rising interest rates and inflation, whereas contractions are associated with lower inflation and interest rates. Supply-driven expansions are associated with lower inflation and interest rates, whereas supply-driven contractions are associated with rising inflation and interest rates.

EXAMPLE 10

Investment Strategy Based on AD and AS Curves

An analyst is evaluating the possibility of investing in China, Italy, Mexico, or Brazil. What are the equity and fixed-income investment opportunities in these countries based on the following events?

1. The Chinese government announced a spending plan of US$1.2 trillion, or 13% of GDP. In addition, the central bank of China eased monetary policy, resulting in a surge of lending.

Solution to 1:

Stimulative fiscal and monetary policies should result in a demand-driven expansion. Investors should reduce investments in fixed-income securities and defensive companies and invest in cyclical companies and commodities. As a result, the prospects for growth-oriented equity investments look favorable in China.

2. The Italian government announced a decline in labor productivity, and it expects this trend to continue into the future.

Solution to 2:

A decline in labor productivity will result in a decline in AS; that is, the AS curve will shift to the left. This scenario is typically a poor investment environment. Investors should reduce investments in both fixed-income and equity securities and invest in commodities. Entry into Italian stocks and bonds does not look attractive.

3. In response to rising inflationary pressure, the Mexican central bank tightened monetary policy, and the government announced tax increases and spending cuts to balance the budget.

Solution to 3:

The policy measures put in place by the Mexican government and central bank will cause a drop in AD and likely result in a recession. Investors should increase their investments in fixed-income securities because interest rates will most likely decline as the recession deepens. This scenario is a poor environment for equity securities.

4. A major discovery of oil off the coast of Brazil lowered oil prices, while the Brazilian government announced a major increase in spending on public infrastructure to stimulate the economy.

Solution to 4:

In this situation, both the AD and AS curves will shift. The increase in spending on public infrastructure will shift the AD curve to the right, resulting in higher aggregate expenditures and prices. Lower oil prices will shift the AS curve to the right, resulting in higher GDP but lower prices. Thus, GDP will clearly increase, but the effect on prices and inflation is indeterminate. As a result, investors should increase their investment in equity securities; however, the effect on fixed-income securities is unclear.

ECONOMIC GROWTH AND SUSTAINABILITY

☐ describe sources, measurement, and sustainability of economic growth

☐ describe the production function approach to analyzing the sources of economic growth

☐ define and contrast input growth and growth of total factor productivity as components of economic growth

Understanding sources of economic growth is crucial for practitioners involved in various types of investment decision making. Economic growth is calculated as the annual percentage change in real GDP or the annual change in real per capita GDP:

- Growth in real GDP measures how rapidly the total economy is expanding.
- Per capita GDP, defined as real GDP divided by population, measures the standard of living in each country and the ability of the average person to buy goods and services.

Exhibit 22 illustrates growth in GDP in selected regions since 1990. It shows that although total GDP doubled in Latin America during the period, GDP per capita in the region increased by only about 50%, as a result of population growth.

Exhibit 22: Real GDP Growth and Per Capita GDP Growth for Selected Regions

In PPP (constant 2017 US$ billion)

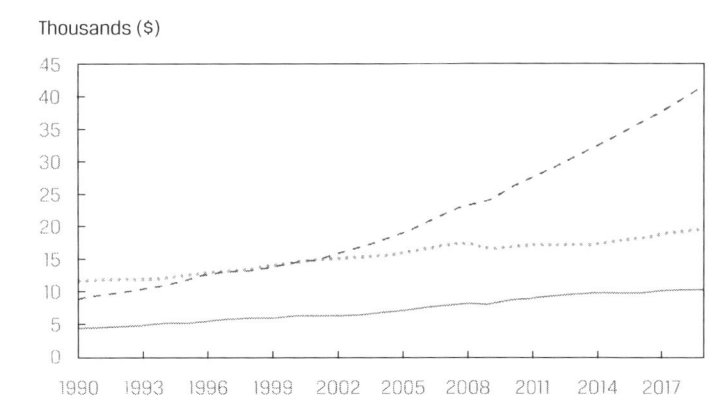

GDP per Capita, PPP (constant 2017 US$)

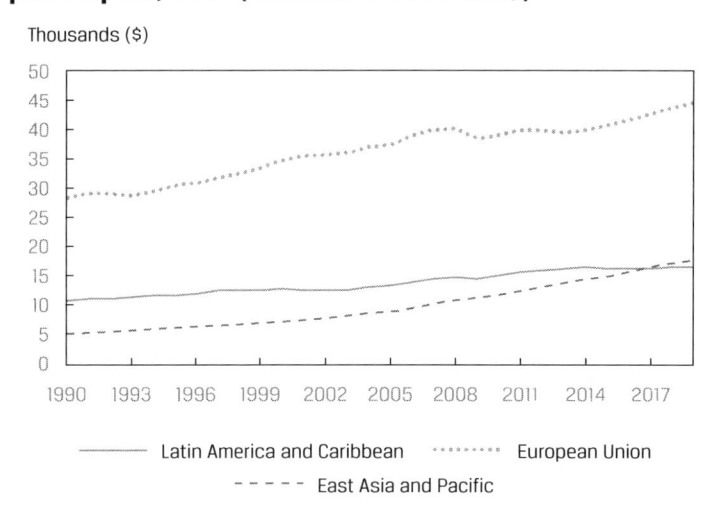

[Chart showing GDP per Capita in thousands of dollars from 1990 to 2017 for Latin America and Caribbean, European Union, and East Asia and Pacific]

Note: PPP is Purchasing Power Parity.
Source: World Bank data.

Economic growth is important because rapid growth in per capita real GDP can transform a poor nation into a wealthy one. Even small differences in the growth rate of per capita GDP, if sustained over time, have a large effect on an economy's standard of living. Nevertheless, there is a limit to how fast an economy can grow. Faster growth is not always better for an economy because there are costs associated with excess growth, such as higher inflation, potential environmental damage, and the lower consumption and higher savings needed to finance the growth.

These costs raise the issue of sustainable growth, which requires an understanding of the concept of potential GDP. Recall that potential GDP measures the economy's productive capacity and is the level of real GDP that an economy could produce if capital and labor are fully employed. In order to grow over time, an economy must add to its productive capacity. Thus, the **sustainable rate of economic growth** is measured by the rate of increase in the economy's productive capacity or potential GDP. It is important to note that economists cannot directly measure potential output. Instead, they estimate it using a variety of techniques that we will discuss.

For global investors, estimating the sustainable rate of economic growth for an economy is important in valuing a variety of assets. Growth in potential GDP matters for long-run equity market appreciation and for individual industries and company forecasts. Potential GDP can be used to gauge inflationary pressures, determine credit quality, and assess the likelihood of a change in central bank policy, all of which are relevant for fixed income investors. Economic growth in large economies or whole regions is also useful for forecasting demand for commodities.

The Production Function and Potential GDP

We focus on the simplest form of what is known as the neoclassical or Solow growth model, the framework used to understand and analyze the underlying sources of growth for an economy. The model shows that the economy's productive capacity and potential GDP increase for two reasons:

1. accumulation of such inputs as capital, labor, and raw materials used in production, and
2. discovery and application of new technologies that make the inputs in the production process more productive—that is, able to produce more goods and services for the same amount of input.

The Production Function

The model is based on a **production function** that provides the quantitative link between the levels of output that the economy can produce and the inputs used in the production process, given the state of technology. A two-factor production function with labor and capital as the inputs is expressed mathematically as

$$Y = AF(L,K),$$

where Y denotes the level of aggregate output in the economy, L is the quantity of labor or number of workers in the economy, K is the capital stock or the equipment and structures used to produce goods and services, and A represents **total factor productivity** (TFP). TFP is a scale factor that captures the exogenous effect of technological change and other factors that raise output beyond the measured contribution of the capital and labor inputs. Like potential GDP, TFP is not directly observed in the economy but instead is estimated.

The production function shows that output in the economy depends on inputs and the level of technology. The economy's capacity to produce goods grows when these inputs increase and/or technology advances. The more technologically advanced an economy is, the more output it is able to produce from a given amount of inputs.

The Model Assumptions

The neoclassical model makes three assumptions about the production function that provide a link to microeconomics. First, it assumes that the production function has constant returns to scale. This means that if all the inputs in the production process are increased by the same percentage, then output will rise by that percentage. Thus, doubling all inputs would double output. Second, the model assumes that the production function exhibits **diminishing marginal productivity** with respect to any individual input. Finally, the model assumes no positive or negative externalities are associated with the use of the inputs. These assumptions play an important role in assessing the contribution of labor and capital to economic growth. Marginal productivity looks at the extra output produced from a one-unit increase in an input if the other inputs are unchanged. It applies to any input as long as the other inputs are held constant. For example, if we have a factory of a fixed size and we add more workers to the factory, the marginal productivity of labor measures how much additional output each additional worker will produce.

Diminishing marginal productivity means that at some point the extra output obtained from each additional unit of the input will decline. In the prior example, if we hire more workers at the existing factory (fixed capital input in this case), output will rise by a smaller and smaller amount with each additional worker.

In the case of capital, if we add more and more capital to a fixed number of workers, the amount of additional output contributed by each additional amount of capital will fall. Thus, if capital grows faster than labor, capital will become less productive, resulting in slower and slower growth. Diminishing marginal productivity of capital has two major implications for potential GDP and long-term growth:

1. Long-term sustainable growth cannot rely solely on **capital deepening investment** that increases the stock of capital relative to labor. More generally, increasing the supply of some input(s) relative to other inputs will lead to diminishing returns and cannot be the basis for sustainable growth.

2. Given that developing countries have relatively less capital, their productivity of capital is high. All else the same, the growth rates of developing countries should exceed those of developed countries. As a result, there should be a **convergence** of incomes between developed and developing countries over time.

Because of the assumption of diminishing returns to capital, the only way to sustain growth in potential GDP per capita in the long run is through growth in TFP. This results in an upward shift in the production function: The economy produces more goods and services using the same level of labor and capital inputs. In terms of the formal production function $Y = AF(L,K)$, this dynamic is reflected by an increase in the parameter A.

Growth Accounting Equation

Using the production function, Robert Solow developed a model that explained the contribution of labor, capital, and TFP to economic growth. The growth accounting equation shows that the rate of growth of potential output equals growth in TFP plus the weighted average growth rate of labor and capital.

$$\text{Growth in potential GDP} = \text{Growth in TFP} + W_L (\text{Growth in labor}) + W_C (\text{Growth in capital})$$

where W_L and W_C are the relative shares of capital and labor in national income. The capital share is the sum of corporate profits, net interest income, net rental income, and depreciation divided by GDP. The labor share is employee compensation divided by GDP. For many developed countries, W_L and W_C are roughly 0.7 and 0.3, respectively.

The growth accounting equation highlights a key point: The contribution of labor and capital to long-term growth depends on their respective shares of national income. For the United States, because labor's share is higher, an increase in the growth rate of labor will have a significantly larger effect (roughly double) on potential GDP growth than will an equivalent increase in the growth rate of capital.

The growth accounting equation can be further modified to explain growth in per capita GDP. Because it measures the standard of living and purchasing power of the average person in an economy, per capita GDP is more relevant than the absolute level of GDP in comparing economic performance among countries. Transforming the growth accounting equation into per capita terms results in the following equation:

Growth in per capita potential GDP

$= \text{Growth in TFP} + W_C (\text{Growth in capital-to-labor ratio})$

The capital-to-labor ratio measures the amount of capital available per worker and is weighted by the share of capital in national income. Because capital's share in national income in the US economy is 0.3, a 1% increase in the amount of capital available for each worker increases per capita output by only 0.3%.

Sources of Economic Growth

The main determinants of growth are capital, labor, and TFP (the key driver being technology). In the standard neoclassical model discussed earlier, these inputs are measured as part of TFP growth along with technological changes. Using this model, the sources of growth for an economy that determine its capacity to supply goods and services are as shown in Exhibit 23. Note that the amount of labor, measured as total hours worked, is determined by the size of the average hours worked per worker multiplied by the labor force. Labor force itself is a product of working age population and the participation rate (the proportion of working age population choosing to work or seeking work).

Exhibit 23: Sources of Economic Growth

Growth in potential GDP = Growth in TFP + WL (Growth in labor) + WC (Growth in capital)

- Technology
- Human capital
- Public infrastructure
- Natural resources
- Other factors

Working age population × Participation rate

Total hours worked

Labor force × Avgerage hours worked per worker

Physical capital stock

Technology

The most important factor affecting economic growth is technology, especially in developed countries. Technology refers to the process a company uses to transform inputs into outputs. Technological advances are discoveries that make it possible to produce more or higher-quality goods and services with the same resources or inputs. At the same time, technological progress results in the creation of new goods and services. Finally, technological progress improves how efficiently businesses are organized and managed.

Technological advances allow an economy to overcome the limits imposed by diminishing marginal returns. Thus, an economy will face limits to growth if it relies exclusively on expanding the inputs or factors of production. One of the key drivers of growth in developed countries is the information technology (IT) sector, whose growth has been driven by technological innovation that has caused the price of key technologies, such as semiconductors, to fall dramatically. The steep declines in prices have encouraged investment in IT at the expense of other assets. The sector has grown very fast and has made a significant contribution to economic growth, employment, and exports.

Countries can innovate through expenditures, both public and private, on research and development (R&D). Expenditures on R&D and the number of patents issued, although not directly measuring innovation, provide some useful insight into innovative performance. Countries can also acquire new technology through imitation or copying the technology developed elsewhere. The embodiment of technology in capital goods can also enable relatively poor countries to catch up to the technology leaders.

TFP is often used as a proxy for technological progress and organizational innovation. TFP is the amount by which output would rise because of improvements in the production process. It is not directly observed and is calculated as a residual, the difference between the growth rate of potential output and the weighted average growth rate of capital and labor. Specifically,

TFP growth

= Growth in potential GDP − [W_L (Growth in labor) + W_C (Growth in capital)]

The interpretation of the TFP as a pure technology measure is incorrect. Given the measurement and estimation difficulties, TFP will measure not only technological change but also the effect of other inputs into the production process such as human capital, public infrastructure, and natural resources. In addition to the other inputs, TFP measures the effect of externalities and spillover effects, omitted inputs, organizational efficiencies, and institutional and governance factors. Nevertheless, it is a useful indicator of the underlying technological forces.

Labor Supply

Growth in the number of people available for work (quantity of workforce) is an important source of economic growth and partially accounts for the superior growth performance of the US economy versus the European and Japanese economies. Most developing countries, such as China, India, and Mexico, have a large potential labor supply. We can measure the potential size of the labor input as the total number of hours available for work, which is given by

Total hours worked = Labor force × Average hours worked per worker

The **labor force** is defined as the portion of the working age population (over the age of 16) that is employed or available for work but not working (unemployed). The contribution of labor to overall output is also affected by changes in the average hours worked per worker. The average number of hours worked is highly sensitive to the business cycle. The long-term trend, however, has been toward a shorter work week in the advanced countries. This development is the result of legislation, collective bargaining agreements, and the growth of part-time and temporary work.

Human Capital

In addition to the quantity of labor (the "L" in the earlier mentioned production function), the quality of the labor force is important. Human capital reflects the accumulated knowledge and skill that workers acquire from education, training, and life experience. It measures the quality of the workforce, and we treat it as part of TFP. In general, better-educated and skilled workers will be more productive and more adaptable to changes in technology.

An economy's human capital is increased through investment in education and on-the-job training. Like physical capital, investment in education is costly. Studies show, however, that education offers a significant return—that is, people with more education earn higher wages. Moreover, education may also have a spillover or externality effect: Increasing the educational level of one person not only raises that person's output but also the output of those around her. The spillover effect operates through the link between education and advances in technology. Education not only improves the quality of the labor force but also encourages growth through innovation. Investment in health is also a major contributor to human capital, especially in developing countries.

Physical Capital Stock

The physical **capital stock** (accumulated amount of buildings, machinery, and equipment used to produce goods and services) increases from year to year as long as net investment (gross investment less depreciation of capital) is positive. Thus, countries with a higher rate of investment should have a growing physical capital stock and a higher rate of GDP growth.

Exhibit 24 shows the level of business investment as a share of GDP across a selection of 18 developed and developing economies. The exhibit shows significant variation across countries. As is evident in Exhibit 24, the correlation between investment (as a percentage of GDP) and economic growth in the subsequent period (19 years after 2000 and 9 years after 2010) is high. Economies that devote a large share of GDP to investment, such as China, India, and South Korea (numerical data not shown), have high growth rates. Ireland, Europe's fastest-growing economy from 2010–2018, has among the highest investment-to-GDP ratios in Europe. Economies that devote a smaller share of GDP to investment, such as Brazil and Mexico, have slower growth rates. The data helps explain why the Chinese economy has expanded so

Economic Growth and Sustainability

rapidly, achieving an annual GDP growth rate of nearly 10% over the last two decades. Investment spending in China on new factories, equipment, and infrastructure as a percentage of GDP is the highest in the world.

Exhibit 24: Business Investment as a Percentage of GDP and GDP Growth in the Subsequent Period

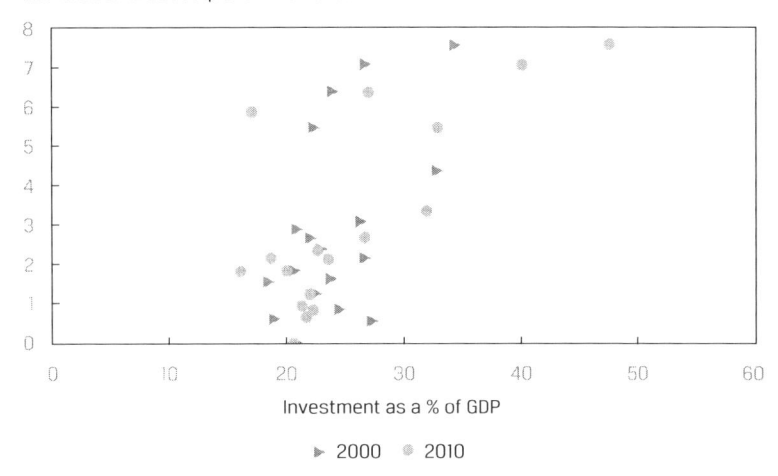

Notes: The term "investment" is represented by non-residential gross fixed capital formation as a share of GDP used. GDP growth is the average annual real GDP growth in the decade following the year of the investment as a percentage of GDP data.

Sources: GDP: OECD National Accounts Statistics (database), April 2019. Gross fixed capital: World Development Indicator, ne.gdi.totl.zs.

Natural Resources

Raw materials are an essential input to growth and include everything from available land to oil to water. Historically, consumption of raw materials has increased as economies have grown. There are two categories of natural resources:

1. **Renewable resources** are those that can be replenished, such as a forest. For example, if a tree is cut, a seedling can be planted and a new forest harvested in the future.
2. **Non-renewable resources** are finite resources that are depleted once they are consumed. Oil and coal are examples.

Natural resources account for some of the differences in growth among countries. Today, such countries as Brazil and Australia, as well as those in the Middle East, have relatively high per capita incomes because of their resource base. Countries in the Middle East have large pools of oil. Brazil has an abundance of land suitable for large-scale agricultural production, making it a major exporter of coffee, soybeans, and beef.

Although natural resources are an important factor in growth, they are not necessary for a country to achieve a high level of income provided it can acquire the requisite inputs through trade. Countries in eastern Asia, such as Japan and South Korea, have in the past experienced rapid economic growth but own few natural resources. It is also important to note that having plentiful natural resources may hurt an economy's growth, a topic that will be explored at a later stage.

Public Infrastructure

Roads, water systems, mass transportation, airports, and utilities are all examples of public infrastructure or public capital. Even if the infrastructure assets are privately owned or operated, the economic impact will be the same. Infrastructure assets have few substitutes and generate significant economies of scale, so they have the characteristics of a natural monopoly. A key feature of public capital is that it creates **externalities**. Externalities are spillover effects of production and consumption activities onto others who are not directly involved in a particular transaction, activity, or decision. In the case of public infrastructure, the externalities complement the production of private sector goods and services. The full benefit of public infrastructure investment may extend beyond its direct expenditure because it boosts the productivity of private capital.

Other Factors Driving Growth

Researchers have focused on the positive externalities associated with research and development and public education. Research and development efforts by one firm spill over and affect the stock of knowledge available to all firms, raising potential GDP growth. Thus, external or social benefits arise from increased spending on research and development that go beyond the benefit for the individual firm. The key point for economic growth is that there may be constant or increasing returns to the inputs, and thus the economy is no longer constrained by diminishing marginal productivity.

Externalities also have a negative effect on growth, with pollution being the primary example. Air and water quality in advanced countries have improved significantly over the last few decades, and there is a strong negative correlation between per capita GDP and pollution. But these success stories largely reflect the local economic effects of economic growth. The environmental problems we face today are global in nature and affect the entire planet. The burning of fossil fuels releases carbon dioxide into the atmosphere, causing a greenhouse effect that raises the earth's overall temperature. Climate change is closely linked to economic growth, because carbon dioxide emissions rise with economic growth. These emissions impose a cost on the global economy in terms of economic activity, food production, health, and habitability.

Without government action, individuals and firms may have no incentive to reduce these negative externalities. The more global the pollution problem, the less any single country benefits from reducing its emissions. Moreover, nations face an important trade-off on emissions: Reducing emissions today may result in lower short-term growth, but not reducing emissions today will negatively affect long-term sustainable GDP growth. Policy measures that create incentives to reduce the carbon intensity of output are the potential solution.

In addition to the aforementioned factors, a country's economic environment can play an important role in influencing economic growth. Lack of appropriate institutions and a poor legal and political environment restrain growth, especially in the developing countries. Factors such as internal competitive structure; poorly developed financial markets; a country's openness to trade; and its political stability, property rights, and rule of law can influence innovative activity and economic growth.

> **EXAMPLE 11**
>
> ## Sources of Growth for Westerland
>
> Westerland is an advanced economy with a high capital-to-labor ratio. Working-age population growth has been close to zero for the last decade. During the same period, annual GDP growth has slowed to about 1%. More than 70% of

Westerland's electricity is produced by renewable energy resources. The nation has reduced carbon dioxide emissions by 25% over the last decade. Policymakers hope to raise Westerland's sustainable rate of growth or its potential GDP.

Explain how the following factors are a potential source of growth for Westerland.

1. Tax reductions are proposed on business investment and R&D.

Solution to 1:

Because Westerland is an advanced economy operating at a high level of capital per worker, diminishing returns to capital are likely to be significant. If this is the case, additions to capital will have little effect on growth and are not a significant source of growth. In contrast, incentives encouraging increased R&D expenditures by increasing the growth rate of TFP and technological change are a potential source of growth.

2. Labor market incentives are planned to create flexible work schedules and develop policies for maternity/parental leave and childcare.

Solution to 2:

Westerland is facing a demographic challenge because slow population growth will limit its potential growth rate. To offset this issue, the country can encourage immigration and/or increase its workforce participation rate. The objective of creating flexible work schedules and developing policies for parental leave and childcare is to raise the labor force participation rate (note that Working age population × Participation rate × Average hours worked gives L, the amount of labor). In the short run, the labor market incentives will increase the growth rate in the labor supply and thus are a potential source of growth. After the initial response to these incentives, however, the labor force participation rate will level off. As a result, the policies will have no long-term effect on the labor input and will not increase sustainable growth.

3. Westerland plans to further reduce its carbon dioxide emissions, but global carbon dioxide emissions are expected to rise significantly as global GDP growth accelerates.

Solution to 3:

Westerland has successfully reduced its carbon dioxide emissions and plans further reduction, probably at the cost of slower GDP growth. Nevertheless, it still faces the negative effects of climate change despite its own effort to reduce emissions. This dynamic highlights climate change as a classic example of a negative externality that no single country can solve and requires global cooperation. This international burden sharing presents a stumbling block for success.

Measures of Sustainable Growth

Measuring how fast an economy can grow is an important exercise. Economists project potential GDP in order to forecast the economy's sustainable growth path. Potential GDP is an unobserved concept that is approximated using a number of alternative methods. Note that estimates of the economy's potential growth can change as new data become available. Being able to understand such changes is critical for financial analysts, because long-term forecasts for cash flows that companies generate are dependent on the sustainable rate of economic growth.

Labor Productivity

One approach to estimating potential GDP uses the productivity of the labor force, which is generally reliable data. **Labor productivity** consists of the quantity of goods and services (real GDP) that a worker can produce in one hour of work. Our standard of living improves if we produce more goods and services for each hour of work. Labor productivity is calculated as real GDP for a given year divided by the total number of hours worked in that year, counting all workers. We use total hours, rather than the number of workers, to adjust for the fact that not everyone works the same number of hours.

Labor productivity = Real GDP/Aggregate hours

Therefore, we need to understand the forces that make labor more productive. Productivity is determined by the factors that we examined earlier: education and skill of workers (human capital), investments in physical and public capital, natural resources, improvements in technology, and other factors. An increase in any of these factors will increase the productivity of the labor force. The factors determining labor productivity can be derived from the production functions under the assumption of constant returns to scale, where a doubling of inputs causes output to double as well. Dividing the production function by L, we obtain the following:

$Y/L = A\boldsymbol{F}(1, K/L)$,

where Y/L is output per worker, which is a measure of labor productivity. The equation states that labor productivity depends on physical capital per worker (K/L) and total factor productivity, which largely measures technological change (A). TFP is a scale factor that does not depend on the mix of inputs. Changes in TFP are measured as a residual, capturing growth that cannot be attributed to the labor supply and physical capital inputs. On the other hand, as shown in this equation, output per worker depends on both the general level of productivity (reflected in TFP) and the mix of inputs. Increases in either TFP or the capital-to-labor ratio boost output per worker. Because both output and labor input can be observed, labor productivity can be measured directly.

Labor productivity is a key concept for measuring the health and prosperity of an economy and its sustainable rate of growth. An analyst examining the growth prospects for an economy needs to focus on the labor productivity data for that country. Growth of labor productivity over time largely explains the differences in the living standards among countries. Labor productivity growth also helps analysts estimate the long-term sustainable growth rates among countries. The distinction between the level and growth rate of productivity is important to understand.

Level of Labor Productivity

The higher the level of labor productivity, the more goods and services the economy can produce with the same number of workers. The level of labor productivity depends on the accumulated stock of human and physical capital and is much higher in the developed countries.

Growth Rate of Labor Productivity

The growth rate of labor productivity is the percentage increase in productivity over a year. It is among the economic statistics that economists and financial analysts watch most closely. In contrast to the level of productivity, the growth rate of productivity is typically higher in developing countries where human and physical capital is scarce but growing rapidly.

If productivity growth is rapid, it means the same number of workers can produce more and more goods and services. In this case, companies can afford to pay higher future wages and still make a profit. Thus, high rates of productivity growth will translate into rising profits. Rising profits, if not already anticipated by the market, will support higher stock prices.

In contrast, persistently low productivity growth suggests the economy is in bad shape. Without productivity gains, businesses have to either cut wages or boost prices in order to increase profit margins. Low rates of productivity growth should be associated with slow growth in profits and flat or declining stock prices.

EXAMPLE 12

Prospects for Equity Returns in Mexico

1. John Todd, CFA, manages a global mutual fund with nearly 30% of its assets invested in Europe. Because of the low population growth rate, he is concerned about the long-term outlook for the European economies. With potentially slower economic growth in Europe, the environment for equities may be less attractive. Therefore, Todd is considering reallocating some of the assets from Europe to Mexico. Data shows that the level of business investment has been around 24% of GDP, while that of China is more than 40% and that of European countries is close to 20%. The level of productivity for Europe as a whole is more than $60 per hour worked (as of 2018). Data also shows that labor productivity since 2001 in Mexico is growing at about a 0.2% annual rate, below that of Germany, France, and Spain. Do you think that investment opportunities are favorable in Mexico? According to the OECD, the Mexican population increased by 1.1% in 2018, compared with a 0.2% increase in the European Union population (27 countries).

Solution:

Other than the higher population growth rate, the potential sources of growth for Mexico are not favorable. The level of business investment in Mexico is quite low, especially compared with China, and not much higher than that of many of the advanced economies in Europe. The level of labor productivity in Mexico is well below that in most European countries. This is not surprising given that the amount of capital per worker in Mexico is much lower than that in Europe.

What is surprising and of concern is the low rate of labor productivity growth in Mexico. This means that the rightward shift in the aggregate supply curve is greater for the European countries than for Mexico, despite the more favorable demographic trend in the country. In addition, it implies that there is more potential for expanding profit margins in Europe than in Mexico. Thus, the analysis of potential growth does not suggest a favorable outlook for equity returns in Mexico. In this simplified example, in the absence of more favorable considerations—for example, compelling equity valuations—Todd should decide not to reallocate assets from Europe to Mexico.

Measuring Sustainable Growth

Labor productivity data can be used to estimate the rate of sustainable growth of the economy. A useful way to describe potential GDP is as a combination of aggregate hours worked and the productivity of those workers:

Potential GDP = Aggregate hours worked × Labor productivity

Transforming the above equation into growth rates, we obtain the following:

Potential growth rate = Long-term growth rate of aggregate hours worked + Long-term labor productivity growth rate

Thus, potential growth is a combination of the long-term growth rate of the aggregate hours worked and the long-term growth rate of labor productivity. Therefore, if aggregate hours worked are growing at 1% per year and productivity per worker is rising at 2% per year, then potential GDP (adjusted for inflation) is rising at 3% per year.

EXAMPLE 13

Estimating the Rate of Growth in Potential GDP

1. Exhibit 25 provides data on the growth rate in aggregate hours worked and productivity growth for Canada, Germany, Japan, and the United States. Estimate the growth rate of potential GDP for each country by averaging the growth rates for these variables since 2001. Also, describe the role that the labor input plays in determining potential growth for each country.

Exhibit 25: Aggregate Hours Worked and Productivity: Average Annual Growth Rate

	Aggregate Hours Worked		Productivity	
	2011–2018	2001–2010	2011–2018	2001–2010
Canada	0.9%	1.4%	1.0%	0.9%
Germany	0.5	0.2	1.1	0.9
Japan	0.3	−0.2	0.8	1.2
United States	0.7	0.7	1.5	0.8

Solution:

Potential GDP is calculated as the sum of the trend growth rate in the aggregate hours worked (labor input) and the trend growth rate in labor productivity. The growth in the labor input depends on the population growth rate, changes in the labor force participation rate, and changes in hours worked per person. Estimating based on the average for the period from 2001–2018 gives the following data:

Economic Growth and Sustainability

	Projected Growth in Aggregate Hours Worked	Projected Growth in Labor Productivity	Projected Growth in Potential GDP
Canada	1.2%	0.9%	2.1%
Germany	0.3	1.0	1.3
Japan	0.0	1.0	1.0
United States	0.7	1.1	1.8

Note: Rounding used throughout.

Most of the difference between the growth rates in potential GDP among these countries can be explained by the labor input. The most significant result is the difference in the growth rate in aggregate hours in Germany and Japan, in contrast to that in the United States and Canada. The results suggest that Japan's sluggish economic growth is likely to continue because of the lack of growth in the labor input.

EXAMPLE 14

Prospects for Fixed-Income Investments

1. As a fixed income analyst for a large Canadian bank, you are preparing the 2019–2020 forecast and have just received the latest GDP forecast from the OECD for Canada, Germany, Japan, and the United States. The forecast is given in Exhibit 26, along with the potential GDP growth estimates that the analyst has calculated.

Exhibit 26: Projected vs. Potential GDP Growth

	Projected Average Annual GDP Growth (2019–2020)	Projected Growth in Potential GDP
Canada	4.0%	2.1%
Germany	1.5	1.3
Japan	0.0	1.0
United States	3.5	1.8

To evaluate the future prospects for fixed-income investments, analysts must estimate the future rate of inflation and assess the possibility of changes in monetary policy by the central bank. An important indicator for both of these factors is the degree of slack in the economy, which can be measured by comparing the growth rates of actual GDP and potential GDP.

Based on the information in Exhibit 26, evaluate the prospects for fixed-income investments in each country.

> **Solution:**
> In comparing the OECD forecast for GDP growth with the estimated growth rate in potential GDP, there are two cases to consider:
>
> 1. If actual GDP is growing at a faster rate than potential GDP, it signals growing inflationary pressures, and an increased likelihood that the central bank will raise interest rates.
> 2. If actual GDP is growing at a slower rate than potential GDP, it signals growing resource slack, less inflationary pressures, and an increased likelihood that the central bank will reduce rates or leave them unchanged.
>
> Projected and potential GDP for the aforementioned countries can be compared referring to Exhibit 26.
>
> The data suggest that inflationary pressure will grow in the United States and Canada and that both the Federal Reserve and the Bank of Canada will eventually raise interest rates. Thus, the environment for bond investing is not favorable in the United States and Canada, because bond prices are likely to decline.
>
> With Germany growing at close to its potential rate of GDP growth, the rate of inflation should neither rise nor fall. Monetary policy is set by the European Central Bank (ECB), but data on the German economy play a big role in the ECB's decision. Based on the data in Exhibit 26, no change in ECB policy is likely. For bond investors, little change in bond prices is likely in Germany, so investors need to focus on the interest (coupon) income received from the bond.
>
> Finally, growing resource slack in Japan will put downward pressure on inflation and may force the Bank of Japan to keep rates low. Bond prices should rise in this environment.

SUMMARY

- GDP is the market value of all final goods and services produced within a country during a given period.
- GDP can be valued by looking at either the total amount spent on goods and services produced in the economy or the income generated in producing those goods and services.
- GDP counts only final purchases of newly produced goods and services during the current period. Transfer payments and capital gains are excluded from GDP.
- Intermediate goods are excluded from GDP in order to avoid double counting.
- GDP can be measured either from the value of final output or by summing the value added at each stage of the production and distribution process. The sum of the value added by each stage is equal to the final selling price of the good.
- Nominal GDP is the value of production using the prices of the current year. Real GDP measures production using the constant prices of a base year. The GDP deflator equals the ratio of nominal GDP to real GDP.

- Households earn income in exchange for providing—directly or indirectly through ownership of businesses—the factors of production (labor, capital, and natural resources including land). From this income, they consume, save, and pay net taxes.
- Businesses produce most of the economy's output/income and invest to maintain and expand productive capacity. Companies retain some earnings but pay out most of their revenue as income to the household sector and as taxes to the government.
- The government sector collects taxes from households and businesses and purchases goods and services, for both consumption and investment, from the private business sector.
- International trade consists of exports and imports. The difference between the two is net exports. If net exports are positive (negative), then the country spends less (more) than it earns. Net exports are balanced by accumulation of either claims on the rest of the world (net exports > 0) or obligations to the rest of the world (net exports < 0).
- Capital markets provide a link between saving and investment in the economy.
- From the expenditure side, GDP includes personal consumption (C), gross private domestic investment (I), government spending (G), and net exports ($X - M$).
- The major categories of expenditure are often broken down into subcategories. Gross private domestic investment includes both investment in fixed assets (plant and equipment) and the change in inventories. In some countries, government spending on investment is separated from other government spending.
- National income is the income received by all factors of production used in the generation of final output. It equals GDP minus the **capital consumption allowance** (depreciation) and a statistical discrepancy.
- Personal income reflects pre-tax income received by households. It equals national income plus transfers minus undistributed corporate profits, corporate income taxes, and indirect business taxes.
- Personal disposable income equals personal income minus personal taxes.
- Private saving must equal investment plus the fiscal and trade deficits. That is, $S = I + (G - T) + (X - M)$.
- Consumption spending is a function of disposable income. The marginal propensity to consume represents the fraction of an additional unit of disposable income that is spent.
- Investment spending depends on the average interest rate and the level of aggregate income. Government purchases and tax policy are often considered to be exogenous variables determined outside the macroeconomic model. Actual taxes collected depend on income and are, therefore, endogenous—that is, determined within the model.
- Aggregate demand and aggregate supply determine the level of real GDP and the price level.
- The downward slope of the aggregate demand curve arises as the result of three effects: the wealth effect, the interest rate effect, and the real exchange rate effect. The curve is drawn assuming a constant money supply.

- The aggregate demand curve will shift if there is a change in a factor, other than price, that affects aggregate demand. These factors include household wealth, consumer and business expectations, capacity utilization, monetary policy, fiscal policy, exchange rates, and other nations' GDP.

- The aggregate supply curve is the relationship between the quantity of real GDP supplied and the price level, keeping all other factors constant. Movements along the supply curve reflect the effects of price on supply.

- The short-run aggregate supply curve is upward sloping because higher prices result in higher profits and induce businesses to produce more and laborers to work more. In the short run, some prices are sticky, implying that some prices do not adjust to changes in demand.

- In the long run, all prices are assumed to be flexible. The long-run aggregate supply curve is vertical because input costs adjust to changes in output prices, leaving the optimal level of output unchanged. The position of the curve is determined by the economy's level of potential GDP.

- The level of potential output, also called the full employment or natural level of output, is unobservable and difficult to measure precisely. This concept represents an efficient and unconstrained level of production at which companies have enough spare capacity to avoid bottlenecks and there is a balance between the pool of unemployed workers and the pool of job openings.

- The long-run aggregate supply curve will shift because of changes in labor supply, supply of physical and human capital, and productivity/technology.

- The short-run supply curve will shift because of changes in potential GDP, nominal wages, input prices, expectations about future prices, business taxes and subsidies, and the exchange rate.

- Short-term fluctuations in GDP are caused by shifts in aggregate demand and aggregate supply.

- When the level of GDP in the economy is below potential GDP, such a recessionary situation exerts downward pressure on the aggregate price level.

- When the level of GDP is above potential GDP, such an overheated situation puts upward pressure on the aggregate price level.

- Stagflation, a combination of high inflation and weak economic growth, is caused by a decline in short-run aggregate supply.

- Growth in real GDP measures how rapidly the total economy is expanding. Per capita GDP, defined as real GDP divided by population, reflects a country's standard of living. Real GDP growth rates and levels of per capita GDP vary widely among countries.

- The sources of economic growth include the supply of labor, the supply of physical and human capital, raw materials, and technological knowledge.

- Output can be described in terms of a production function. For example, $Y = AF(L,K)$, where L is the quantity of labor, K is the capital stock, and A represents total factor productivity (primarily technology). The function $F(\cdot)$ is assumed to exhibit constant returns to scale but diminishing marginal productivity for each input individually.

- Total factor productivity is a scale factor that reflects the portion of output growth that is not accounted for by changes in the capital and labor inputs. TFP is mainly a reflection of technological change.

- Based on a two-factor production function, Potential GDP growth = Growth in TFP + W_L (Growth in labor) + W_C (Growth in capital), where W_L and W_C (= $1 - W_L$) are the shares of labor and capital in GDP.
- Diminishing marginal productivity implies that
  - increasing the supply of some input(s) relative to other inputs will lead to diminishing returns and cannot be the basis for sustainable growth. In particular, long-term sustainable growth cannot rely solely on capital deepening (i.e., on increasing the stock of capital relative to labor).
  - given the relative scarcity and hence high productivity of capital in developing countries, the growth rate of developing countries should exceed that of developed countries.
- The sustainable rate of economic growth is measured by the rate of increase in the economy's productive capacity or potential GDP.
- The labor supply is determined by both population growth (including immigration) and the labor force participation rate. The capital stock in a country increases with investment. Correlation between long-run economic growth and the rate of investment is high.
- In addition to labor, capital, and technology, human capital—essentially, the quality of the labor force—and natural resources are important determinants of output and growth as are the state of public infrastructure and the institutional, legal and political environment.
- Technological advances are discoveries that make it possible to produce more and/or higher-quality goods and services with the same resources or inputs. Technology is the main factor affecting economic growth in developed countries.
- Externalities and spillover effects are also recognized to play an important role in growth. Positive externalities are associated with research and development and public education. Negative externalities such as pollution have a negative effect on growth.
- Climate change is closely linked to economic growth as carbon dioxide emissions rise with economic growth. These emissions impose a cost on the global economy in terms of economic activity, food production, health and habitability.
- The sustainable rate of growth in an economy is determined by the growth rate of the labor supply plus the growth rate of labor productivity.

REFERENCES

Case, K., J. Quigley, R. Shiller. 2005. "Comparing Wealth Effects: The Stock Market versus the Housing Market." *Advances in Macroeconomics*, vol. 5, no. 1.

Funke, N. 2004. "Is There a Stock Market Wealth Effect in Emerging Markets?" *International Monetary Fund* (March).

PRACTICE PROBLEMS

1. Which of the following statements is the *most* appropriate description of gross domestic product (GDP)?

    A. The total income earned by all households, firms, and the government whose value can be verified

    B. The total amount spent on all final goods and services produced within the economy during a given period

    C. The total market value of resalable and final goods and services produced within the economy during a given period

2. The component *least likely* to be included in a measurement of gross domestic product (GDP) is:

    A. the value of owner occupied rent.

    B. the annual salary of a local police officer.

    C. environmental damage caused by production.

3. Which of the following would be included in Canadian GDP for a given year? The market value of:

    A. wine grown in Canada by US citizens.

    B. electronics made in Japan and sold in Canada.

    C. movies produced outside Canada by Canadian filmmakers.

4. Suppose a painting is produced and sold in 2018 for £5,000. The expenses involved in producing the painting amounted to £2,000. According to the sum-of-value-added method of calculating GDP, the value added by the final step of creating the painting was:

    A. £2,000.

    B. £3,000.

    C. £5,000.

5. Which of the following conditions is *least likely* to increase a country's GDP?

    A. An increase in net exports

    B. Increased investment in capital goods

    C. Increased government transfer payments

6. The *most* accurate description of nominal GDP is:

    A. a measure of total expenditures at current prices.

    B. the value of goods and services at constant prices.

    C. a measure to compare one nation's economy to another.

7. From the beginning to the ending years of a decade, the annual value of final goods and services for country X increased from €100 billion to €300 billion. During that period, the GDP deflator increased from 111 to 200. Over the decade, real GDP for country X increased by approximately:

   A. 50%.

   B. 67%.

   C. 200%.

8. If the GDP deflator values for Year 1 and Year 3 were 190 and 212.8, respectively, which of the following *best* describes the annual growth rate of the overall price level?

   A. 5.8%

   B. 6%

   C. 12%

9. The numerator of the GDP price deflator reflects:

   A. the value of base year output at current prices.

   B. the value of current year output at current prices.

   C. the value of current year output at base year prices.

10. Consider the following data for a hypothetical country:

Account name	Amount ($ trillions)
Consumption	15.0
Capital consumption allowance	1.5
Government spending	3.8
Imports	1.7
Gross private domestic investment	4.0
Exports	1.5

    Based only on the data given, the gross domestic product and national income are respectively *closest* to:

    A. 21.1 and 20.6.

    B. 22.6 and 21.1.

    C. 22.8 and 20.8.

11. In calculating personal income for a given year, which of the following would *not* be subtracted from national income?

    A. Indirect business taxes

    B. Undistributed corporate profits

    C. Unincorporated business net income

12. Equality between aggregate expenditure and aggregate output implies that the

government's fiscal deficit must equal:

   A. Private saving – Investment – Net exports.

   B. Private saving – Investment + Net exports.

   C. Investment – Private saving + Net exports.

13. Because of a sharp decline in real estate values, the household sector has increased the fraction of disposable income that it saves. If output and investment spending remain unchanged, which of the following is *most likely*?

   A. A decrease in the government deficit

   B. A decrease in net exports and increased capital inflow

   C. An increase in net exports and increased capital outflow

14. A GDP deflator less than 1 indicates that an economy has experienced:

   A. inflation.

   B. deflation.

   C. stagflation.

15. In explaining the downward slope of the aggregate demand curve, the interest rate effect suggests that a higher price level will:

   A. lead to lower interest rates, which will lead to higher levels of consumption and investment.

   B. lead to higher interest rates, which will lead to lower levels of consumption and investment.

   C. not affect interest rates and therefore will lead to a higher level of aggregate demand.

16. One of the reasons the aggregate demand curve is downward sloping is because a lower price level means that the real exchange rate:

   A. depreciates, making domestic goods cheaper in other countries and imports less competitive, resulting in a higher level of net exports.

   B. appreciates, making domestic goods more expensive in other countries and imports more competitive, resulting in a higher level of net exports.

   C. appreciates, making the country's exports and imports less competitive and leading to lower net exports.

17. The full employment, or natural, level of output is *best* described as:

   A. the maximum level obtainable with existing resources.

   B. the level at which all available workers have jobs consistent with their skills.

   C. a level with a modest, stable pool of unemployed workers transitioning to new jobs.

18. Which of the following *best* describes the aggregate supply curve in the short run

(one to two years)? The short-run aggregate supply curve is:

- **A.** flat, because output is more flexible than prices in the short run.
- **B.** vertical, because wages and other input prices fully adjust to the price level.
- **C.** upward sloping, because input prices do not fully adjust to the price level in the short run.

19. If wages were automatically adjusted for changes in the price level, the short-run aggregate supply curve would *most likely* be:
    - **A.** flatter.
    - **B.** steeper.
    - **C.** unchanged.

20. The *least likely* cause of a decrease in aggregate demand is:
    - **A.** higher taxes.
    - **B.** a weak domestic currency.
    - **C.** a fall in capacity utilization.

21. Which of the following is *most likely* to cause the long-run aggregate supply curve to shift to the left?
    - **A.** Higher nominal wages
    - **B.** A decline in productivity
    - **C.** An increase in corporate taxes

22. Increased household wealth will *most likely* cause an increase in:
    - **A.** household saving.
    - **B.** investment expenditures.
    - **C.** consumption expenditures.

23. The *most likely* outcome when both aggregate supply and aggregate demand increase is:
    - **A.** a rise in inflation.
    - **B.** higher employment.
    - **C.** an increase in nominal GDP.

24. Which of the following is *least likely* to be caused by a shift in aggregate demand?
    - **A.** Stagflation
    - **B.** A recessionary gap
    - **C.** An inflationary gap

25. Following a sharp increase in the price of energy, the overall price level is *most*

likely to rise in the short run:

   A. and remain elevated indefinitely unless the central bank tightens.

   B. but remain unchanged in the long run unless the money supply is increased.

   C. and continue to rise until all prices have increased by the same proportion.

26. Among developed economies, which of the following sources of economic growth is *most likely* to explain superior growth performance?

    A. Technology

    B. Capital stock

    C. Labor supply

27. Which of the following can be measured directly?

    A. Potential GDP

    B. Labor productivity

    C. Total factor productivity

28. The sustainable growth rate is *best* estimated as:

    A. the weighted average of capital and labor growth rates.

    B. growth in the labor force plus growth of labor productivity.

    C. growth in total factor productivity plus growth in the capital-to-labor ratio.

29. In the neoclassical or Solow growth model, an increase in total factor productivity reflects an increase in:

    A. returns to scale.

    B. output for given inputs.

    C. the sustainable growth rate.

30. Convergence of incomes over time between emerging market countries and developed countries is *most likely* the result of:

    A. total factor productivity.

    B. diminishing marginal productivity of capital.

    C. the exhaustion of non-renewable resources.

SOLUTIONS

1. B is correct. GDP is the total amount spent on all final goods and services produced within the economy during a specific period.

2. C is correct. Byproducts of production processes that have no explicit market value are not included in GDP.

3. A is correct. Canadian GDP is the total market value of all final goods and services produced during a given period within Canada. The wine was produced in Canada and counts toward Canadian GDP.

4. B is correct. The value added by the artist is £5,000 − £2,000 = £3,000.

5. C is correct. Government transfer payments, such as unemployment compensation or welfare benefits, are excluded from GDP.

6. A is correct. Nominal GDP is defined as the value of goods and services measured at current prices. Expenditure is used synonymously with the value of goods and services because aggregate expenditures must equal aggregate output of an economy.

7. B is correct. Real GDP in the first year was €100 billion/1.11 = €90 billion, and in the last year it was €300 billion/2.00 = €150 billion. Thus, (€150 − €90)/€90 = 0.67, or 67%.

8. A is correct: $(212.8/190)^{1/2} - 1 = 0.0583$, or 5.8%.

9. B is correct.

    $$\text{GDP deflator} = \frac{\text{Value of current year output at current year prices}}{\text{Value of current year output at base year prices}} \times 100$$

10. B is correct. GDP = Consumption + Gross private domestic investment + Government spending + (Exports − Imports) = 15 + 4 + 3.8 + (1.5 − 1.7) = 22.6. National income = GDP − CCA = 22.6 − 1.5 = 21.1.

11. C is correct. Unincorporated business net income, also known as proprietor's income, is included in personal income.

12. A is correct. The fundamental relationship among saving, investment, the fiscal balance, and the trade balance is $S = I + (G - T) + (X - M)$. This form of the relationship shows that private saving must fund investment expenditures, the government fiscal balance, and net exports (= net capital outflows). Rearranging gives $G - T = (S - I) - (X - M)$. The government's fiscal deficit $(G - T)$ must equal the private sector's saving/investment balance $(S - I)$ minus net exports.

13. C is correct. The fundamental relationship among saving, investment, the fiscal balance, and the trade balance is $S = I + (G - T) + (X - M)$. Given the levels of output and investment spending, an increase in saving (reduction in consumption) must be offset by either an increase in the fiscal deficit or an increase in net exports. Increasing the fiscal deficit is not one of the choices, so an increase in net exports and a corresponding increase in net capital outflows (increased lending internationally and/or increased international purchases of assets) are the correct response.

14. B is correct. The GDP deflator = Nominal GDP/Real GDP. To obtain a ratio less

than 1, real GDP must exceed nominal GDP, which indicates that prices have decreased and, accordingly, deflation has occurred.

15. B is correct. Assuming a fixed supply of money, a higher price level will lead to a higher price of money. Because the price of money is the interest rate, as the price level increases, the interest rate increases. Higher interest rates will lead to lower consumption and investment.

16. A is correct. A lower price level results in a weaker real exchange rate, making domestic goods cheaper to people in other countries and imports less competitive, resulting in a higher level of net exports.

17. C is correct. At the full employment, or natural, level of output, the economy is operating at an efficient and unconstrained level of production. Companies have enough spare capacity to avoid bottlenecks, and there is a modest, stable pool of unemployed workers (job seekers equal job vacancies) looking for and transitioning into new jobs.

18. C is correct. Because of long-term contracts and other rigidities, wages and other input costs do not fully adjust to changes in the price level in the short run. Given input prices, firms respond to output price changes by expanding or contracting output to maximize profit. Hence, the SRAS is upward sloping.

19. B is correct. The slope of the short-run aggregate supply curve reflects the extent to which wages and other input costs adjust to the overall price level. Automatic adjustment of wages would mitigate the impact of price changes on profitability. Hence, firms would not adjust output as much in response to changing output prices—the SRAS curve would be steeper.

20. B is correct. A weak domestic currency will result in an increase in aggregate demand at each price level—a rightward shift in the AD curve. A weaker currency will cause a country's exports to be cheaper in global markets. Conversely, imports will be more expensive for domestic buyers. Hence, the net exports component of aggregate demand will increase.

21. B is correct. Productivity measures the efficiency of labor and is the amount of output produced by workers during a given period. A decline in productivity implies decreased efficiency. A decline in productivity increases labor costs, decreases profitability, and results in lower output at each output price level—a leftward shift in both the short-run and long-run aggregate supply curves.

22. C is correct. The wealth effect explains the impact of increases or decreases in household wealth on economic activity. Household wealth includes financial and real assets. As asset values increase, consumers save less and spend more out of current income because they will still be able to meet their wealth accumulation goals. Therefore, an increase in household wealth results in a rightward shift in the aggregate demand curve.

23. B is correct. Higher aggregate demand and higher aggregate supply raise real GDP and lower unemployment, meaning employment levels increase.

24. A is correct. Stagflation occurs when output is declining and prices are rising. This dynamic most likely results from a decline in aggregate supply—a leftward shift of the SRAS curve. Depending on the source of the shift, the LRAS may shift too.

25. B is correct. An increase in energy prices will shift the short-run aggregate supply curve (SRAS) to the left, reducing output and increasing prices. If the aggregate

demand curve does not change—in particular, if the central bank does not expand the money supply—slack in the economy will put downward pressure on in input prices, shifting the SRAS back to its original position. In the long run, the price level will be unchanged.

26. A is correct. Technology is the most important factor affecting economic growth for developed countries. Technological advances are very important because they allow an economy to overcome the limits imposed by diminishing marginal returns.

27. B is correct. Labor productivity can be directly measured as output/hour.

28. B is correct. Output growth is equal to the growth rate of the labor force plus the growth rate of labor productivity—that is, output per worker. Unlike total factor productivity, output per worker is observable, so this measure is the most practical way to approach estimation of sustainable growth.

29. B is correct. Total factor productivity is a scale factor primarily reflecting technology. An increase in TFP means that output increases for any level of factor inputs.

30. B is correct. Diminishing marginal productivity of capital means that as a country accumulates more capital per worker, the incremental boost to output declines. Thus, all else equal, economies grow more slowly as they become more capital intensive. Given the relative scarcity and hence high marginal productivity of capital in developing countries, these economies tend to grow more rapidly than developed countries. This dynamic leads to convergence in income levels over time.

LEARNING MODULE 4

Introduction to Business Cycles

by Michele Gambera, PhD, CFA, Milton Ezrati, and Bolong Cao, PhD, CFA.

Michele Gambera, PhD, CFA, is with UBS Asset Management and the University of Illinois at Urbana-Champaign (USA). Milton Ezrati (USA). Bolong Cao, PhD, CFA, is at Ohio University (USA).

LEARNING OUTCOMES	
Mastery	The candidate should be able to:
☐	describe how resource use, consumer and business activity, housing sector activity, and external trade sector activity vary as an economy moves through the business cycle
☐	describe types of unemployment, and compare measures of unemployment
☐	explain inflation, hyperinflation, disinflation, and deflation
☐	explain the construction of indexes used to measure inflation
☐	compare inflation measures, including their uses and limitations
☐	contrast cost-push and demand-pull inflation

INTRODUCTION

A typical economy's output of goods and services fluctuates around its longer-term path. We now turn our attention to those recurring, cyclical fluctuations in economic output. Some of the factors that influence short-term changes in the economy—such as changes in population, technology, and capital—are the same as those that affect long-term sustainable economic growth. But forces that cause shifts in aggregate demand and aggregate supply curves—such as expectations, political developments, natural disasters, and fiscal and monetary policy decisions—influence economies particularly in the short run.

Business cycles are expansions and contractions in economic activity which affect broad segments of the economy. While each cycle is different, analysts and investors must understand expectations and decisions of businesses and households that influence the performance of sectors and companies. These behaviors also impact financial conditions and risk appetite, thus impacting the setting of expectations and choices of portfolio exposures to different investment sectors or styles.

In the sections that follow, we describe consumer behavior, housing sector behavior and external trade sector behavior and how they are affected by business cycles. We then proceed to explain measures and features of unemployment and inflation.

2. CONSUMER BEHAVIOR

> describe how resource use, consumer and business activity, housing sector activity, and external trade sector activity vary as an economy moves through the business cycle

Households represent the largest single sector of most economies. As a result, patterns of household consumption determine overall economic direction more than any other sector. For this reason, the patterns of household consumption are important to a range of practitioners, not just to analysts focusing on companies serving consumers.

Consumer Confidence

Consumer confidence plays a significant role in spending decisions and reflects expectations of future incomes and employment prospects. Beyond direct observations of consumer spending and its mix, practitioners can also gauge future directions of spending by analyzing measures of consumer confidence or sentiment to ascertain how aggressive consumers may be in their spending. Usually, such information is in the form of surveys intended to provide practitioners with a general guide to trends.

Measures of Consumption

Two primary measures of household consumption are retail sales (physical as well as online) and broad-based indicators of consumer spending that also include purchases outside purely retail establishments, such as utilities and household services. Some additional measures make finer distinctions, such as tracking spending, both real and nominal, of a specific group of consumer products. Exhibit 1 shows how consumer spending changes through the economic cycle, and it splits consumer spending into three parts: (1) durable goods, (2) non-durable goods, and (3) services. Spending on durables is the most cyclical part, while spending on non-durables is the least cyclical. Spending on services, which include both more and less cyclical sub-components, in aggregate fits between the durable and non-durable goods categories. It is also worth noting that consumer spending, including that on durables, while cyclical, is less cyclical than investment spending by firms.

Exhibit 1: Consumer Behavior

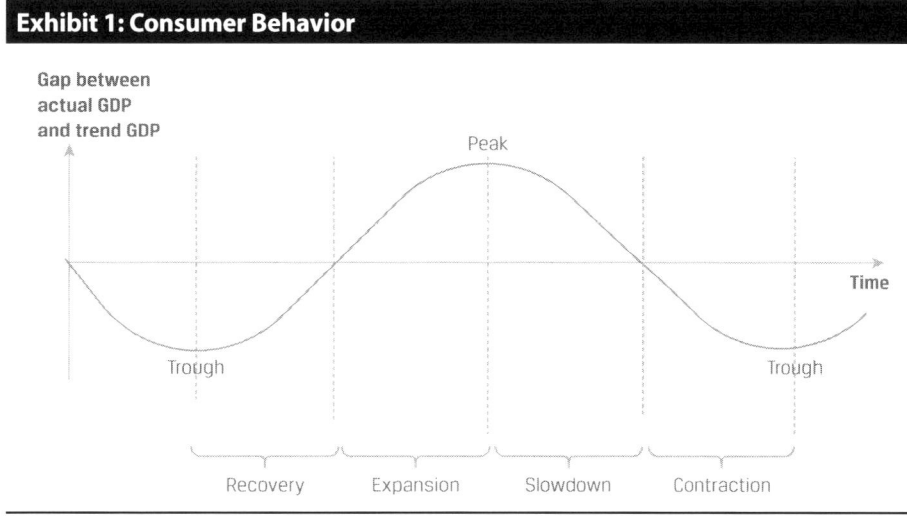

Gap between actual GDP and trend GDP

(Curve showing business cycle with Trough → Recovery → Peak → Expansion → Slowdown → Contraction → Trough over Time)

Phase of the Cycle	Recovery	Expansion	Slowdown	Contraction
Incomes, employment, and confidence	Unemployment remains above average. Layoffs slow. Businesses rely on overtime before moving to hiring. Consumer confidence starts improving.	Hiring restarts. Unemployment rate stabilizes and starts falling. Consumers experience rising incomes, healthy employment prospects, and greater confidence.	Businesses continue hiring but at a slower pace. Unemployment rate continues to fall. Incomes are still growing. Consumers remain confident.	Businesses first cut hours of overtime prior to freezing hiring and starting layoffs. Employment levels decline, and consumer confidence weakens.
Spending on consumer durables (autos, motorcycles, appliances, furniture)	Spending limited as households postpone spending.	Spending increases.	Spending above average.	Purchases postponed; spending decreasing.
Consumer non-durables (i.e., medicines, food, household products)	Spending shows little change through the cycle.			
Services (entertainment, outdoor eating, communications, personal services)	Spending below average.	Spending increases.	Spending above average.	Spending declines.

Analysts often compare trends in durable purchases with those in the other categories to understand the economy's progress through the cycle. Because durable goods purchases usually replace items with longer useful lives, households usually postpone such purchases during economic downturns. Therefore, a weakness in durables spending may be an early indication of general economic weakness, and an increase in such spending may signal a more general cyclical recovery.

Income Growth

Growth in income is normally a good indicator of consumption prospects, and, albeit not as timely as consumer surveys, household income figures are widely available in most countries. Especially relevant is after-tax income, known as disposable income. Some analysts chart consumer spending based on a concept termed permanent income. Permanent income excludes temporary income (windfall or sudden, unexpected) and unsustainable losses and gains and tries to capture the income flow on which households believe they can rely. The basic level of consumption reflects this notion of permanent income. However, spending on durables tends to rise and fall with disposable income, regardless of the source, not just permanent income.

Saving Rates

Consumer spending patterns frequently diverge from trends in income, no matter how income is measured. An analysis of the saving rates can assist practitioners in this regard. Changes in saving rates can capture consumers' intent to reduce spending out of current income. The saving rate may also reflect future income uncertainties perceived by consumers (precautionary savings). Therefore, a higher saving rate may indicate consumers' ability to spend despite possible lower income in the future. A rise in the saving rate, usually measured as a percentage of income, may indicate caution among households and signal economic weakening. At the same time, the greater the stock of savings in the household sector and the wider the gap between ongoing income and spending, the greater the capacity for households to increase their spending. So, although unusually high savings may at first say something negative about the cyclical outlook, they point longer-term to the potential for recovery.

EXAMPLE 1

Consumer Behavior

1. Durable goods have the most pronounced cyclical behavior because:
   - **A.** they have a longer useful life.
   - **B.** their purchase cannot be delayed.
   - **C.** they are needed more than non-durable goods or services.

Solution to 1:

A is correct. Durable goods are usually big ticket items, the life span of which can be extended with repairs and without incurring high replacement costs. So, consumers tend to delay replacement when the economic outlook is not favorable.

2. Permanent income provides a better guide to:
   - **A.** saving rates.
   - **B.** spending on services.
   - **C.** spending on durable goods.

Solution to 2:

B is correct. Households adjust consumption of discretionary goods and services based on the perceived permanent income level rather than temporary earning fluctuations. Saving rates and durable goods consumption are more related to the short-term uncertainties caused by recessions.

HOUSING SECTOR BEHAVIOR

3

☐ describe how resource use, consumer and business activity, housing sector activity, and external trade sector activity vary as an economy moves through the business cycle

Housing sector activity includes new and existing home sales and residential construction activity. It is a small part of the overall economy compared to consumer spending, but because housing activity experiences dramatic swings, it often counts more in overall economic movements than the sector's relatively small size might suggest. In many countries, such as the United States and the United Kingdom, changing property values are closely related to consumer wealth and confidence.

Available Statistics

Many economies offer statistics on a range of housing activities, including the inventory of unsold homes on the market and average or median price of homes (sometimes recorded by type of housing unit and sometimes as the price per square foot or square meter). The relationships in this area typically follow fairly regular cyclical patterns.

Sensitivity to Interest Rates and Relationship to Credit Cycle

Because many home buyers finance their purchase with a loan (called a mortgage in some countries), the sector is especially sensitive to interest rates. Home buying and consequently construction activity expand in response to lower loan interest rates and contract in response to higher loan interest rates.

Beyond such interest rate effects, housing also follows its own internal cycle, seen as part of the credit cycle. When housing prices are low relative to average incomes, and especially when mortgage rates are also low, the cost of owning a house falls and demand for housing increases. Often indicators of the cost of owning a house are available to compare household incomes with the cost of supporting an average house, both its price and the expense of a typical mortgage. Commonly, housing prices and mortgage rates rise disproportionately as expansionary cycles mature, bringing on an increase in relative housing costs even as household incomes rise. The resulting slowdown of house sales can lead to a cyclical downturn first in buying and then, as the inventory of unsold houses builds, in actual construction activity.

These links, clear as they are, are far from mechanical. If housing prices have risen rapidly in the recent past, for instance, many people will buy to gain exposure to the expected further price gains even as the purchase in other respects becomes harder to rationalize. Such behavior can extend the cycle upward and may later result in a more severe correction. This result occurs because "late buying" activity invites overbuilding. The large inventory of unsold homes eventually puts downward pressure on real estate prices, catching late buyers, who have stretched their resources. This pattern occurred in many countries during the 2008–2009 global financial crisis.

The Role of Demographics

Cyclical behavior in housing occurs around the long-run growth trend in housing determined by demographics, such as family and household formation. Where data on family formation are unavailable, analysts can gauge the rate of family formation by assessing the age structure of the population, as household formation commonly occurs in the 25- to 40-year-old age group. Adjusted for older people who are vacating existing homes, such calculations serve as an indicator of underlying, longer-term, secular housing demand.

Impact on the Economic Cycle

Although such measures have little to do with business cycles, they do offer a gauge, along with affordability, of how quickly the housing market can correct excess and return to growth. As some faster-growing developing economies experience urbanization (people moving from the countryside to cities), they witness fast growth in demand for housing units. Such housing demand may quickly reverse any cyclical weakness in the economy, more so than in such economies as Italy or Japan where net new family formation is relatively slight.

> **EXAMPLE 2**
>
> ### Housing Sector Behavior
>
> 1. Housing is more sensitive than other sectors of the economy to:
>   - **A.** interest rates.
>   - **B.** permanent income.
>   - **C.** government spending.
>
> ### Solution to 1:
>
> A is correct. Because real estate purchases are usually financed with mortgage loans, interest rate changes directly influence the monthly payment amounts.
>
> 2. Apart from questions of affordability, house buying is affected by:
>   - **A.** the rate of family formation.
>   - **B.** expectation of housing price increases.
>   - **C.** both the rate of family formation and expectation of housing price increases.
>
> ### Solution to 2:
>
> C is correct. Family formation constitutes the actual need for housing, whereas buying on the expectation of housing price increases reflects the fact that real estate has investment value.

4. EXTERNAL TRADE SECTOR BEHAVIOR

☐ describe how resource use, consumer and business activity, housing sector activity, and external trade sector activity vary as an economy moves through the business cycle

The external trade sector varies tremendously in size and importance from one economy to another. In such places as Singapore or smaller open economies, such as Lithuania, where almost all inputs are imported and the bulk of the economy's output finds its way to the export market, trade (the sum of both exports and imports) easily exceeds GDP. External conditions, especially the stage of the cycle in key export regions and in primary trading partners, play a crucial role. In other places, such as Brazil or the United States, external trade assumes a much smaller part of GDP. Since the 1970s, global trade has risen substantially, so the business cycles of the large economies in the world can be more easily transmitted to other economies.

Cyclical Fluctuations of Imports and Exports

Typically, imports rise, all else equal, with the pace of domestic GDP growth because rising domestic demand increases purchases of goods and services, by consumers and business, from abroad. Thus, imports respond to the domestic cycle. Exports are more dependent on cycles in the rest of the world. If these external cycles are strong, all else equal, exports will grow even if the domestic economy should experience a decline in growth. To understand the impact of exports, financial analysts need to understand the strength of the major trading partners of the economy under consideration. The net effect of trade may offset cyclical weakness and, depending on the importance of exports to the economy, could erase it altogether. For these reasons, such differences can mean the pattern of external trade balances is entirely different from the rest of the domestic economic cycle. Exhibit 2 provides a short summary.

Exhibit 2: External Trade

Phase of the Cycle (domestic economy)	Recovery	Expansion	Slowdown	Contraction
Exports	Driven by external demand			
Imports (*assuming exchange rate remains unchanged)	Imports below average, start to increase.	Imports increase.	Imports peak and start to decline.	Imports in decline to below-average levels.

The Role of the Exchange Rate

The currency exchange rate also has an independent effect that can move trade in directions strikingly different from the domestic economic cycle. When a nation's currency appreciates (the currency gains in strength relative to other currencies), foreign goods are cheaper than domestic goods to the domestic population, prompting, all else equal, a relative rise in imports. At the same time, such currency appreciation makes that nation's exports more expensive in global markets and may reduce exports. Currency depreciation has the opposite effect. Although currency moves may be volatile and on occasion extreme, they have a significant effect on trade and the balance of payments only when they cumulate in a single direction for some time. Moves from one month or quarter to the next, however great, have a minimal effect until they persist. Thus, cumulative currency movements that take place over a period of years will have an impact on trade flows that will persist even if the currency subsequently moves in the opposite direction for a temporary period.

Overall Effect on Exports and Imports

Financial analysts need to consider a wide range of variables, both in the domestic economy and abroad, to assess relative GDP growth rates and then factor in currency considerations to ascertain whether they reinforce or counteract other cyclical forces. Generally, GDP growth differentials in global economic growth rates between countries have the most immediate and straightforward effects: Domestic changes in economic activity raise or reduce imports, and foreign economic activity changes raise or reduce exports. Currency moves have a more complex and, despite the interim short-term currency moves, a more gradual effect.

EXAMPLE 3

External Trade

1. Imports most clearly respond to:
    - **A.** the level of exports.
    - **B.** domestic industrial policy.
    - **C.** the domestic GDP growth rate.

Solution to 1:

C is correct. As a part of aggregate demand, imports reflect the domestic needs for foreign goods, which vary together with domestic economic growth.

2. Exports generally respond to the:
    - **A.** government expenditure.
    - **B.** global GDP growth rates.
    - **C.** domestic GDP growth rates.

Solution to 2:

B is correct. Exports reflect the foreign demands on domestic output, which depend on the conditions of the global economy.

EXAMPLE 4

Investment Implications

1. A junior portfolio manager is reviewing portfolio holdings. He focuses on three specific companies that he was tasked with reviewing. He has just received an analysis of the stage of the business cycle from a team of the firm's economists. To set the context of his analysis, he needs to understand the behavior of the three companies as they have exposures to different parts of the economy. One is focused on consumer goods (electronics and small vehicles) sold on the local market; one is focused on equipment sold to domestic companies; and one makes household and personal care consumer products, which it sells both domestically and abroad.

    Which of the these three companies' financial performance fluctuates with the business cycle of their domestic economy the *most*?

- **A.** Consumer goods company
- **B.** Business equipment company
- **C.** Producer of household and personal care products

Solution:

B is correct. Business investment fluctuates more than consumer spending and exports. A and C are incorrect because although consumer goods companies are impacted by the cycle, they are impacted less than companies exposed to business investment.

UNEMPLOYMENT

☐ describe types of unemployment, and compare measures of unemployment

Many governments and central banks have economic policy objectives related to limiting the rate at which citizens are unemployed and containing price inflation (i.e., preserving the purchasing power of a domestic currency). In general, unemployment is at its highest somewhat after the recovery has started and is at its lowest somewhat after the peak of the economy.

An overheated economy often leads to inflation when unemployment is very low. Workers ask for higher wages because they expect prices of goods and services to keep going up; at the same time, they have market power against employers because there are few available workers to be hired. The upward pressure on wages coupled with the impact of wage escalator clauses (automatic increases in wages as the consumer price index grows) trigger a price–wage inflationary spiral. This issue was a particular problem in industrialized countries during the 1960s and 1970s and to a degree remains relevant today.

A key aspect in this process is inflation expectations. Because inflation expectations are high, the request for higher wages is stronger, which induces employers to increase prices in advance to keep their profit margins stable. This avalanche process grows with time. Central banks act, sometimes drastically, to slow down the economy and reset inflationary expectations throughout the economy at a low level so that if everyone expects low inflation, the inflationary spiral itself will stop. These actions may trigger a deep recession. Therefore, whenever a financial analyst sees signs of a price–wage spiral in the making, a reasonable response would be to consider the effect of both high inflation and sharp tightening of monetary policy.

This example shows that measures of labor market conditions are important in assessing whether an economy is at risk of cyclical downturn.

The following are definitions of a few terms used to summarize the state of the labor market:

- **Employed**: The number of people with a job. This figure normally does not include people working in the informal sector (e.g., street vendors, illegal workers).
- **Labor force**: The number of people who either have a job or are actively looking for a job. This number excludes retirees, children, stay-at-home parents, full-time students, and other categories of people who are neither employed nor actively seeking employment.

- **Unemployed**: People who are actively seeking employment but are currently without a job. Some special subcategories include:
  - **Long-term unemployed**: People who have been out of work for a long time (more than three to four months in many countries) but are still looking for a job.
  - **Frictionally unemployed**: People who are not working at the time of filling out the statistical survey because they are taking time to search for a job that matches their skills, interests, and other preferences better than what is currently available, or people who have left one job and are about to start another job. The frictionally unemployed includes people who have voluntarily left their previous positions to change their jobs—in other words, they are "between jobs"—and those new entrants or re-entrants into the labor force who have not yet found work. Frictional unemployment is short-term and transitory in nature.
- **Unemployment rate**: The ratio of unemployed to labor force.
  - **Participation rate**: (or activity ratio): The ratio of labor force to total population of working age (i.e., those between 16 and 64 years of age).
- **Underemployed**: A person who has a job but either has the qualifications to work at a significantly higher-paying job or works part-time but desires a full-time position. For example, a lawyer who is out of work and takes a job in a bookstore could call herself underemployed. This lawyer would not count as unemployed for the computation of the unemployment rate (she does have a job, even if it may not be her highest-paying job). Although the unemployment rate statistic is criticized for not taking the issue of underemployment into account, it may be difficult to classify whether a person is truly underemployed—for example, the lawyer may find legal work too stressful and prefers working at the bookstore.
- **Discouraged worker**: A person who has stopped looking for a job. Perhaps because of a weak economy, the discouraged worker has given up seeking employment. Discouraged workers are statistically outside the labor force (similar to children and retirees), which means they are not counted in the official unemployment rate. During prolonged recessions, the unemployment rate may actually decrease because many discouraged workers stop seeking work. It is important to observe the participation rate together with the unemployment rate to understand if unemployment is decreasing because of an improved economy or because of an increase in discouraged workers. Discouraged workers and underemployed people may be considered examples of "hidden unemployment."
- **Voluntarily unemployed**: A person voluntarily outside the labor force, such as a jobless worker refusing an available vacancy for which the wage is lower than their threshold or those who retired early.

The Unemployment Rate

The unemployment rate is certainly the most quoted measure of joblessness; it attempts to measure those who do not have a job, but would work if they could find one, generally stated as a percentage of the overall labor force. In the United States, the indicator emerges from a monthly survey of households by the US Bureau of Labor Statistics. The survey asks how many household members have jobs and how many of working age do not have jobs but are seeking work. Other statistical bureaus rely on other sources for the calculation, using claims for unemployment assistance, for instance, or their equivalent. Some statistical bureaus measure the labor force simply as those of working age, regardless of whether they are ready or willing to work. These differences can make precise international comparisons problematic. One solution is to use the International Labour Organization (ILO) statistics that try to measure unemployment using consistent methodologies.

Although these various unemployment measures provide insight to the state of the economy, they are inaccurate in pointing to cyclical directions for two primary reasons, both of which make unemployment a lagging economic indicator of the business cycle.

One reason is that the unemployment rate is backward looking—that is, it lags the cycle—because the labor force expands and declines in response to the economic environment. Compounding the inaccuracy, discouraged workers cease searching for work when times get hard, reducing the number typically counted as unemployed and making the job market look stronger than it really is. Conversely, when the job market picks up, these people return to the search; however, because they seldom find work immediately, they at least initially raise the calculation of those unemployed, giving the false impression of the lack of recovery in the jobs market, when, in fact, it is the improvement that brought these people back into the labor force. Sometimes this cyclical flow of new job seekers is so great that the unemployment rate actually rises even as the economic recovery gains momentum. Those agencies that measure the labor force in terms of the working-age population avoid this bias because the working-age population measure is unaffected by economic conditions in the labor market. But this approach introduces biases of its own, such as counting as unemployed those people who have severe disabilities and could never seek work.

Another reason the unemployment indicator tends to lag the cycle comes from the typical reluctance of businesses to lay off people. The reluctance may stem from a desire to retain good workers for the long run, or it may reflect constraints written into labor contracts that make layoffs expensive. The reluctance makes the various measures of unemployment rise more slowly as the economy slides into recession than they otherwise might. Then as the recovery develops, a business waits to hire until it has fully employed the workers it has kept on the payroll during the recession; this delay causes decreases in the unemployment rate to lag the cycle.

Overall Payroll Employment and Productivity Indicators

To get a better picture of the employment cycle, practitioners often rely on more straightforward measures of payroll growth. By measuring the size of payrolls, practitioners sidestep such issues as the ebb and flow of discouraged workers. These statistics, however, have biases of their own. It is hard, for instance, to count employment in smaller businesses, which may be significant drivers of employment growth. Still, there is a clear indication of economic trouble when payrolls shrink and a clear indication of recovery when they rise.

The examination of other measures can also assist in understanding the employment situation and its use in determining cyclical directions. Two additional measures are hours worked, especially overtime, and the use of temporary workers. A business does not want to make mistakes with full-time staff, either hiring or firing. Thus, at the first signs of economic weakness, managers cut back hours, especially overtime. Such movements can simply reflect minor month-to-month production shifts, but if followed by cutbacks in part-time and temporary staff, the picture gives a strong signal of economic weakness, especially if confirmed by other independent indicators. Similarly, on the cyclical upswing, a business turns first to increases in overtime and hours. If a business then increases temporary staffing, it gives a good signal of economic recovery long before any movement in rehiring full-time staff again.

Productivity measures also offer insight into this cyclical process. Because productivity is usually measured by dividing output by hours worked, a business's tendency to keep workers on the payroll even as output falls usually prompts a reduction in measured productivity. If measures are available promptly enough, this sign of cyclical weakness might precede even the change in hours. This drop in productivity precedes any change in full-time payrolls. Productivity also responds promptly when business conditions improve and the business first begins to utilize its underemployed workers, which occurs earlier than any upturn in full-time payrolls.

On a more fundamental level, productivity can also pick up in response to technological breakthroughs or improved training techniques. As already mentioned, such changes affect potential GDP. If strong enough, they can negatively affect employment trends, keeping them slower than they would be otherwise by relieving the need for additional staff to increase production. But these influences usually unfold over decades and mean little to cyclical considerations, which, at most, unfold over years. What is more, there are few statistical indicators to gauge the onset of technological change, confining analysts to the use of anecdotal evidence or occasional longitudinal studies.

EXAMPLE 5

Analyzing Unemployment

1. At the peak of the business cycle, if the unemployment rate is low, the majority of the unemployed are *most likely*:

    A. discouraged workers.
    B. long-term unemployed.
    C. frictionally unemployed.

Solution to 1:

C is correct. At the peak of a business cycle, the labor market is usually tight, and people become unemployed largely because they are either "between jobs" or they have entered or reentered the labor force but have not yet found work.

2. As an economy starts to recover from a trough in the business cycle, the unemployment rate is *most likely* to:

    A. continue to rise with a decline in the number of discouraged workers.
    B. start to decline with an increase in the number of discouraged workers.
    C. continue to rise with an increase in the number of discouraged workers.

Solution to 2:

A is correct. As the economy starts to recover, discouraged workers return to the labor force and start looking for jobs, which increases both the number of unemployed and the size of the labor force. The unemployment rate rises because the rise in the unemployed population is proportionately larger than the increase in the size of the labor force. B and C are incorrect because an increase in the number of discouraged workers typically occurs when the economy is contracting.

3. An analyst observes that the unemployment rate is high and rising, whereas productivity and hours worked have declined. The analyst is *most likely* to conclude that the labor market is signaling the:

   A. end of a recession.
   B. deepening of a recession.
   C. peak of the business cycle.

Solution to 3:

B is correct. High and rising unemployment, declining hours worked, and falling productivity are all signs of a weak economy getting weaker. When the economy first slows down, businesses cut back employees' hours. As the recession deepens, they then lay off employees, leading to a higher unemployment rate. Yet, because workforce turnover is costly for businesses, the scale of the layoff can be less than the decline in output, resulting in a decline in productivity. A is incorrect because toward the end of a recession, businesses are hesitant to increase hiring and instead use more overtime, increasing both productivity and the hours worked. C is incorrect because at the peak of a business cycle, the unemployment rate is usually low and the level of hours worked is high.

INFLATION

- explain inflation, hyperinflation, disinflation, and deflation
- explain the construction of indexes used to measure inflation
- compare inflation measures, including their uses and limitations
- contrast cost-push and demand-pull inflation

In general, the inflation rate is pro-cyclical (that is, it goes up and down *with* the cycle), but with a lag of a year or more.

Inflation refers to a sustained rise in the overall level of prices in an economy. Economists use various price indexes to measure the overall price level, also called the aggregate price level. The inflation rate is the percentage change in a price index—that is, the speed of overall price level movements. Investors follow the inflation rate closely not only because it can help to infer the state of the economy, but also because an unexpected change may result in a change in monetary policy, which can have a large and immediate impact on asset prices. In developing countries, very high inflation rates can lead to social unrest or even shifts of political power, which constitutes political risk for investments in those economies.

Central banks, the monetary authority in most economies, monitor the domestic inflation rates closely when conducting monetary policy. Monetary policy determines interest rates and the available quantities of money and loans in an economy. A high inflation rate combined with fast economic growth and low unemployment usually indicates the economy is overheating, which may trigger some policy movements to cool it down. However, if a high inflation rate is combined with a high level of unemployment and a slowdown of the economy—an economic state known as stagflation (stagnation plus inflation)—the economy will typically be left to correct itself because no short-term economic policy is deemed effective.

Deflation, Hyperinflation, and Disinflation

Various terms are related to the levels and changes of the inflation rate:

- **Deflation**: A sustained decrease in aggregate price level, which corresponds to a negative inflation rate—that is, an inflation rate of less than 0%.
- **Hyperinflation**: An extremely fast increase in aggregate price level, which corresponds to an extremely high inflation rate—for example, 500% to 1,000% per year.
- **Disinflation**: A decline in the inflation rate, such as from around 15% or 20% to 5% or 6%. Disinflation is very different from deflation because even after a period of disinflation, the inflation rate remains positive and the aggregate price level keeps rising (although at a slower speed).

Inflation means that the same amount of money can purchase less real goods or services in the future. So, the value of money or the purchasing power of money decreases in an inflationary environment. When deflation occurs, the value of money actually increases. Because most debt contracts are written in fixed monetary amounts, the liability of a borrower also rises in real terms during deflation. As the price level falls, the revenue of a typical company also falls during a recession. Facing increasing real debt, a company that is short of cash usually cuts its spending, investment, and workforce sharply. Less spending and high unemployment further exacerbate the economic contraction. To avoid getting too close to deflation, the consensus on the preferred inflation rate is around 2% per year for developed economies. Deflation occurred in the United States during the Great Depression and briefly during the recession following the global financial crisis of 2008–2009. Since the late 1990s, Japan has experienced several episodes of deflation.

Hyperinflation usually occurs when large scale government spending is not backed by real tax revenue and the monetary authority accommodates government spending by increasing the money supply. Hyperinflation may also be caused by the shortage of supply created during or after a war, economic regime transition, or prolonged economic distress of an economy caused by political instability. During hyperinflation, people are eager to change their cash into real goods because prices are rising very fast. As a result, money changes hands at an extremely high frequency. The government also has to print more money to support its increased spending. As more cash chases a limited supply of goods and services, the rate of price increases accelerates. Because the basic cause for hyperinflation is too much money in circulation, regaining control of the money supply is the key to ending hyperinflation.

Measuring Inflation: The Construction of Price Indexes

Because the inflation rate is measured as the percentage change of a price index, it is important to understand how a price index is constructed so that the inflation rate derived from that index can be accurately interpreted. A price index represents the average prices of a basket of goods and services, and various methods can be used to average the different prices. Exhibit 3 shows a simple example of the change of a consumption basket over time.

Inflation

Exhibit 3: Consumption Basket and Prices over Two Months

Time	January 2019		February 2019	
Goods	Quantity	Price	Quantity	Price
Rice	50 kg	¥3/kg	70 kg	¥4/kg
Gasoline	70 liters	¥4.4/liter	60 liters	¥4.5/liter

For January 2019, the total value of the consumption basket is:

Value of rice + Value of gasoline = (50 × 3) + (70 × 4.4) = ¥458.

A price index uses the relative weight of a good in a basket to weight the price in the index. Therefore, the same consumption basket in February 2019 is worth:

Value of rice + Value of gasoline = (50 × 4) + (70 × 4.5) = ¥515.

The price index in the base period is usually set to 100. So, if the price index in January 2019 is 100, then the price index in February 2019 is

$$\text{Price index in February 2019} = \frac{515}{458} \times 100 = ¥112.45 \text{ and}$$

$$\text{Inflation rate} = \frac{112.45}{100} - 1 = 0.1245 = 12.45\%.$$

A price index created by holding the composition of the consumption basket constant is called a Laspeyres index. Most price indexes around the world are Laspeyres indexes because the survey data on the consumption basket are only available with a lag. In many countries, the basket is updated every five years. Because most price indexes are created to measure the cost of living, however, simply using a fixed basket of goods and services has three serious biases:

- Substitution bias: As the price of one good or service rises, people may substitute it with other goods or services that have a lower price. This substitution will result in an upward bias in the measured inflation rate based on a Laspeyres index.

- Quality bias: As the quality of the same product improves over time, it satisfies people's needs and wants better. One such example is the quality of cars. Over the years, the prices of cars have been rising while the safety and reliability of cars have been enhanced. If not adjusted for quality, the measured inflation rate will experience another upward bias.

- New product bias: New products are frequently introduced, but a fixed basket of goods and services will not include them. In general, this situation again creates an upward bias in the inflation rate.

It is relatively easy to resolve the quality bias and new product bias. Many countries adjust for the quality of the products in a basket, a practice called hedonic pricing. New products can be introduced into the basket over time. The substitution bias can be somewhat resolved by using the chained price index formula.

Price Indexes and Their Usage

Most countries use a consumer price index (CPI) specific to the domestic economy to track inflation. Exhibit 4 shows the different weights for various categories of goods and services in the consumer price indexes of different countries.

Exhibit 4: The Consumption Basket of Different Consumer Price Indexes

Country	China	India	India	Germany	United States	United States
Name of Index	CPI	CPI(UNME)	CPI(Urban)[c]	HICP	CPI-U	PCE
Year[a]	2016[b]	1984/85	2012	2017/18	2017/18	2009
Category (%):						
Food and Beverage	30	47.1	37.7	14	15.3	13.4
Housing and Utility	21	21.9	27.2	31.7	37.9	17.3
Furniture	6	2	3.9	5	4.2	3.4
Apparel	7.5	7	5.6	4.5	3.3	3.3
Medical Care	8	2.5	4.8	4.4	7.7	16.9
Transportation and Communication	13	5.2	9.7	16.5	15.3	9.3[d]
Education and Recreation	10.5	6.8	7.6	12.3	9.1	8.9[e]
Others	4	7.5	3.5	11.6	7.2	27.6

[a] *The base year of the weights, where it is appropriate.*
[b] *Weights for China are not released publicly. Imputed numbers given as of 2018 are from the Reserve Bank of Australia.*
[c] *India redefined the CPI bundle in 2012 for urban consumers.*
[d] *Includes only transportation expenditures by consumers.*
[e] *Includes only recreational expenditures by consumers.*
Sources: Government websites and authors' calculations.

As shown in Exhibit 4, in different countries the consumer price indexes have different names and different weights on various categories of goods and services. For example, food weights are higher in the CPI for China and India but less for the developed countries; a greater proportion of income of the average consumer goes to food in the developing countries of China and India than in the developed countries shown in Exhibit 4. For India, the weights across categories change dramatically over time as the country has developed. Weights across the categories change across time in developed countries too, but these changes tend to be much smaller. The scope of the index is also different among countries. For China and Germany, the surveys used to collect data for CPI cover both urban and rural areas. The CPI for the United States covers only urban areas using a household survey, which is why it is called the CPI-U. On the other hand, using business surveys, the personal consumption expenditure (PCE) price index covers all personal consumption in the United States.

The producer price index (PPI) is another important inflation measure. The PPI reflects the price changes experienced by domestic producers in a country. Because price increases may eventually pass through to consumers, the PPI can influence the future CPI. The items in the PPI include fuels, farm products (such as grains and meat), machinery and equipment, chemical products (such as drugs and paints), transportation equipment, metals, pulp and paper, and so on. These products are usually further grouped by stage-of-processing categories: crude materials, intermediate materials, and finished goods. Similar to the CPI, scope and weights vary among countries. The differences in the weights can be much more dramatic for the PPI than for the CPI because different countries may specialize in different industries. In some countries, the PPI is called the wholesale price index (WPI).

As an important inflation indicator, many economic activities are indexed to a certain price index. For example, in the United States, Treasury Inflation-Protected Securities (TIPS) adjust the bond's principal according to the US CPI-U index. The terms of labor contracts and commercial real estate leases may adjust periodically according to the CPI. Recurring payments in business contracts can be linked to the PPI or its sub-indexes for a particular category of products.

Central banks usually use a consumer price index to monitor inflation. For example, the European Central Bank (ECB), the central bank for the European Union (EU), focuses on the Harmonised Index of Consumer Prices (HICP). Each member country in the EU first reports its own individual HICP, and then Eurostat, the statistical office for the EU, aggregates the country-level HICPs with country weights. But there are exceptions. The Reserve Bank of India follows the inflation in India using a WPI. Because food items only represent about 27% in the India WPI (much lower than the 70% in the India rural CPI), the rural CPIs can rise faster than the WPI when there is high food price inflation. Besides the weight differences, the wholesale prices in the WPI also understate market prices because they do not consider retail margins (markups). The choice of inflation indicator may also change over time. The central bank of the United States, known as the Federal Reserve Board (the Fed), once focused on the CPI-U produced by the Bureau of Labor Statistics under the US Department of Labor. Because the CPI-U has the previously discussed upward biases, however, the Fed switched in 2000 to the PCE index, produced by the Bureau of Economic Analysis under the US Department of Commerce. The PCE index also has the advantage that it covers the complete range of consumer spending rather than just a basket.

HEADLINE AND CORE INFLATION

Headline inflation refers to the inflation rate calculated based on the price index that includes all goods and services in an economy. **Core inflation** usually refers to the inflation rate calculated based on a price index of goods and services except food and energy. Policy makers often choose to focus on the core inflation rate when reading the trend in the economy and making economic policies as they try to avoid overreaction to short-term fluctuations in food and energy prices that may not have a significant impact on future headline inflation.

Besides tracking inflation, financial analysts also use the price index to deflate GDP (i.e., to eliminate the price effect in nominal GDP data so as to identify trends in real economic growth). Many countries publish a particular price index, called the GDP deflator, for that purpose. Sub-indexes are also commonly available and may prove more valuable to an analyst with an interest in a particular industry or company.

EXAMPLE 6

Inflation

1. Which of the following statements regarding the movements of overall price levels is *most* accurate?

   A. Disinflation means that the overall price level declines.
   B. Deflation occurs when the inflation rate turns negative.
   C. When the price of chicken rises, the inflation rate will increase.

Solution to 1:

B is correct. When the inflation rate falls below zero—that is, the overall price level declines—the economy is experiencing deflation. A is incorrect, because disinflation indicates that the overall price level is rising but at a slower pace. C is incorrect because inflation measures are designed to reflect changes in the overall price level. Consumption baskets in modern economies usually contain a large number of goods and services, thus the price of a particular product usually cannot significantly influence the overall price level.

2. Deflation can exacerbate a recession because firms may reduce their investments and hiring when:

   A. the slower pace of inflation lowers aggregate demand.
   B. their revenues decline but their debt burden rises in real terms.
   C. the prices of their products continue to fall because of intense competition.

Solution to 2:

B is correct. As the prices of the output of firms fall, the firms receive lower revenues. Because the nominal amount of debt that firms carry is usually fixed, lower general price levels lead to higher debt balances in real terms. These two forces push firms closer to default, so they may scale back spending on investments and labor, which further lowers the aggregate demand and pushes the general price level even lower. In macroeconomic analysis, it is usually the changes in aggregate demand that influence inflation instead of the reverse causality. Furthermore, neither inflation fluctuations nor aggregate demand shifts explain the potential damaging effect of deflation. Price decline attributable to the competitive environment is a microeconomic phenomenon that is not sufficient to explain the macroeconomic impact of deflation.

3. Which one of the following economic phenomena related to inflation cannot be determined by using observations of the inflation rate alone?

   A. Deflation
   B. Stagflation
   C. Hyperinflation

Solution to 3:

B is correct. A high inflation rate alone does not indicate stagflation, which happens if high unemployment occurs together with high inflation.

4. If a price index is calculated based on a fixed basket of goods, in an inflationary environment the inflation rate calculated based on this index over time will:

   A. overstate the actual cost of living.
   B. understate the actual cost of living.
   C. track the actual cost of living quite closely.

Solution to 4:

A is correct. Upward biases, such as the substitution bias or quality bias, will overstate the actual cost of living.

5. To adjust nominal economic growth for general price level changes in a country, an analyst would prefer to use:

   A. the CPI.
   B. the GDP deflator.
   C. the Personal Consumption Expenditures (PCE) index.

Solution to 5:

B is correct. The GDP deflator reflects the prices of the goods and services produced domestically. Both the CPI and PCE indexes are constructed using consumption baskets, and the components of a consumption basket can be very different from the components of output of that same country.

6. To estimate the trends in sales and production costs of a given industry, an analyst would prefer to collect data on:

    A. the sub-indexes of the wholesale price index (WPI) for that industry.
    B. the sub-indexes of both the CPI and WPI that are relevant to the industry.
    C. the sub-indexes of the CPI relevant to the output and inputs of that industry.

Solution to 6:

B is correct. A sub-index of the CPI reflects the market price changes of the products of an industry, whereas a sub-index of the WPI reflects the price changes of the inputs of an industry. The different composition of outputs and inputs of an industry need to be appropriately accounted for when selecting a price series. Furthermore, the WPI may not take the markups set by the industry into account.

7. Compared with core inflation, headline inflation:

    A. has an upward bias.
    B. is more subject to short-term market conditions.
    C. can more accurately predict future inflation.

Solution to 7:

B is correct. Headline inflation is heavily influenced by food and energy price fluctuations, which are affected by short-term supply and demand changes in these markets. These market conditions may not persist. It is also possible for an economy to absorb the price changes so that they will not have a long-lasting impact on the headline inflation rate. This means headline inflation contains a great deal of noise and is not a reliable predictor of future inflation trends. The biases in various inflation measures are inherent in the index construction methodology and are not related to the price movements of the goods and services.

Explaining Inflation

Economists describe two types of inflation: cost-push, in which rising costs, usually wages, compel businesses to raise prices generally, and demand-pull, in which increasing demand raise prices generally, which then are reflected in a business's costs as workers demand wage hikes to catch up with the rising cost of living. Whatever the sequence by which prices and costs rise in an economy, the fundamental cause is the same: excessive demands—either for raw materials, finished goods, or labor—that outstrip the economy's ability to respond. The initial signs appear in the areas with the greatest constraints: the labor market, the commodity market, or some area of final output. Even before examining particular cost and price measures, when considering inflation, practitioners look to indicators that might reveal when the economy faces such constraints.

Cost-Push Inflation

Considering cost-push inflation, analysts may look at commodity prices because commodities are an input to production. But because wages are the single biggest cost to businesses, practitioners focus most particularly on wage-push inflation, which is tied to the labor market. Because the object is to gauge demand for labor relative to capacity, the unemployment rate is key, as well as measures of the number of workers available to meet the economy's expanding needs. Obviously, the higher the unemployment rate, the lower the likelihood that shortages will develop in labor markets, whereas the lower the unemployment rate, the greater the likelihood shortages will drive up wages. Because the unemployment rate generally only counts people who are looking for work, some practitioners argue that it fails to account for the economy's full labor potential. They state that a tight labor market will bring people out in search of work and ease any potential wage strains. To account for this issue and to modify the unemployment rate indicator, these practitioners also look at the participation rate of people in the labor force, arguing that it gives a fuller and more accurate picture of potential than the unemployment rate.

Analysis in this area recognizes that not all labor is alike. Structural factors related to training deficiencies, cultural patterns in all or some of the population, inefficiencies in the labor market, and the like can mean that the economy will effectively face labor shortages long before the unemployment rate reaches very low figures. This effective unemployment rate, below which pressure emerges in labor markets, is frequently referred to as the **non-accelerating inflation rate of unemployment** (NAIRU) or, drawing on the work of the Nobel Prize winner Milton Friedman, the **natural rate of unemployment** (NARU). Of course, these rates vary from one economy to another and over time in a single economy. It is this rate rather than full employment that determines when an economy will experience bottlenecks in the labor market and wage-push inflationary pressures.

Take, for example, the technology sector. It has grown so rapidly in some economies that training in the labor force cannot keep up with demand. This sector can, therefore, face shortages of trained workers and attendant wage pressures even though the economy as a whole seems to have considerable slack in the overall labor market. Until training (supply) catches up with demand, that economy may experience wage and inflation pressure at rates of unemployment that in other places and circumstances might suggest ample slack in the labor market and much less wage-push pressure.

Assessments of wage-push inflation also consider direct observations of wage trends that, when they accelerate, might force businesses to raise prices (initiating the wage-price spiral mentioned earlier in this reading). Statistical agencies provide a wide array of wage-cost indicators, such as hourly wage gauges, weekly earnings, and overall labor costs, including the outlays for benefits. Some of these indicators include the effects of special overtime pay or bonuses, and others do not. And although these measures give an idea of the cost to businesses and hence the kind of wage-push inflationary pressure, a complete picture only emerges when practitioners examine such trends alongside productivity measures.

Productivity, or output per hour, is an essential part of wage-push inflation analysis because the output available from each worker determines the number of units over which businesses can spread the cost of worker compensation. The greater each worker's output per hour, the lower the price businesses need to charge for each unit of output to cover hourly labor costs. And by extension, the faster output per hour grows, the faster labor compensation can expand without putting undue pressure on businesses' costs per unit of output. The equation for this **unit labor cost** (ULC) indicator, as it is called, is as follows:

ULC = W/O,

where

ULC = unit labor costs

O = output per hour per worker

W = total labor compensation per hour per worker

Many factors can affect labor productivity across time and between economies. The cyclical swings have already been described, as have the effects of technology and training. The pace of development also tends to increase worker productivity because the more sophisticated equipment, systems, and technologies workers have at their disposal, the higher their output per hour. Whatever causes the productivity growth, if it fails to keep up with worker compensation, unit costs to a business rise, and as a business tries to protect its profit margins, prices generally come under increasing upward pressure. Generally, this situation occurs because heavy demand for labor relative to available labor resources has pushed up compensation faster than productivity. Practitioners use a variety of indicators to identify cost- or wage-push inflationary pressure.

EXAMPLE 7

Unemployment Too High

1. Which of the following is **not** a problem with the NARU and NAIRU?

   A. They only work in monetarist models.

   B. They may change over time given changes in technology and economic structure.

   C. They do not account for bottlenecks in segments of the labor market (e.g., college graduates).

Solution:

A is correct. The NARU and NAIRU are the unemployment rates at which the inflation rate will not rise because of a shortage of labor. This concept does not tie to a particular school of macroeconomic models.

Demand-Pull Inflation

The search for indicators from the demand-pull side of the inflation question brings practitioners back to the relationship between actual and potential real GDP and industrial capacity utilization. The higher the rate of capacity utilization or the closer actual GDP is to potential, the more likely an economy will suffer shortages, bottlenecks, a general inability to satisfy demand, and hence, price increases. The more an economy operates below its potential or the lower the rate of capacity utilization, the less such supply pressure will exist and the greater likelihood of a slowdown in inflation, or outright deflation. In addition to these macro indicators, practitioners will also look for signs of inflationary pressure in commodity prices—in part because they are a cost to business, but more as a general sign of excess demand. For an individual economy, observations of commodity prices could be misleading because commodities trade in a global market and accordingly reflect global economic conditions more than those in an individual economy.

Taking a different perspective, Monetarists contend that inflation is fundamentally a monetary phenomenon. A surplus of money, they argue, will inflate the money price of everything in the economy. Stated in terms of straightforward supply and demand relationships, a surplus of money would bring down its value just as a surplus in any market would bring down the price of the product in excess. Because the price of money is stated in terms of the products it can buy, its declining value would have an expression in generally higher prices—that is, in inflation. This Monetarist argument, as it is called, finds a simpler expression in the old saying: "Inflation results when too much money chases too few goods." Although it seems distant from other explanations of inflation, in practice it is not that distinct. Excess money causes inflationary pressure by increasing liquidity, which ultimately causes a rapid rise in demand. In this sense, the Monetarist argument is a special case under the more general heading of demand-pull concepts of inflation. The practical distinction between the monetarist and other approaches is in identifying the initial cause of the demand excess.

Practitioners can track this effect by examining various money supply indicators, usually provided by the central bank. To detect inflationary or deflationary pressure, practitioners note acceleration or deceleration in monetary growth based on past trends. Obviously in the absence of a special explanation, acceleration signals the potential for inflationary pressure. In applying this approach, practitioners also compare monetary growth with the growth of the nominal economy, represented by nominal GDP. If monetary growth is outpacing the growth of the nominal economy, there is deemed to be inflationary potential. This is especially the case if monetary growth has also accelerated from its trend. There is a disinflationary or deflationary potential if monetary growth lags the economy's rate of expansion, especially if it has also decelerated from its trend.

> **INFLATION AND VELOCITY**
>
> Some practitioners view the likelihood of inflationary pressure from the vantage point of the ratio of nominal GDP to money supply, commonly called the "velocity of money." If this ratio remains stable around a constant or a historical trend, they see reason to look for relative price stability. If velocity falls, it could suggest a surplus of money that might have inflationary potential, but much depends on why it has declined. If velocity has fallen because a cyclical correction has brought down the GDP numerator relative to the money denominator, then practitioners view prospects as more likely to lead to a cyclical upswing to reestablish the former relationship than inflationary pressure. If velocity has fallen, however, because of an increase in the money denominator, then inflationary pressure becomes more likely. If velocity rises, financial analysts might be concerned about a shortage of money in the economy and disinflation or deflation.

Inflation Expectations

Beyond demand-pull, monetary, and cost-push inflation considerations, practitioners also need to account for the effect of inflation expectations. Once inflation becomes embedded in an economy, businesses, workers, consumers, and economic actors of every kind begin to expect it and build those expectations into their actions. This reaction, in turn, creates an inflationary momentum of its own. Such expectations give inflation something of a self-sustaining character and cause it to persist in an economy even after its initial cause has disappeared. High inflation rates persisted in the 1970s and early 1980s in Europe and the United States on the basis of expectations—even after these economies had sunk into recession. The resulting slow or negative economic growth combined with high unemployment and rising inflation was termed "stagflation."

Inflation

Measuring inflation expectations is not easy. Some practitioners gauge expectations by relying on past inflation trends and on the assumption that market participants largely extrapolate their past experiences. In some markets, surveys of inflation expectations are available, although these are often biased by the way the questions are asked. Another indicator of inflation expectations becomes available when governments issue bonds, such as Treasury Inflation-Protected Securities (TIPS), that adjust in various ways to compensate holders for inflation. By comparing the interest available on these bonds with other government bonds that do not offer such inflation-linked adjustments, practitioners can gauge the general level of inflation expectations among market participants and factor it into their own inflation forecasts and strategies.

For example, if today's yield on the 10-year nominal bond of a certain country is 3.5% and the yield on the 10-year inflation-protected bond of the same country is 1.5%, we infer that the market is pricing in a 3.5% − 1.5% = 2% average annual inflation over the next 10 years. However, this calculation needs to be treated with caution because the market for inflation-linked bonds is relatively small and thus yields can be influenced by other factors, such as the very strong demand from US pension funds seeking to match their liabilities.

EXAMPLE 8

Inflation

1. To examine whether there is inflationary pressure caused by rising costs, an analyst will *most likely* gather data on:

    A. the growth rates of money supply and nominal GDP.

    B. the unemployment rate, the NAIRU, and productivity growth.

    C. commodity prices, past inflation trends, and expected inflation surveys.

Solution to 1:

B is correct. Comparing the current unemployment rate with the NAIRU and productivity growth with the wage growth can help an analyst determine whether inflation may be rising because of higher costs (cost-push inflation). Comparing the monetary growth with nominal GDP growth is helpful to determine whether high demand is creating inflationary pressure (demand-pull inflation). Commodity price increases could be an indicator of either cost-push or demand-pull inflation but may contain limited information in some situations. Past inflation trends and surveys on inflation expectations can help to gauge expected inflation rates; inflation expectations can be a driver of inflation even in the absence of the original underlying cause.

2. The most recent macroeconomic data for an economy are given in the following table:

Variable	Value
Hourly wage growth rate	3.4%
Unit labor cost growth rate	−0.25%
Nominal GDP growth rate	3.4%

Variable	Value
Money supply growth rate	6.7%
Implied inflation rate from government issued inflation-linked securities	2.2%

Based on the information in the table, an analyst will conclude that current inflation pressure in this economy is *most likely* caused by:

A. rising wages.

B. rising inflation expectations.

C. bottlenecks in increasing supply to satisfy demand.

Solution to 2:

C is correct. The table shows that growth in the money supply has outpaced nominal GDP growth, which can result in too much money chasing too few goods. In other words, inflation pressure results from demand beyond the economy's current capacity to produce. Although the wage rate is rising, the negative unit labor cost growth rate indicates an increase in productivity. Thus, it is unlikely the economy will experience cost-push inflation. The implied inflation rate is very modest, which is unlikely to lead to a rising inflation rate.

3. Cost-push inflation *most likely* occurs when:

   A. unemployment rates are low.

   B. unemployment rates are high.

   C. unemployment is either high or low.

Solution to 3:

A is correct. When unemployment is below the NAIRU, there is a shortage of labor that pushes up labor cost.

4. Unit labor costs measure:

   A. hourly wage rates.

   B. total labor compensation per hour.

   C. a combination of hourly wages and output.

Solution to 4:

C is correct. Unit labor costs reflect the labor cost in each unit of output.

5. Demand-pull inflation:

   A. is a discredited concept.

   B. depends on the movements in commodity prices.

   C. reflects the state of economic activity relative to potential.

Solution to 5:

C is correct. When the economy is operating above its potential capacity allowed by the resources available, inflation will start to rise.

6. Monetarists believe inflation:
   A. reflects the growth of money.
   B. is driven by the level of interest rates.
   C. is largely a cost-push phenomenon.

Solution to 6:

A is correct. Monetarists emphasize the role of money growth in determining the inflation rate, especially in the long run. As Milton Friedman famously put it: "Inflation is always and everywhere a monetary phenomenon."

7. The inflationary potential of a particular inflation rate depends on the economy's NAIRU or NARU, which, in turn, depends in part on:
   A. the intensity of past cyclical swings.
   B. the bargaining power of trade unions.
   C. the skill set of the labor force relative to the economy's industrial mix.

Solution to 7:

C is correct. If the skill set of a large part of the labor force cannot satisfy the hiring need from the employers, the NAIRU of such an economy can be quite high.

8. Which of the following is *not* a problem with the NARU and NAIRU?
   A. They are not observable directly.
   B. They work only in monetarist models.
   C. They change over time given changes in technology and economic structure.

Solution to 8:

B is correct. The NAIRU or NARU reflects the potential of an economy and thus cannot be directly observed from the economic data. They also change over time depending on technological progress and social factors.

SUMMARY

- Business cycles are recurrent expansions and contractions in economic activity affecting broad segments of the economy.
- Business cycles are a fundamental feature of market economies, but their amplitude and/or length vary considerably.
- Business cycles can be split into many different phases. The investment industry typically refers to four phases of the cycle: recovery, expansion, slowdown, and contraction, with the peak in output occurring during the slowdown phase and the trough in output occurring in the recovery phase.
- Classical cycle refers to fluctuations in the level of economic activity when measured by GDP in volume terms.

- Growth cycle refers to fluctuations in economic activity around the long-term potential trend growth level with a focus on how much actual economic activity is below or above trend growth in economic activity.
- Growth rate cycle refers to fluctuations in the growth rate of economic activity.
- Credit cycles describe the changing availability—and pricing—of credit. When the economy is strong or improving, the willingness of lenders to extend credit, and on favorable terms, is high. When the economy is weak or weakening, lenders pull back, or "tighten" credit, by making it less available and more expensive, contributing to asset values, further economic weakness and higher defaults.
- Credit cycles are relevant due to the importance of credit in the financing of construction and the purchase of property.
- The extent of business cycle fluctuations and the duration of recessions and recoveries are often shaped by linkages between business and credit cycles.
- Key economic variables change through the business cycle. The level of business investment shows significant changes over the cycle.
- Employment levels follow the cycle with a delay as companies initially use overtime before hiring after the onset of recovery and then reduce overtime before reducing employment as the economy passes its peak and enters contraction.
- Consumer spending, the largest component of output, follows cyclical patterns as workers make decisions based on their levels of income, wage growth, and employment outlook.
- Spending on consumer durables is the most cyclical consumer activity, followed by services and consumer staples, which are less affected by the cyclicality of the economy.
- The size of inventories is small relative to the size of the economy, but they have a much greater effect on economic growth than justified by their relatively small aggregate size relative to the economy as a whole.
- Inventory–sales ratio measures the inventories available for sale to the level of sales. Analysts pay attention to inventories to gauge the position of the economy in the cycle.
- Neoclassical and Real Business Cycle (RBC) theories focus on fluctuations of aggregate supply (AS). If AS shifts left because of an input price increase or right because of a price decrease or technical progress, the economy will gradually converge to its new equilibrium. Government intervention is generally not necessary because it may exacerbate the fluctuation or delay the convergence to equilibrium.
- Keynesian theories focus on fluctuations of aggregate demand (AD). If AD shifts left, Keynesians advocate government intervention to restore full employment and avoid a deflationary spiral.
- Monetarists argue that the timing of the impact from government policies is uncertain, and it is generally better to let the economy find its new equilibrium unassisted while ensuring that the money supply is kept growing at an even pace.
- Economic indicators are statistics on macroeconomic variables that help in understanding which stage of the business cycle an economy is at. Of particular importance are the leading indicators, which suggest where the economy is likely to be in the near future. No economic indicator is perfect, and many of these statistics are subject to periodic revisions.

- Leading economic indicators have turning points that usually precede those of the overall economy. They include survey-based indicators, such as (ISM), new orders, and average consumer expectations. They also include average weekly hours, initial claims for unemployment insurance, new building permits, stock market indexes, and the difference between yields on short-term and long-term bonds.
- Coincident economic indicators have turning points that are usually close to those of the overall economy. They are believed to have value for identifying the economy's present state. They include industrial production indexes, manufacturing and trade sales indexes, aggregate real personal income, and non-agricultural employment.
- Lagging economic indicators have turning points that take place later than those of the overall economy; they change after a trend has been established. They include average duration of unemployment, inventory–sales ratio, change in unit labor costs, average bank prime lending rate, commercial and industrial loans outstanding, ratio of consumer installment debt to income, and change in consumer price index for services.
- Policy makers and market practitioners use real-time monitoring of economic and financial variables to continuously assess current conditions and produce a nowcast. Nowcasting produces an estimate of the present state of the economy. It is useful because the actual data on such measures as GDP are only published with delay, after the end of the time period under consideration.
- The unemployed are those people who are actively seeking employment but are currently without a job.
- The long-term unemployed are those who have been out of work for a long time (more than three to four months in many countries) but are still looking for a job.
- The frictionally unemployed are those people who are not working at the time of filling out the statistical survey because they are taking time to search for a job that matches their skills, interests, and other preferences better than what is currently available, or people who have left one job and are about to start another job.
- There are different types of inflation. Hyperinflation indicates a high (e.g., 100% annual) and increasing rate of inflation; deflation indicates a negative inflation rate (prices decrease); imported inflation is associated with increasing cost of inputs that come from abroad; demand inflation is caused by constraints in production that prevent companies from making as many goods as the market demands (it is sometimes called wartime inflation, because in times of war, goods tend to be rationed).
- Inflation is measured by many indexes. Consumer price indexes reflect the prices of a basket of goods and services that are typically purchased by a normal household. Producer price indexes measure the cost of a basket of raw materials, intermediate inputs, and finished products. GDP deflators measure the price of the basket of goods and services produced within an economy in a given year. Core indexes exclude volatile items, such as agricultural products and energy, whose prices tend to vary more than those of other goods.
- Price levels are affected by real factors and monetary factors. Real factors include aggregate supply (an increase in supply leads to lower prices) and aggregate demand (an increase in demand leads to higher prices). Monetary factors include the supply of money (i.e., more money circulating, if the

economy is in equilibrium, will lead to higher prices) and the velocity of money (i.e., higher velocity, if the economy is in equilibrium, will lead to higher prices).

- Economists describe two types of inflation: cost-push, in which rising costs, usually wages, compel businesses to raise prices generally, and demand-pull, in which increasing demand raises prices generally, which then are reflected in a business's costs as workers demand wake hikes to catch up with the rising cost of living.

PRACTICE PROBLEMS

1. A decrease in a country's total imports is *most likely* caused by:
   A. an increase in the pace of domestic GDP growth.
   B. a cyclical downturn in the economies of primary trading partners.
   C. persistent currency depreciation relative to primary trading partners.

2. A decrease in both the labor force participation ratio and the unemployment rate is *most likely* caused by:
   A. an increase in discouraged workers.
   B. an increase in underemployed workers.
   C. a decrease in voluntarily unemployed persons.

3. The treasury manager of a large company has recently left his position to accept a promotion with a competitor six months from now. A statistical employment survey conducted now should categorize the status of the former treasury manager as:
   A. underemployed.
   B. voluntarily unemployed.
   C. frictionally unemployed.

4. The discouraged worker category is defined to include people who:
   A. are overqualified for their job.
   B. could look for a job but choose not to.
   C. currently look for work without finding it.

5. The category of persons who would be *most likely* to be harmed by an increase in the rate of inflation is:
   A. homeowners with fixed 30-year mortgages.
   B. retirees relying on a fixed annuity payment.
   C. workers employed under contracts with escalator clauses.

6. The term that describes when inflation declines but nonetheless remains at a positive level is:
   A. deflation.
   B. stagflation.
   C. disinflation.

7. Deflation is *most likely* to be associated with:
   A. a shortage of government revenue.

B. substantial macroeconomic contraction.

C. explicit monetary policy to combat inflation.

8. The *least likely* consequence of a period of hyperinflation is the:

   A. reduced velocity of money.

   B. increased supply of money.

   C. possibility of social unrest.

The following information relates to questions 9-10

Exhibit 1: Consumption Baskets and Prices over Two Months				
	November 2010		December 2010	
Goods	Quantity	Price	Quantity	Price
Sugar	70 kg	€0.90/kg	120 kg	€1.00/kg
Cotton	60 kg	€0.60/kg	50 kg	€0.80/kg

9. Assuming the base period for 2010 consumption is November and the initial price index is set at 100, then the inflation rate after calculating the December price index as a Laspeyres index is *closest to*:

   A. 19.2%.

   B. 36.4%.

   C. 61.6%.

10. For the December consumption basket in Exhibit 1, the value of the Paasche index is *closest to*:

    A. 116.

    B. 148.

    C. 160.

11. A central bank will *most likely* allow the economy to self-correct in periods of:

    A. high inflation, fast economic growth, and low unemployment.

    B. low inflation, slow economic growth, and high unemployment.

    C. high inflation, slow economic growth, and high unemployment.

12. Disinflation is *best* described as a:

    A. decline in price levels.

Practice Problems

   B. negative inflation rate.

   C. decline in the inflation rate.

13. The characteristic of national consumer price indexes that is *most likely* shared across major economies worldwide is:

   A. the geographic areas covered in their surveys.

   B. the weights they place on covered goods and services.

   C. their use in the determination of macroeconomic policy.

14. Of the following statements regarding the Producer Price Index (PPI), which is the *least likely*? The PPI:

   A. can influence the future CPI.

   B. category weights can vary more widely than analogous CPI terms.

   C. is used more frequently than CPI as a benchmark for adjusting labor contract payments.

15. The following presents selected commodity price data for July–August 20X0:

	July 20X0		August 20X0	
Goods	Quantity	Price	Quantity	Price
Milk	18 liters	€1.00/liter	17 liters	€1.00/liter
Orange juice	6 liters	€2.00/liter	4 liters	€2.50/liter

   Given the consumption basket and prices presented, which type of price index will result in the highest calculated inflation rate over a two-month time period?

   A. One that uses a current consumption basket

   B. One that uses a constant consumption basket

   C. One reflecting substitutions made by consumers over time

16. The inflation rate *most likely* relied on to determine public economic policy is:

   A. core inflation.

   B. headline inflation.

   C. index of food and energy prices.

17. What is the *most* important effect of labor productivity in a cost-push inflation scenario?

   A. Rising productivity indicates a strong economy and a bias towards inflation.

   B. The productivity level determines the economy's status relative to its "natural rate of unemployment."

   C. As productivity growth proportionately exceeds wage increases, product price increases are less likely.

18. A product is part of a price index based on a fixed consumption basket. If, over

time, the product's quality improves while its price stays constant, the measured inflation rate is *most likely*:

A. unaffected.

B. biased upward.

C. biased downward.

19. A price index of goods and services that excludes food and energy is *most likely* used to calculate:

    A. core inflation.

    B. the GDP deflator.

    C. headline inflation.

20. An economist expects the following:

    - The decline in the unemployment rate will result in higher revenues for home retailers.
    - A tighter labor market will put upward pressure on wages, compelling home retailers to raise prices.

    Which type of inflation *best* corresponds to the economist's expectations?

    A. Stagflation

    B. Cost-push inflation

    C. Demand-pull inflation

SOLUTIONS

1. C is correct. When a nation's currency depreciates, domestic goods seem cheaper than foreign goods, placing downward pressure on demand for imports. When the depreciation persists for some time, the country's total imports are likely to decrease.

2. A is correct. Discouraged workers have given up seeking employment and are statistically outside the labor force. Therefore, an increase in discouraged workers will decrease the labor force and thus the labor participation ratio, which is the ratio of labor force to total working age population. Additionally, an increase in discouraged workers will decrease the unemployment rate because discouraged workers are not counted in the official unemployment rate.

3. C is correct. Frictionally unemployed people are not working at the time of the employment survey but have recently left one job and are about to start another job. The frictionally unemployed have a job waiting for them and are not 100% unemployed, it is just that they have not started the new job yet. Although the treasury manager has left his current employment, he has accepted a new position at another firm that starts in six months.

4. B is correct. Discouraged workers are defined as persons who have stopped looking for work and are outside the labor force.

5. B is correct. With inflation, a fixed amount of money buys fewer goods and services, thus reducing purchasing power.

6. C is correct. Disinflation is known as a reduction of inflation from a higher to lower, but still above zero, level.

7. B is correct. Deflation is connected to a vicious cycle of reduced spending and higher unemployment.

8. A is correct. In hyperinflation, consumers accelerate their spending to beat price increases, and money circulates more rapidly.

9. A is correct. The Laspeyres index is calculated with these inputs:
   - November consumption bundle: 70 × 0.9 + 60 × 0.6 = 99
   - December consumption bundle: 70 × 1 + 60 × 0.8 = 118
   - December price index: (118/99) × 100 = 119.19
   - Inflation rate: (119.19/100) − 1 = 0.1919 = 19.19%

10. A is correct. The Paasche index uses the current product mix of consumption combined with the variation of prices. For December, its value is

    (120 × 1 + 50 × 0.8)/(120 × 0.9 + 50 × 0.6) = (160/138) × 100 = 115.9.

11. C is correct. This scenario is often referred to as stagflation. Here, the economy is likely to be left to self-correct because no short-term economic policy is thought to be effective.

12. C is correct. Disinflation is a decline in the inflation rate—for example, from 7% to 4%.

13. C is correct. Central banks typically use consumer price indexes to monitor inflation and evaluate their monetary policies.

14. C is correct. The CPI is typically used for this purpose, while the PPI is more closely connected to business contracts.

15. B is correct. The inflation rate calculated by using a constant consumption basket (the Laspeyres index) is 10%, derived as follows:

    July 20X0 consumption basket = (18 × €1) + (6 × €2) = €30

    August 20X0 consumption basket = (18 × €1) + (6 × €2.5) = €33

    Value of the Laspeyres index (I_L) = (€33/€30) × 100 = €110

    Inflation rate = (110/100) − 1 = 0.10 = 10%

    The inflation rate calculated using a current consumption basket (the Paasche index) is 8%, derived as follows:

    July 20X0 consumption basket = (17 × €1) + (4 × €2) = €25

    August 20X0 consumption basket = (17 × €1) + (4 × €2.5) = €27

    Value of the Paasche index (I_P) = (€27/€25) × 100 = €108

    Inflation rate = (108/100) − 1 = 0.08 = 8%

    The inflation rate calculated by "chaining" the monthly prices of consumption baskets as they change over time (the Fisher index) is derived as follows:

    Value of the Fisher index = $\sqrt{I_P \times I_L}$

    Value of the Fisher Index = $\sqrt{€110 \times €108}$ = €108.99

    Inflation rate = (108.99/100) − 1 = 0.0899 = 8.99%

16. A is correct. Core inflation is less volatile since it excludes food and energy prices and therefore will not be as likely to lead to policy overreactions when serving as a target.

17. C is correct. For productivity, or output per hour, the faster that it can grow, the further that wages can rise without putting pressure on business costs per unit of output.

18. B is correct. As the quality of a product improves, it satisfies people's needs and wants better. The measured inflation rate is skewed higher than otherwise unless an adjustment is made for the increase in the quality of the good. Even if the good's price had increased over time, the improvements in quality would still bias the measured inflation rate upward.

19. A is correct. A price index of goods and services that excludes food and energy is used to calculate core inflation. Policy makers often use core inflation when reading the trend in the economy and making economic policies. The reason is because policy makers are trying to avoid overreaction to short-term fluctuations in prices as a result of short-term changes in supply and demand.

20. B is correct. Cost-push inflation refers to the situation in which rising costs, usually wages, compel businesses to raise prices.

LEARNING MODULE 5

Monetary and Fiscal Policy

by Andrew Clare, PhD, and Stephen Thomas, PhD.

Andrew Clare, PhD, and Stephen Thomas, PhD, are at Cass Business School (United Kingdom).

LEARNING OUTCOMES

Mastery	The candidate should be able to:
☐	compare monetary and fiscal policy
☐	describe functions and definitions of money
☐	explain the money creation process
☐	describe theories of the demand for and supply of money
☐	describe the Fisher effect
☐	contrast the costs of expected and unexpected inflation

1. INTRODUCTION TO MONETARY AND FISCAL POLICY

☐ compare monetary and fiscal policy

The economic decisions of households can have a significant impact on an economy. For example, a decision on the part of households to consume more and to save less can lead to an increase in employment, investment, and ultimately profits. Equally, the investment decisions made by corporations can have an important impact on the real economy and on corporate profits. But individual corporations can rarely affect large economies on their own, just as the decisions of a single household concerning consumption will have a negligible impact on the wider economy.

By contrast, the decisions made by governments can have an enormous impact on even the largest and most developed of economies for two main reasons. First, the public sectors of most developed economies normally employ a significant proportion of the population, and they are usually responsible for a significant proportion of spending in an economy. Second, governments are also the largest borrowers in world debt markets.

Government policy is ultimately expressed through its borrowing and spending activities. The two types of government policy that can affect the macroeconomy and financial markets include monetary policy and fiscal policy.

Monetary policy refers to central bank activities that are directed toward influencing the quantity of money and credit in an economy.[1] By contrast, **fiscal policy** refers to the government's decisions about taxation and spending. Both monetary and fiscal policies are used to regulate economic activity over time. They can be used to accelerate growth when an economy starts to slow or to moderate growth and activity when an economy starts to overheat. In addition, fiscal policy can be used to redistribute income and wealth.

The overarching goal of both monetary and fiscal policy is normally the creation of an economic environment where growth is stable and positive and inflation is stable and low. Crucially, the aim is therefore to steer the underlying economy so that it does not experience economic booms that may be followed by extended periods of low or negative growth and high levels of unemployment. In such a stable economic environment, households can feel secure in their consumption and saving decisions, while corporations can concentrate on making sound investment decisions, regular coupon payments to bond holders, and profits for their shareholders.

The challenges to achieving this overarching goal are many. Not only are economies frequently buffeted by shocks (such as oil price jumps), but some economists believe that natural cycles in the economy also exist. Moreover, there are plenty of examples from history where government policies—either monetary, fiscal, or both—have exacerbated an economic expansion that eventually led to damaging consequences for the real economy, financial markets, and investors.

This reading focuses on the relationship between money, interest rates and inflation.

Before we can begin to understand how monetary and fiscal policies are implemented and how they affect interest rates and inflation, we must examine the functions and role of **money**. We can then explore the special role that **central banks** play in today's economies.

EXAMPLE 1

Monetary and Fiscal Policy

1. Which of the following statements *best* describes monetary policy? Monetary policy:

    A. involves the setting of medium-term targets for broad money aggregates.

    B. involves the manipulation by a central bank of the government's budget deficit.

    C. seeks to influence the macro economy by influencing the quantity of money and credit in the economy.

Solution to 1:

C is correct. Choice A is incorrect because, although the setting of targets for monetary aggregates is a possible *tool* of monetary policy, monetary policy itself is concerned with influencing the overall, or macro, economy.

---

1 Central banks can implement monetary policy almost completely independent of government interference and influence at one end of the scale, or simply as the agent of the government at the other end of the scale.

2. Which of the following statements *best* describes fiscal policy? Fiscal policy:

   A. is used by governments to redistribute wealth and incomes.
   B. is the attempt by governments to balance their budgets from one year to the next.
   C. involves the use of government spending and taxation to influence economy activity.

Solution to 2:

C is correct. Note that governments may wish to use fiscal policy to redistribute incomes and balance their budgets, but the overriding goal of fiscal policy is usually to influence a broader range of economic activity.

MONEY: FUNCTIONS, CREATION, AND DEFINITION

2

☐ describe functions and definitions of money
☐ explain the money creation process

To understand the nature, role, and development of money in modern economies, it is useful to think about a world without money—where to purchase any good or service, an individual would have to "pay" with another good or service. An economy where such economic agents as households, corporations, and even governments pay for goods and services in this way is known as a **barter economy**. There are many drawbacks to such an economy. First, the exchange of goods for other goods (or services) would require both economic agents in the transaction to want what the other is selling. It might also be impossible to undertake transactions where the goods are indivisible—that is, where one agent wishes to buy a certain amount of another's goods, but that agent only has one indivisible unit of another good that is worth more than the good that the agent is trying to buy. Another problem occurs if economic agents do not wish to exchange all of their goods on other goods and services. Finally, in a barter economy, there are many measures of value: the price of oranges in terms of pears or of pears in terms of bread. A barter economy has no common measure of value that would make multiple transactions simple.

The Functions of Money

The most generic definition of money is that it is any generally accepted medium of exchange. A **medium of exchange** is any asset that can be used to purchase goods and services or to repay debts. When this medium of exchange exists, a farmer wishing to sell wheat for wine does not need to identify a wine producer in search of wheat. Instead, he can sell wheat to those who want wheat in exchange for money. The farmer can then exchange this money for wine with a wine producer, who in turn can exchange that money for the goods or services that she wants.

However, for money to act as this liberating medium of exchange, it must possess the following qualities:

   i. readily acceptable
   ii. have a known value

iii. easily divisible

iv. have a high value relative to its weight

v. difficult to counterfeit

Given the qualities that money needs to have, it is clear why precious metals (particularly gold and silver) often fulfilled the role of medium of exchange in early societies, and as recently as the early part of the twentieth century. Precious metals were acceptable as a medium of exchange because they had a known value, were easily divisible, had a high value relative to their weight, and could not be easily counterfeited.

Thus, precious metals were capable of acting as a medium of exchange. But they also fulfilled two other useful functions that are essential for the characteristics of money. Because precious metals like gold had a high value relative to their bulk and were not perishable, they could act as a **store of wealth**. However, their ability to act as a store of wealth not only depended on the fact that they did not perish physically over time, but also on the belief that others would always value precious metals. The value from year to year of precious metals depended on people's continued demand for them in ornaments, jewellery, and so on. For example, people were willing to use gold as a store of wealth because they believed that it would remain highly valued. However, if gold became less valuable to people relative to other goods and services year after year it would not be able to fulfill that role and as such might also lose its status as a medium of exchange.

Another important characteristic of money is that it can be used as a universal unit of account. As such, it can create a single unitary **measure of value** for all goods and services. In an economy where gold and silver are the accepted medium of exchange, all prices, debts, and wealth can be recorded in terms of their gold or silver coin exchange value.

In summary, money fulfills three important functions; it:

- acts as a medium of exchange;
- provides individuals with a way of storing wealth; and
- provides society with a convenient measure of value.

Paper Money and the Money Creation Process

Although precious metals like gold and silver fulfilled the required functions of money relatively well for many years, and although carrying gold coins around was easier than carrying around one's physical produce, it was not necessarily a safe way to conduct business.

A crucial development in the history of money was the **promissory note**. The process began when individuals began leaving their excess gold with goldsmiths, who would look after it for them. In turn the goldsmiths would give the depositors a receipt, stating how much gold they had deposited. Eventually these receipts were traded directly for goods and services, rather than there being a physical transfer of gold from the goods buyer to the goods seller. Of course, both the buyer and seller had to trust the goldsmith because the goldsmith had all the gold and the goldsmith's customers had only pieces of paper. These depository receipts represented a promise to pay a certain amount of gold on demand. This paper money therefore became a proxy for the precious metals on which it was based; that is, it was directly related to a physical commodity. Many of these early goldsmiths evolved into banks, taking in excess wealth and in turn issuing promissory notes that could be used in commerce.

In taking in other people's gold and issuing depository receipts and later promissory notes, it became clear to the goldsmiths and early banks that not all the gold that they held in their vaults would be withdrawn at any one time. Individuals were willing to buy and sell goods and services with the promissory notes, but the majority of the gold that backed the notes just sat in the vaults—although its ownership would change with the flow of commerce over time. A certain proportion of the gold that was not being withdrawn and used directly for commerce could therefore be lent to others at a rate of interest. By doing this, the early banks created money.

The process of **money creation** is a crucial concept for understanding the role that money plays in an economy. Its potency depends on the amount of money that banks keep in reserve to meet the withdrawals of its customers. This practice of lending customers' money to others on the assumption that not all customers will want all of their money back at any one time is known as **fractional reserve banking**.

We can illustrate how it works through a simple example. Suppose that the bankers in an economy come to the view that they need to retain only 10 percent of any money deposited with them. This is known as the **reserve requirement**.[2] Now consider what happens when a customer deposits €100 in the First Bank of Nations. This deposit changes the balance sheet of First Bank of Nations, as shown in Exhibit 1, and it represents a liability to the bank because it is effectively loaned to the bank by the customer. By lending 90 percent of this deposit to another customer the bank has two types of assets: (1) the bank's reserves of €10, and (2) the loan equivalent to €90. Notice that the balance sheet still balances; €100 worth of assets and €100 worth of liabilities are on the balance sheet.

Now suppose that the recipient of the loan of €90 uses this money to purchase some goods of this value and the seller of the goods deposits this €90 in another bank, the Second Bank of Nations. The Second Bank of Nations goes through the same process; it retains €9 in reserve and loans 90 percent of the deposit (€81) to another customer. This customer in turn spends €81 on some goods or services. The recipient of this money deposits it at the Third Bank of Nations, and so on. This example shows how money is created when a bank makes a loan.

Exhibit 1: Money Creation via Fractional Reserve Banking

First Bank of Nations

Assets		Liabilities	
Reserves	€10	Deposits	€100
Loans	€90		

Second Bank of Nations

Assets		Liabilities	
Reserves	€9	Deposits	€90
Loans	€81		

Third Bank of Nations

Assets		Liabilities	
Reserves	€8.1	Deposits	€81
Loans	€72.9		

This process continues until there is no more money left to be deposited and loaned out. The total amount of money 'created' from this one deposit of €100 can be calculated as:

---

2 This is an example of a *voluntary* reserve requirement because it is self-imposed.

$$\text{New deposit/Reserve requirement} = €100/0.10 = €1{,}000 \qquad (1)$$

It is the sum of all the deposits now in the banking system. You should also note that the original deposit of €100, via the practice of reserve banking, was the catalyst for €1,000 worth of economic transactions. That is not to say that economic growth would be zero without this process, but instead that it can be an important component in economic activity.

The amount of money that the banking system creates through the practice of fractional reserve banking is a function of 1 divided by the reserve requirement, a quantity known as the **money multiplier**.[3] In the case just examined, the money multiplier is 1/0.10 = 10. Equation 1 implies that the smaller the reserve requirement, the greater the money multiplier effect.

In our simplistic example, we assumed that the banks themselves set their own reserve requirements. However, in some economies, the central bank sets the reserve requirement, which is a potential means of affecting money growth. In any case, a prudent bank would be wise to have sufficient reserves such that the withdrawal demands of their depositors can be met in stressful economic and credit market conditions.

Later, when we discuss central banks and central bank policy, we will see how central banks can use the mechanism just described to affect the money supply. Specifically, the central bank could, by purchasing €100 in government securities credited to the bank account of the seller, seek to initiate an increase in the money supply. The central bank may also lend reserves directly to banks, creating excess reserves (relative to any imposed or self-imposed reserve requirement) that can support new loans and money expansion.

EXAMPLE 2

Money and Money Creation

1. To fulfill its role as a medium of exchange, money should:

    A. be a conservative investment.

    B. have a low value relative to its weight.

    C. be easily divisible and a good store of value.

Solution to 1:

C is correct. Money needs to have a known value and be easily divisible. It should also be readily acceptable, difficult to counterfeit, and have a high value relative to its weight.

2. If the reserve requirement for banks in an economy is 5 percent, how much money could be created with the deposit of an additional £100 into a deposit account?

    A. £500

    B. £1,900

    C. £2,000

---

3 This quantity, known as the simple money multiplier, represents a maximum expansion. To the extent that banks hold excess reserves or that money loaned out is not re-deposited, the money expansion would be less. More complex multipliers incorporating such factors are developed in more advanced texts.

> **Solution to 2:**
>
> C is correct. To calculate the increase in money from an additional deposit in the banking system, use the following expression: new deposit/reserve requirement.
>
> 3. Which of the following functions does money normally fulfill for a society? It:
>
>   A. acts as a medium of exchange only.
>   B. provides economic agents with a means of storing wealth only.
>   C. provides society with a measure of value, acts as a medium of exchange, and acts as a store of wealth.
>
> **Solution to 3:**
>
> C is correct. Money needs to be able to fulfill the functions of acting as a measure of value, a medium of exchange, and a means of storing wealth.

Definitions of Money

The process of money creation raises a fundamental issue: What is money? In an economy with money but without promissory notes and fractional reserve banking, money is relatively easy to define: Money is the total amount of gold and silver coins in circulation, or their equivalent. The money creation process above, however, indicates that a broader definition of money might encompass all the notes and coins in circulation *plus* all bank deposits.

More generally, we might define money as any medium that can be used to purchase goods and services. Notes and coins can be used to fulfill this purpose, and yet such currency is not the only means of purchasing goods and services. Personal cheques can be written based on a bank chequing account, while debit cards can be used for the same purpose. But what about time deposits or savings accounts? Nowadays transfers can be made relatively easily from a savings account to a current account; therefore, these savings accounts might also be considered as part of the stock of money. Credit cards are also used to pay for goods and services; however, there is an important difference between credit card payments and those made by cheques and debit cards. Unlike a cheque or debit card payment, a credit card payment involves a deferred payment. Basically, the greater the complexity of any financial system, the harder it is to define money.

The monetary authorities in most modern economies produce a range of measures of money. But generally speaking, the money stock consists of notes and coins in circulation, plus the deposits in banks and other financial institutions that can be readily used to make purchases of goods and services in the economy. In this regard, economists often speak of the rate of growth of **narrow money** and/or **broad money**. By narrow money, they generally mean the notes and coins in circulation in an economy, plus other very highly liquid deposits. Broad money encompasses narrow money but also includes the entire range of liquid assets that can be used to make purchases.

Because financial systems, practice, and institutions vary from economy to economy, so do definitions of money; thus, it is difficult to make international comparisons. Still, most central banks produce both a narrow and broad measure of money, plus some intermediate ones too.

3 MONEY: QUANTITY THEORY, SUPPLY AND DEMAND, FISHER EFFECT

> ☐ describe theories of the demand for and supply of money
> ☐ describe the Fisher effect

In this section, we explore the important relationship between money and the price level. This relationship is best expressed in the **quantity theory of money**, which asserts that total spending (in money terms) is proportional to the quantity of money. The theory can be explained in terms of Equation 2, known as the **quantity equation of exchange**:

$$M \times V = P \times Y \tag{2}$$

where M is the quantity of money, V is the velocity of circulation of money (the average number of times in a given period that a unit of currency changes hands), P is the average price level, and Y is real output. The expression is really just an accounting identity. Effectively, it says that over a given period, the amount of money used to purchase all goods and services in an economy, $M \times V$, is equal to the monetary value of this output, $P \times Y$. If the velocity of money is approximately constant—which is an assumption of quantity theory—then spending $P \times Y$ is approximately proportional to M. The quantity equation can also be used to explain a consequence of **money neutrality**. If money neutrality holds, then an increase in the money supply, M, will not affect Y, real output, or the speed with which money changed hands, V, because if real output is unaffected, there would be no need for money to change hands more rapidly.[4] However, it will cause the aggregate price level, P, to rise.

The simple quantity theory gave rise to the equally simple idea that the price level, or at least the rate of inflation, could be controlled by manipulating the rate of growth of the money supply. Economists who believe this are referred to as **monetarists**. They argue that there is a causal relationship running from money growth to inflation. In the past, some governments have tried to apply this logic in their efforts to control inflation. However, it is possible that causality runs the other way—that is, from real activity to the money supply. This means that the quantity of money in circulation is determined by the level of economic activity, rather than vice versa.

The Demand for Money

The amount of wealth that the citizens of an economy choose to hold in the form of money—as opposed to bonds or equities—is known as the demand for money. There are three basic motives for holding money:

- transactions-related;
- precautionary; and
- speculative.

---

4 Note that the full version of the quantity theory of money uses the symbol T rather than Y to indicate transactions because money is used not just for buying goods and services but also for financial transactions. We will return to this point in the discussion of quantitative easing.

Money balances that are held to finance transactions are referred to as **transactions money balances**. The size of the transactions balances will tend to increase with the average value of transactions in an economy. Generally speaking, as gross domestic product (GDP) grows over time, transactions balances will also tend to grow; however, the ratio of transactions balances to GDP remains fairly stable over time.

As the name suggests, **precautionary money balances** are held to provide a buffer against unforeseen events that might require money. These balances will tend to be larger for individuals or organizations that enter into a high level of transactions over time. In other words, a precautionary buffer of $100 for a company that regularly enters into transactions worth millions of dollars might be considered rather small. When we extend this logic to the overall economy, we can see that these precautionary balances will also tend to rise with the volume and value of transactions in the economy, and therefore, GDP as well.

Finally, the **speculative demand for money** relates to the demand to hold speculative money balances based on the potential opportunities or risks that are inherent in other financial instruments (e.g., bonds). **Speculative money balances** consist of monies held in anticipation that other assets will decline in value. But in choosing to hold speculative money balances rather than bonds, investors give up the return that could be earned from the bond or other financial assets. Therefore, the speculative demand for money will tend to fall as the returns available on other financial assets rises. However, it will tend to rise as the perceived risk in other financial instruments rises. In equilibrium, individuals will tend to increase their holdings of money relative to riskier assets until the marginal benefit of having a lower risk portfolio of wealth is equal to the marginal cost of giving up a unit of expected return on these riskier assets. In aggregate then, speculative balances will tend to be inversely related to the expected return on other financial assets and directly related to the perceived risk of other financial assets.

EXAMPLE 3

Money

1. The transactions demand for money refers to the demand to hold money:

    A. as a buffer against unforeseen events.

    B. to use in the purchase of goods and services.

    C. based on the opportunity or risks available on other financial instruments.

Solution to 1:

B is correct. The transactions demand for money refers to the amount of money that economic agents wish to hold to pay for goods and services.

2. The speculative demand for money will tend to:

    A. fall as the perceived risk on other assets rises.

    B. rise as the expected returns on other assets fall.

    C. be inversely related to the transactions demand for money.

Solution to 2:

B is correct. If the expected return on other assets falls, then the opportunity cost of holding money also falls and can, in turn, lead to an increase in the speculative demand for money.

3. What is the difference between narrow and broad money? Broad money:

   A. is limited to those liquid assets most commonly used to make purchases.

   B. can be used to purchase a wider range of goods and services than narrow money.

   C. encompasses narrow money and refers to the stock of the entire range of liquid assets that can be used to make purchases.

Solution to 3:

C is correct. This is the definition of broad money. Broad money encompasses narrow money.

The Supply and Demand for Money

We have now discussed definitions of money, its relationship with the aggregate price level, and the demand for it. We now discuss the interaction between the supply of and demand for money.

As with most other markets, the supply of money and the demand to hold it will interact to produce an equilibrium price for money. In this market, the price of money is the nominal interest rate that could be earned by lending it to others. Exhibit 2 shows the supply and demand curves for money. The vertical scale represents the rate of interest; the horizontal scale plots the quantity of nominal money in the economy. The supply curve (MS) is vertical because we assume that there is a fixed nominal amount of money circulating at any one time. The demand curve (MD) is downward sloping because as interest rates rise, the speculative demand for money falls. The supply and demand for money are both satisfied at an equilibrium interest rate of I_0. I_0 is the rate of interest at which no excess money balances exist.

Exhibit 2: The Supply and Demand for Money

Nominal Rate of Interest

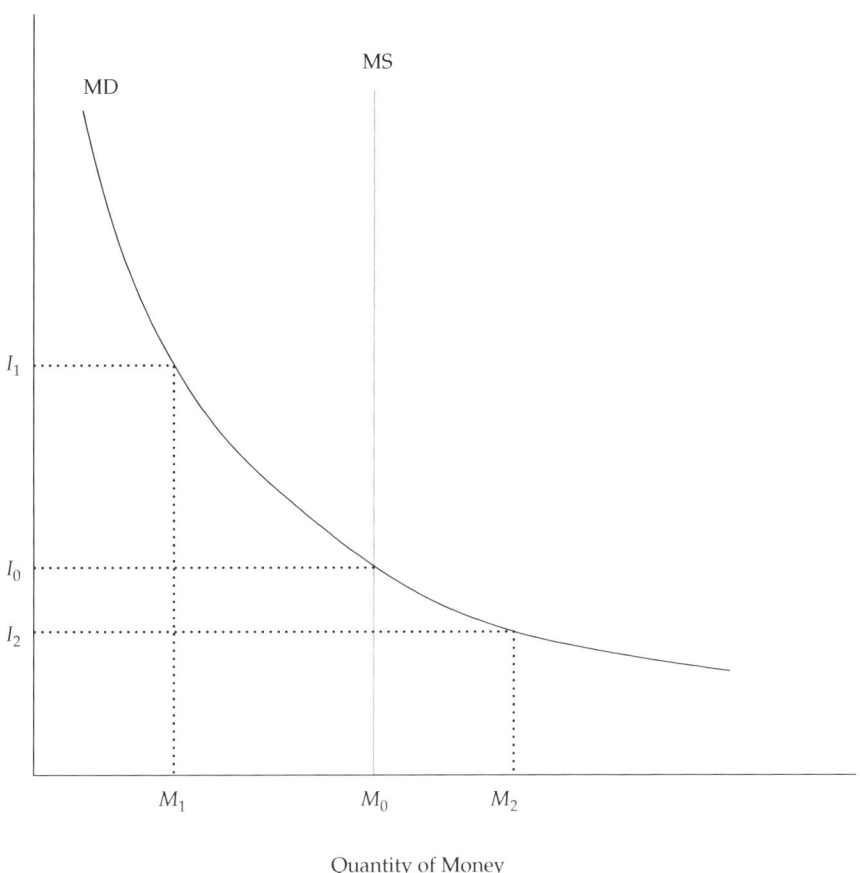

Quantity of Money

To see why I_0 is the equilibrium rate of interest where there are no excess money balances, consider the following. If the interest rate on bonds were I_1 instead of I_0, there would be excess supply of money ($M_0 - M_1$). Economic agents would seek to buy bonds with their excess money balances, which would force the price of bonds up and the interest rate back down to I_0. Similarly, if bonds offered a rate of interest, I_2, there would be an excess demand for money ($M_2 - M_0$). Corporations and individuals would seek to sell bonds so that individuals could increase their money holdings, but in doing so, the price of bonds would fall and the interest rate offered on them would rise until it reached I_0. Interest rates effectively adjust to bring the market into equilibrium. In this simple example, we have also assumed that the supply of money and bonds is fixed as economic agents readjust their holdings. In practice, this may not be true, but the dynamics of the adjustment process described here essentially still hold.

Exhibit 2 also reemphasises the relationship between the supply of money and the aggregate price level, which we first encountered when discussing the quantity theory of money. Suppose that the central bank increases the supply of money from M_0 to M_2, so that the vertical supply curve shifts to the right. Because the increase in the supply of money makes it more plentiful and hence less valuable, its price (the interest rate) falls as the price level rises.

This all sounds very simple, but in practice the effects of an increase in the money supply are more complex. The initial increase in the money supply will create excess supply of cash. People and companies could get rid of the excess by loaning the money to others by buying bonds, as implied above, but they might also deposit it in a bank or simply use it to buy goods and services. But an economy's capacity to produce goods and services depends on the availability of real things: notably, natural resources, capital, and labour—that is, factors of production supplied either directly or indirectly by households. Increasing the money supply does not change the availability of these real things. Thus, some economists believe that the long-run impact of an exogenous increase in the supply of money is an increase in the aggregate price level.

The Fisher Effect

The **Fisher effect** is directly related to the concept of money neutrality. Named after the economist Irving Fisher, the Fisher effect states that the real rate of interest in an economy is stable over time so that changes in nominal interest rates are the result of changes in expected inflation. Thus, the nominal interest rate (R_{nom}) in an economy is the sum of the required real rate of interest (R_{real}) and the expected rate of inflation (π^e) over any given time horizon:

$$R_{nom} = R_{real} + \pi^e \tag{3}$$

According to money neutrality, over the long term the money supply and/or the growth rate in money should not affect R_{real} but will affect inflation and inflation expectations.

EXAMPLE 4

Interest Rates and the Supply of Money

1. According to the quantity equation of exchange, an increase in the money supply can lead to an:

    A. increase in the aggregate price level, regardless of changes in the velocity of circulation of money.

    B. increase in the aggregate price level as long as the velocity of circulation of money rises sufficiently to offset the increase in the money supply.

    C. increase in the aggregate price level as long as the velocity of circulation of money does not fall sufficiently to offset the increase in the money supply and real output is unchanged.

Solution to 1:

C is correct. If the velocity of circulation of money does not change with an increase in the money supply and real output is fixed, then the aggregate price level should increase. If the velocity of circulation of money falls sufficiently, or if real output rises sufficiently, then the increase in money may have no impact on prices.

2. The nominal interest rate comprises a real rate of interest:

    A. plus a risk premium only.

    B. plus a premium for expected inflation only.

    C. and compensation for both expected inflation and risk.

Solution to 2:

C is correct. Investors demand a real rate of interest, compensation for expected inflation and a risk premium to compensate them for uncertainty.

> 3. An expansion in the money supply would *most likely*:
>
>   **A.** lead to a decline in nominal interest rates.
>
>   **B.** lead to an increase in nominal interest rates.
>
>   **C.** reduce the equilibrium amount of money that economic agents would wish to hold.
>
> ## Solution to 3:
>
> A is correct. Increasing the supply of money, all other things being equal, will reduce its "price," that is, the interest rate on money balances.

THE COSTS OF INFLATION   4

☐ contrast the costs of expected and unexpected inflation

Huge efforts have been put into controlling inflation since the major economies experienced such high levels of inflation in the 1970s. From the early 1970s then, inflation has been seen as a very bad thing. But why? What are the costs of inflation? The debate around the "costs" of inflation really centers on the distinction between **expected inflation** and **unexpected inflation**. Expected inflation is clearly the level of inflation that economic agents expect in the future. Unexpected inflation can be defined as the level of inflation that we experience that is either below or above that which we expected; it is the component of inflation that is a surprise.

To demonstrate the significant costs of inflation, consider the following. Imagine a world where inflation is high but where all prices (including asset prices) in an economy are perfectly indexed to inflation. In such a world, would economic agents care about inflation? Probably not. If the average price of goods and services rose by 10 percent, people's salaries (and all other prices) would rise by the same amount, which would therefore make economic agents indifferent to the rise in prices.

In practice, however, all prices, wages, salaries, rents, and so forth are not indexed, in which case economic agents would certainly need to think about inflation more carefully. But what if inflation in this world where prices are no longer perfectly indexed is high, but perfectly predictable? In this alternative, imaginary world, economic agents would have to think about inflation, but not too hard as long as they were capable of calculating the impact of the known inflation rate on all future prices. So, if everyone knew that inflation was going to be 10 percent over the next year, then everyone could bargain for a 10 percent increase in their salaries to accommodate this, and companies could plan to put up the prices of their goods and services by 10 percent. In this world, an expectation of 10 percent inflation would become a self-fulfilling prophecy.

However, economic agents would worry about inflation in a world where all prices were not indexed and, crucially, where inflation was high and unpredictable. In fact, this is a crude description of the inflationary backdrop in many developed economies over the 1970s and 1980s, including the United States, France, the United Kingdom, Italy, and Canada.

Arguably it is **unexpected inflation** that is most costly. Inflation that is fully anticipated can be factored into wage negotiations and priced into business and financial contracts. But when inflation turns out to be higher than is anticipated, then borrowers benefit at the expense of lenders because the real value of their borrowing declines. Conversely, when inflation is lower than is anticipated, lenders benefit at the expense of borrowers because the real value of the payment on debts rises. Furthermore, if inflation is very uncertain or very volatile, then lenders will ask for a premium to compensate them for this uncertainty. As a result, the costs of borrowing will be higher than would otherwise have been the case. Higher borrowing costs could in turn reduce economic activity, for example, by discouraging investment.

It is also possible that **inflation uncertainty** can exacerbate the economic cycle. Inflation uncertainty is the degree to which economic agents view future rates of inflation as hard to forecast. Take for example the case of an imaginary television manufacturer. Suppose one day that the manufacturer looks out at the market for televisions and sees that the market price of televisions has risen by 10 percent. Armed with this information, the manufacturer assumes that there has been an increase in demand for televisions or maybe a reduction in supply. So, to take advantage of the new, higher prices, the manufacturer extends the factory, employs more workers, and begins to produce more televisions.

Having now increased the output of the factory, the manufacturer then attempts to sell the extra televisions that the factory has produced. But to its horror, the manufacturer finds out that there is no extra demand for televisions. Instead, the 10 percent rise in television prices was caused by a generalized 10 percent increase in all consumer prices across the economy. The manufacturer realizes that it has surplus stock, surplus factory capacity, and too many workers. So, it cuts back on production, lays off some of the workforce, and realizes that it won't need to invest in new plant or machinery for a long time.

This example emphasizes the potentially destabilizing impact of unexpected inflation. It demonstrates how unanticipated inflation can reduce the information content of market prices for economic agents. If we scale this example up, it should not be too difficult to imagine how unanticipated increases or decreases in the general price level could help to exacerbate—and in some extreme cases cause—economic booms and busts.

Over the last two to three decades the consensus among economists has been that unanticipated and high levels of inflation can have an impact on real things like employment, investment and profits, and therefore that controlling inflation should be one of the main goals of macroeconomic policy.

SUMMARY

In this reading, we have sought to explain the practices of both monetary and fiscal policy. Both can have a significant impact on economic activity, and it is for this reason that financial analysts need to be aware of the tools of both monetary and fiscal policy, the goals of the monetary and fiscal authorities, and most important the monetary and fiscal policy transmission mechanisms.

- Governments can influence the performance of their economies by using combinations of monetary and fiscal policy. Monetary policy refers to central bank activities that are directed toward influencing the quantity of money and credit in an economy. By contrast, fiscal policy refers to the government's decisions about taxation and spending. The two sets of policies affect the economy via different mechanisms.

- Money fulfills three important functions: It acts as a medium of exchange, provides individuals with a way of storing wealth, and provides society with a convenient measure of value. Via the process of fractional reserve banking, the banking system can create money.

- The amount of wealth that the citizens of an economy choose to hold in the form of money—as opposed to, for example, bonds or equities—is known as the demand for money. There are three basic motives for holding money: transactions-related, precautionary, and speculative.

- The addition of 1 unit of additional reserves to a fractional reserve banking system can support an expansion of the money supply by an amount equal to the money multiplier, defined as 1/reserve requirement (stated as a decimal).

- The nominal rate of interest is comprised of three components: a real required rate of return, a component to compensate lenders for future inflation, and a risk premium to compensate lenders for uncertainty (e.g., about the future rate of inflation).

- Central banks take on multiple roles in modern economies. They are usually the monopoly supplier of their currency, the lender of last resort to the banking sector, the government's bank and the bank of the banks, and they often supervise banks. Although they may express their objectives in different ways, the overarching objective of most central banks is price stability.

- The ultimate challenge for central banks as they try to manipulate the supply of money to influence the economy is that they cannot control the amount of money that households and corporations put in banks on deposit, nor can they easily control the willingness of banks to create money by expanding credit. Taken together, this also means that they cannot always control the money supply. Therefore, there are definite limits to the power of monetary policy.

- Fiscal policy involves the use of government spending and revenue raising (taxation) to impact a number of aspects of the economy: the overall level of aggregate demand in an economy and hence the level of economic activity; the distribution of income and wealth among different segments of the population; and hence ultimately the allocation of resources between different sectors and economic agents.

- The tools that governments use in implementing fiscal policy are related to the way in which they raise revenue and the different forms of expenditure. Governments usually raise money via a combination of direct and indirect taxes. Government expenditure can be current on goods and services or can take the form of capital expenditure, for example, on infrastructure projects.

- As economic growth weakens, or when it is in recession, a government can enact an expansionary fiscal policy—for example, by raising expenditure without an offsetting increase in taxation. Conversely, by reducing expenditure and maintaining tax revenues, a contractionary policy might reduce economic activity. Fiscal policy can therefore play an important role in stabilizing an economy.

PRACTICE PROBLEMS

1. As the reserve requirement increases, the money multiplier:
   A. increases.
   B. decreases.
   C. remains the same.

2. Which is the *most* accurate statement regarding the demand for money?
   A. Precautionary money demand is directly related to GDP.
   B. Transactions money demand is inversely related to returns on bonds.
   C. Speculative demand is inversely related to the perceived risk of other assets.

3. The following exhibit shows the supply and demand for money:

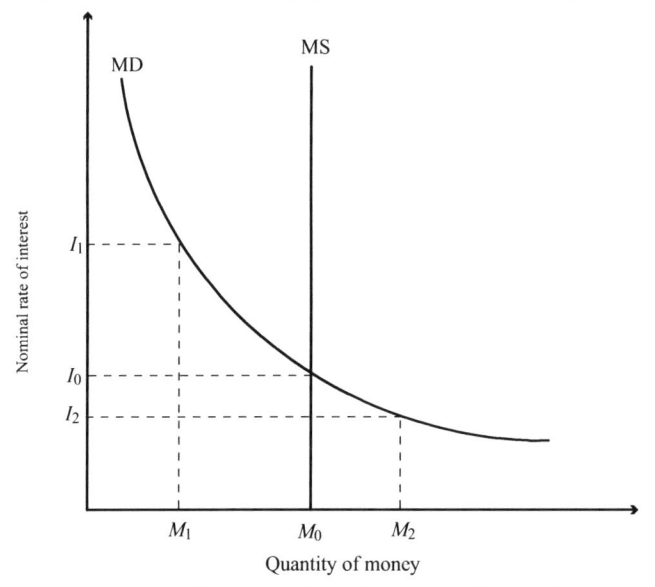

   There is an excess supply of money when the nominal rate of interest is:
   A. I_0.
   B. I_1.
   C. I_2.

4. According to the theory of money neutrality, money supply growth does *not* affect variables such as real output and employment in:
   A. the long run.
   B. the short run.
   C. the long and short run.

5. Which of the following *best* describes a fundamental assumption when monetary policy is used to influence the economy?
   A. Financial markets are efficient.

Practice Problems

    B. Money is not neutral in the short run.

    C. Official rates do not affect exchange rates.

6. Monetarists are *most likely* to believe:
   A. there is a causal relationship running from inflation to money.

   B. inflation can be affected by changing the money supply growth rate.

   C. rapid financial innovation in the market increases the effectiveness of monetary policy.

7. The proposition that the real interest rate is relatively stable is *most* closely associated with:
   A. the Fisher effect.

   B. money neutrality.

   C. the quantity theory of money.

8. Which of the following equations is a consequence of the Fisher effect?
   A. Nominal interest rate = Real interest rate + Expected rate of inflation.

   B. Real interest rate = Nominal interest rate + Expected rate of inflation.

   C. Nominal interest rate = Real interest rate + Market risk premium.

9. Central banks would typically be *most* concerned with costs of:
   A. low levels of inflation that are anticipated.

   B. moderate levels of inflation that are anticipated.

   C. moderate levels of inflation that are not anticipated.

SOLUTIONS

1. B is correct. There is an inverse relationship between the money multiplier and the reserve requirement. The money multiplier is equal to 1 divided by the reserve requirement.

2. A is correct. Precautionary money demand is directly related to GDP. Precautionary money balances are held to provide a buffer against unforeseen events that might require money. Precautionary balances tend to rise with the volume and value of transactions in the economy, and therefore rise with GDP.

3. B is correct. When the interest rate on bonds is I_1 there is an excess supply of money (equal to $M_0 - M_1 > 0$). Economic agents would seek to buy bonds with their excess money balances, which would force the price of bonds up and the interest rate down to I_0.

4. A is correct. According to the theory of money neutrality, an increase in the money supply ultimately leads to an increase in the price level and leaves real variables unaffected in the long run.

5. B is correct. If money were neutral in the short run, monetary policy would not be effective in influencing the economy.

6. B is correct. By definition, monetarists believe prices may be controlled by manipulating the money supply.

7. A is correct. The Fisher effect is based on the idea that the real interest rate is relatively stable. Changes in the nominal interest rate result from changes in expected inflation.

8. A is correct. The Fisher effect implies that changes in the nominal interest rate reflect changes in expected inflation, which is consistent with Nominal interest rate = Real interest rate + Expected rate of inflation.

9. C is correct. Low levels of inflation have higher economic costs than moderate levels, all else equal; unanticipated inflation has greater costs than anticipated inflation.

LEARNING MODULE 6

International Trade and Capital Flows

by Usha Nair-Reichert, PhD, and Daniel Robert Witschi, PhD, CFA.

Usha Nair-Reichert, PhD, is at Georgia Institute of Technology (USA). Daniel Robert Witschi, is at Dreyfus Sons & Co Ltd, PhD, CFA (Switzerland).

LEARNING OUTCOMES

Mastery	The candidate should be able to:
☐	compare gross domestic product and gross national product
☐	describe benefits and costs of international trade
☐	contrast comparative advantage and absolute advantage
☐	compare the Ricardian and Heckscher–Ohlin models of trade and the source(s) of comparative advantage in each model
☐	describe the balance of payments accounts including their components
☐	explain how decisions by consumers, firms, and governments affect the balance of payments

1. INTRODUCTION & INTERNATIONAL TRADE: BASIC TERMINOLOGY

☐ compare gross domestic product and gross national product

Global investors must address two fundamentally interrelated questions: where to invest and in what asset classes? Some countries may be attractive from an equity perspective because of their strong economic growth and the profitability of particular domestic sectors or industries. Other countries may be attractive from a fixed income perspective because of their interest rate environment and price stability. To identify markets that are expected to provide attractive investment opportunities, investors must analyze cross-country differences in such factors as expected GDP growth rates, monetary and fiscal policies, trade policies, and competitiveness. From a longer term perspective investors also need to consider such factors as a country's stage of economic and financial market development, demographics, quality and quantity of physical and human capital (accumulated education and training of workers), and area(s) of comparative advantage.[1]

This reading provides a framework for analyzing a country's trade and capital flows and their economic implications. International trade can facilitate economic growth by increasing the efficiency of resource allocation, providing access to larger capital and product markets, and facilitating specialization based on comparative advantage. The flow of financial capital (funds available for investment) between countries with excess savings and those where financial capital is scarce can increase liquidity, raise output, and lower the cost of capital. From an investment perspective, it is important to understand the complex and dynamic nature of international trade and capital flows because investment opportunities are increasingly exposed to the forces of global competition for markets, capital, and ideas.

This reading defines basic terminology and describes patterns and trends in international trade and capital flows. It also discusses the benefits of international trade, distinguishes between absolute and comparative advantage, and explains two traditional models of comparative advantage. The reading also introduces and describes the balance of payments, which summarizes a country's economic transactions with the rest of the world. A summary of key points and practice problems conclude the reading.

International Trade

The following sections describe the role, importance, and possible benefits and costs of international trade. Before beginning those discussions, we define some basic terminology used in this area.

Basic Terminology

The aggregate output of a nation over a specified time period is usually measured as its gross domestic product or its gross national product. Gross domestic product (GDP) measures the market value of all final goods and services produced by factors of production (such as labor and capital) located within a country/economy during a given period of time, generally a year or a quarter. Gross national product (GNP), however, measures the market value of all final goods and services produced by factors of production (such as labor and capital) supplied by citizens of a country, regardless of whether such production takes place within the country or outside of the country. The difference between a country's GDP and its GNP is that GDP includes, and GNP excludes, the production of goods and services by foreigners within that country, whereas GNP includes, and GDP excludes, the production of goods and services by its citizens outside of the country.

Imports are goods and services that a domestic economy (i.e., households, firms, and government) purchases from other countries. **Exports** are goods and services that a domestic economy sells to other countries.

The **terms of trade** are defined as the ratio of the price of exports to the price of imports, representing those prices by export and import price indexes, respectively. The terms of trade capture the relative cost of imports in terms of exports. If the

---

1 Comparative advantage refers to a country's ability to produce a good at a relatively lower cost than other goods it produces, as compared with another country. It will be more precisely defined and illustrated in the next section.

prices of exports increase relative to the prices of imports, the terms of trade have improved because the country will be able to purchase more imports with the same amount of exports.[2]

Net exports is the difference between the value of a country's exports and the value of its imports (i.e., value of exports minus imports). If the value of exports equals the value of imports, then trade is balanced. If the value of exports is greater (less) than the value of imports, then there is a **trade surplus (deficit)**. When a country has a trade surplus, it lends to foreigners or buys assets from foreigners reflecting the financing needed by foreigners running trade deficits with that country. Similarly, when a country has a trade deficit, it has to borrow from foreigners or sell some of its assets to foreigners.

Autarky is a state in which a country does not trade with other countries. This means that all goods and services are produced and consumed domestically. The price of a good or service in such an economy is called its **autarkic price**. An autarkic economy is also known as a **closed economy** because it does not trade with other countries. An **open economy**, in contrast, is an economy that trades with other countries. If there are no restrictions on trade, then members of an open economy can buy and sell goods and services at the price prevailing in the world market, the **world price**. An open economy can provide domestic households with a larger variety of goods and services, give domestic companies access to global markets and customers, and offer goods and services that are more competitively priced. In addition, it can offer domestic investors access to foreign capital markets, foreign assets, and greater investment opportunities. For capital intensive industries, such as automobiles and aircraft, manufacturers can take advantage of economies of scale because they have access to a much larger market. **Free trade** occurs when there are no government restrictions on a country's ability to trade. Under free trade, global aggregate demand and supply determine the equilibrium quantity and price of imports and exports. Government policies that impose restrictions on trade, such as tariffs and quotas (discussed later in the reading), are known as **trade protection** and prevent market forces (demand and supply) from determining the equilibrium price and quantity for imports and exports.

PATTERNS AND TRENDS IN INTERNATIONAL TRADE AND CAPITAL FLOWS

2

☐ describe benefits and costs of international trade

The importance of trade in absolute and relative terms (trade-to-GDP ratio) is illustrated in Exhibit 1 through Exhibit 3. Exhibit 1 shows that trade as a percentage of regional GDP increased in all regions of the world during 1970–2006. Developing countries in Asia had the fastest growth in trade, increasing from less than 20 percent of GDP in 1970 to more than 70 percent of GDP in 2006.

---

2 Although the prices of imports and exports are each stated in currency units, the currency units cancel out when we take the ratio, so the terms of trade reflect the relative price of imports and exports in real (i.e., quantity) terms: units of imports per unit of exports. To see this, note that if one unit of imports costs P_M currency units and one unit of exports is priced at P_X currency units, then the country can buy P_X/P_M (= Terms of trade) units of imports for each unit of exports.

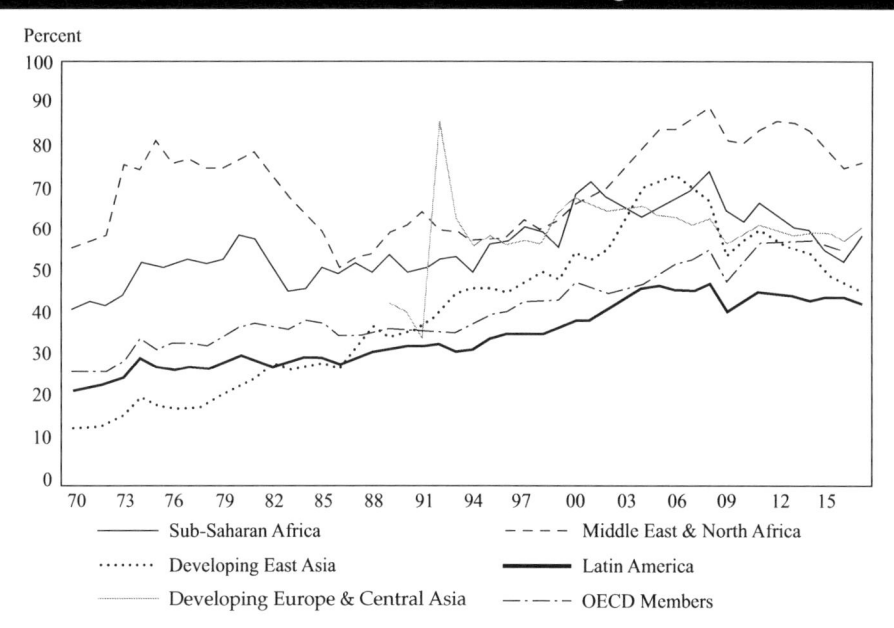

Exhibit 1: Trade in Goods and Services (Percent of Regional GDP)

Note: Developing East Asia and Developing Europe & Central Asia exclude all World Bank designated "High Income" countries in these regions.

Source: World Development Indicators.

Exhibit 2 indicates that trade as a percentage of GDP and the GDP growth rate increased in most regions of the world during 1990–2009. However, data for 2010-2016 indicates a decline that, although consistent with the worldwide economic downturn, varied across country groups. High-income countries that are members of the Organisation for Economic Co-Operation and Development (OECD) experienced a growth rate of 2.4 percent during 2000–2006, but had a growth rate of only 1.1 percent in between 2010-2016. The corresponding numbers for growth in non-OECD high-income countries are 5.0 percent and 2.0 percent, respectively; for lower-middle-income countries, they are 7.7 percent and 3.3 percent, respectively. The 2009 World Development Report affirmed the link between trade and growth and noted evidence that all rich and emerging economies are oriented to being open to trade. More specifically, the report indicated:

> ...When exports are concentrated in labor-intensive manufacturing, trade increases the wages for unskilled workers, benefiting poor people. It also encourages macroeconomic stability, again benefiting the poor, who are more likely to be hurt by inflation. And through innovation and factor accumulation, it enhances productivity and thus growth. There may be some empirical uncertainty about the strength of trade's relationship with growth. But essentially all rich and emerging economies have a strong trade orientation. (World Bank 2009)

Of course, trade is not the only factor that influences economic growth. Research has also identified such factors as the quality of institutions, infrastructure, and education; economic systems; the degree of development; and global market conditions (World Trade Organization 2008).

Exhibit 2: Trade Openness and GDP Growth

Country Group	Trade as Percent of GDP (averaged over the period)				Average GDP growth (%)			
	1980–1989	1990–1999	2000–2009	2010–2016	1980–1989	1990–1999	2000–2009	2010–2016
World	75.4	77.9	91.6	94.1	3.1%	2.5%	3.2%	2.1%
High income:								
All	40.7	42.8	53.6	61.3	3.1%	2.5%	1.5%	1.1%
OECD	36.5	39.1	48.7	56.0	3.1%	2.4%	1.3%	1.1%
Non-OECD	126.3	116.5	134.9	138.8	3.9%	3.4%	3.4%	2.0%
Low and middle income:								
All	30.2	42.3	56.3	52.7	3.4%	2.6%	5.5%	3.0%
Middle	30.0	42.2	56.2	52.6	3.4%	2.6%	5.5%	3.0%
Upper middle	28.9	41.5	55.7	51.5	2.1%	2.4%	5.5%	2.9%
Lower middle	33.7	44.7	57.9	56.3	6.0%	3.0%	5.5%	3.3%
Low	52.9	54.1	63.5	66.9	2.6%	1.9%	4.4%	2.3%

Note: Averages indicate the average of the annual data for the period covered.
Source: World Bank.

Exhibit 3 presents trade and foreign direct investment as a percentage of GDP for select countries for 1990-2017. **Foreign direct investment** (FDI) refers to direct investment by a firm in one country (the *source country*) in productive assets in a foreign country (the *host country*). When a firm engages in FDI, it becomes a **multinational corporation** (MNC) operating in more than one country or having subsidiary firms in more than one country. It is important to distinguish FDI from **foreign portfolio investment** (FPI), which refers to shorter-term investment by individuals, firms, and institutional investors (e.g., pension funds) in such foreign financial instruments as foreign stocks and foreign government bonds. Exhibit 3 shows that trade as a percentage of GDP for the world as a whole increased from 39 percent in 1990 to 57 percent in 2010. In Argentina, trade as a percentage of GDP increased from 15 percent in 1990 to 35 percent in 2010, while in India during this same period it increased from 16 percent to almost 50 percent. Among the more advanced economies, trade expanded sharply in Germany (from 46 percent to 87 percent between 1990 and 2017), but in the United States trade expanded more modestly (from 20 percent to 27 percent).

Exhibit 3: Increasing Global Interdependence: FDI and Trade as a Percentage of GDP

Country	Type of Flow	1990	2000	2010	2017
World	Trade	38.9	51.3	56.9	56.2*
	FDI: Net Inflows	0.9	4.4	2.7	2.4
	FDI: Net Outflows	1.3	4.1	2.6	2.0
Argentina	Trade	15.0	22.6	35.0	25.0
	FDI: Net Inflows	1.3	3.7	2.7	1.9
	FDI: Net Outflows	0.0	0.3	0.2	0.2

Country	Type of Flow	1990	2000	2010	2017
Germany	Trade	46.0	61.4	79.3	86.9
	FDI: Net Inflows	0.2	12.7	2.5	2.1
	FDI: Net Outflows	1.4	5.0	4.3	3.4
India	Trade	15.7	27.2	49.7	40.6
	FDI: Net Inflows	0.1	0.8	1.7	1.5
	FDI: Net Outflows	0.0	0.1	1.0	0.4
United States	Trade	19.8	25.0	28.2	26.6*
	FDI: Net Inflows	0.8	3.4	1.7	1.8
	FDI: Net Outflows	1.0	1.8	2.3	2.2

Trade figures for 2016.
Source: World Development Indicators.

The increasing importance of multinational corporations is also apparent in Exhibit 3. Net FDI inflows and outflows increased as a percentage of GDP between 1990 and 2000 for each of the countries shown. Trade between multinational firms and their subsidiaries (i.e., intra-firm trade) has become an important part of world trade. For example, 46 percent of US imports occur between related parties (Bernard, Jensen, Redding, and Schott 2010). Globalization of production has increased the productive efficiency of manufacturing firms because they are able to decompose their value chain into individual components or parts, and then outsource their production to different locations where these components can be produced most efficiently.[3] For example, in 2016 Apple's iPhone 6s was manufactured with components sourced from several locations around the world: the camera, display and storage were manufactured in Japan; the RAM and A9 processor were manufactured in South Korea; the modem, battery, Wi-Fi module, radio frequency transceiver and chassis were manufactured in China; and much of the hardware and software was designed in the United States while the phone itself was assembled in China.[4] Foreign direct investment and outsourcing have increased business investment in these economies and provided smaller and less developed economies the opportunity to participate in international trade. For example, in 2016 Intel had 10 fabrication plants and 101 assembly and testing sites in 8 countries/regions. These trends indicate the increasing global interdependence of economies, although the degree of interdependence varies. Greater interdependence also means that economies are now more exposed to global competition. As a result, they must be more flexible in their production structure in order to respond effectively to changes in global demand and supply.

---

[3] Hill and Hult (2019) explain the idea of the firm as a value chain: "The operations of the firms can be thought of as a value chain composed of a series of distinct value creation activities including production, marketing and sales, materials management, R&D, human resources, information systems, and firm infrastructure." Production itself can be broken down into distinct components and each component outsourced separately.

[4] "Here's where all the components of your iPhone come from" Skye Gould and Antonio Villas-Boas (12 April 2016). https://www.businessinsider.com/where-iphone-parts-come-from-2016-4

COMPARATIVE ADVANTAGE AND THE GAINS FROM TRADE: ABSOLUTE AND COMPARATIVE ADVANTAGE

☐ contrast comparative advantage and absolute advantage

Up to this point, we have not been precise about what it means for a country to have a comparative advantage in the production of specific goods and services. In this section, we define comparative advantage, distinguish it from the notion of absolute advantage, and demonstrate the gains from trading in accordance with comparative advantage. We then explain two traditional models of trade—the Ricardian and Heckscher–Ohlin models—and the source of comparative advantage in each model.

Gains from Trade: Absolute and Comparative Advantage

A country has an **absolute advantage** in producing a good (or service) if it is able to produce that good at a lower cost or use fewer resources in its production than its trading partner. For example, suppose a worker in Brazil can produce either 20 pens or 40 pencils in a day. A worker in Vietnam can produce either 10 pens or 60 pencils. A Vietnamese worker produces 60 pencils a day while a Brazilian worker produces only 40 pencils a day. Hence, Vietnam produces pencils at a lower cost than Brazil, and has an absolute advantage in the production of pencils. Similarly, Brazil produces pens at a lower cost than Vietnam, and hence has an absolute advantage in the production of pens. A country has a **comparative advantage** in producing a good if its opportunity cost of producing that good is less than that of its trading partner. In our example, the opportunity cost of producing an extra pen in Vietnam is 6 pencils. It is the opportunity forgone: namely, the number of pencils Vietnam would have to give up to produce an extra pen. If Brazil does not trade and has to produce both pens and pencils, it will have to give up 2 pencils in order to produce a pen. Similarly, in Vietnam each pen will cost 6 pencils. Hence, the opportunity cost of a pen in Brazil is 2 pencils, whereas in Vietnam it is 6 pencils. Brazil has the lower opportunity cost and thus a comparative advantage in the production of pens. Vietnam has a lower opportunity cost (1 pencil costs 1/6th of a pen) than Brazil (1 pencil costs 1/2 a pen) in the production of pencils and thus has a comparative advantage in the production of pencils. Example 1 further illustrates these concepts.

EXAMPLE 1

Absolute and Comparative Advantages

Suppose there are only two countries, India and the United Kingdom. India exports cloth to the United Kingdom and imports machinery. The output per worker per day in each country is shown in Exhibit 4:

Exhibit 4: Output per Worker per Day

	Machinery	Cloth (yards)
United Kingdom	4	8
India	2	16

> Based only on the information given, address the following:
>
> 1. Which country has an absolute advantage in the production of:
>   A. machinery?
>   B. cloth?
> 2. Do the countries identified in Question 1 as having an absolute advantage in the production of A) machinery and B) cloth also have a comparative advantage in those areas?
>
> ## Solution to 1A:
>
> The United Kingdom has an absolute advantage in the production of machinery because it produces more machinery per worker per day than India.
>
> ## Solution to 1B:
>
> India has an absolute advantage in the production of cloth because it produces more cloth per worker per day than the United Kingdom.
>
> ## Solution to 2A and 2B:
>
> In both cases, the answer is "yes." In the case of machinery, the opportunity cost of a machine in the United Kingdom is 2 yards of cloth (8 ÷ 4 or 1 machine = 2 yards cloth). This amount is the autarkic price of machines in terms of cloth in the United Kingdom. In India, the opportunity cost of a machine is 8 yards of cloth (16 ÷ 2 or 1 machine = 8 yards cloth). Thus, the United Kingdom has a comparative advantage in producing machines. In contrast, the opportunity cost of a yard of cloth in the United Kingdom and in India is 1/2 and 1/8 of a machine, respectively. India has a lower opportunity cost (1/8 of a machine) and, therefore, a comparative advantage in the production of cloth.

It is important to note that even if a country does not have an absolute advantage in producing any of the goods, it can still gain from trade by exporting the goods in which it has a comparative advantage. In Example 1, if India could produce only 6 yards of cloth per day instead of 16 yards of cloth, the United Kingdom would have an *absolute* advantage in both machines and cloth. However, India would still have a *comparative* advantage in the production of cloth because the opportunity cost of a yard of cloth in India, 1/3 of a machine in this case, would still be less than the opportunity cost of a yard of cloth in the United Kingdom (1/2 of a machine as before).

Let us now illustrate the gains from trading according to comparative advantage. In Example 1, if the United Kingdom could sell a machine for more than 2 yards of cloth and if India could purchase a machine for less than 8 yards of cloth, both countries would gain from trade. Although it is not possible to determine the exact world price without additional details regarding demand and supply conditions, both countries would gain from trade as long as the world price for machinery in terms of cloth is between the autarkic prices of the trading partners. In our example, this price corresponds to a price of between 2 and 8 yards of cloth for a machine. *The further away the world price of a good or service is from its autarkic price in a given country, the more that country gains from trade.* For example, if the United Kingdom was able to sell a machine to India for 7 yards of cloth (i.e., closer to India's autarkic price), it would gain 5 yards of cloth per machine sold to India compared with its own autarkic price (with no trade) of 1 machine for 2 yards of cloth. However, if the United Kingdom was able to sell a machine to India for only 3 yards of cloth (closer to the UK autarkic price), it would gain only 1 yard of cloth per machine sold to India compared with its own autarkic price.

Comparative Advantage and the Gains from Trade: Absolute and Comparative Advantage

A country's comparative advantage can change over time as a result of structural shifts in its domestic economy, shifts in the global economy, the accumulation of physical or human capital, new technology, the discovery of such natural resources as oil, and so on. For example, an increase in skilled labor in China has led several multinational companies to establish R&D facilities in China to benefit from its highly educated workforce.

EXAMPLE 2

Changes in Comparative Advantage

Exhibit 5 shows how South Korea's comparative advantage changed over time as a result of an export-oriented development strategy it adopted during the 1960s.[5] The challenges of foreign competition created a "virtuous circle" that was self-reinforcing. South Korea's changing comparative advantage was the result of government policy, an increasingly skilled and productive workforce, and proactive firms that learned and adapted new technology.

Exhibit 5: Changes in Structure of South Korea's Exports, 1980–2015 (Percentage Shares)

	1980	1985	1990	1995	2000	2005	2010	2015
Agricultural products	6.8%	4.0%	3.8%	3.2%	2.3%	1.8%	2.0%	2.0%
Fuels and mining products	1.0%	3.1%	1.6%	2.7%	6.1%	6.9%	8.9%	8.1%
Manufactures	69.3%	74.2%	76.9%	81.8%	82.2%	86.9%	86.5%	87.5%
Chemicals	3.3%		3.2%	6.4%	7.3%	9.3%	10.3%	10.9%
Pharmaceuticals			0.1%	0.2%	0.2%	0.2%	0.3%	0.4%
Machinery and transport equipment	15.7%		32.4%	46.9%	53.2%	58.4%	55.5%	57.7%
Office and telecom equipment	7.5%	9.9%	18.2%	23.8%	31.1%	27.9%	20.3%	20.5%
Integrated circuits & electronic components			6.8%	13.9%	13.1%	9.3%	9.1%	10.7%
Textiles	9.8%	6.8%	7.7%	8.8%	6.7%	3.5%	2.3%	2.0%
Clothing	13.1%	11.9%	10.0%	3.5%	2.7%	0.9%	0.3%	0.4%

Source: World Trade Organization, WTO Statistics Database.

1. How has South Korea's structure of exports changed over time?

Solution to 1:

In 1980, agriculture and clothing accounted for 6.8 percent and 13 percent of South Korea's exports, respectively. By 2015, the corresponding figures were 2.0 percent and 0.4 percent. In contrast, by 2015 machinery and transport equipment were almost 60% of South Korea's merchandise exports, up from only about 16% in 1980. Manufactures as a whole were 87.5%, up from 69% in 1980.

---

5 Wikipedia: Trade Policy of South Korea. In 1962, South Korea first introduced an export promotion policy targeted at labor intensive industries like textiles and clothing. By the 1970s, this plan had shifted focus to heavy industries and chemicals as the main export targets. As South Korea developed in the 1980s and early 1990s, export policies shifted toward consumer products, electronics, and high tech in particular.

2. How did increased foreign competition impact the economy?

Solution to 2:

The challenges of foreign competition created a "virtuous circle" that was self-reinforcing. Success in export markets increased the confidence of South Korean firms and led to greater success in exports through increased productivity, higher-quality products, acquisition of new skills, and adoption of technologies.

3. What were the factors that helped to change South Korea's comparative advantage?

Solution to 3:

The factors that helped change South Korea's comparative advantage included government policy, an increasingly skilled and productive workforce, and proactive firms that learned and adapted new technology.

From an investment perspective, it is critical for analysts to be able to examine a country's comparative and absolute advantages and to analyze changes in them. It is also important to understand changes in government policy and regulations, demographics, human capital, demand conditions, and other factors that may influence comparative advantage and production and trade patterns. This information can then be used to identify sectors, industries within those sectors, and companies within those industries that will benefit.

4 RICARDIAN AND HECKSCHER–OHLIN MODELS OF COMPARATIVE ADVANTAGE

☐ compare the Ricardian and Heckscher–Ohlin models of trade and the source(s) of comparative advantage in each model

A discussion of absolute and comparative advantage and the gains from specialization would be incomplete without a discussion of two important theories of trade, the Ricardian Model and the Heckscher–Ohlin Model. These models are based on cross-country differences in technology and in factor endowments, respectively. These theoretical models are based on several assumptions, some of which may not be fully satisfied in the real world; nonetheless they provide extremely useful insights into the determinants and patterns of trade.

Adam Smith argued that a country could gain from trade if it had an absolute advantage in the production of a good. David Ricardo extended Smith's idea of the gains from trade by arguing that even if a country did not have an absolute advantage in the production of any good, it could still gain from trade if it had a comparative advantage in the production of a good. In the Ricardian model, labor is the only (variable) factor of production. Differences in labor productivity, reflecting underlying differences in technology, are the source of comparative advantage and hence the key driver of trade in this model. A country with a lower opportunity cost in the production of a good has a comparative advantage in that good and will specialize in its production. In our two-country model, if countries vary in size, the smaller country may specialize completely, but may not be able to meet the total demand for the product. Hence, the

Ricardian and Heckscher–Ohlin Models of Comparative Advantage

larger country may be incompletely specialized, producing and exporting the good in which it has a comparative advantage but still producing (and consuming) some of the good in which it has a comparative disadvantage. It is important to recognize that although differences in technology may be a major source of comparative advantage at a given point in time, other countries can close the technology gap or even gain a technological advantage. The shift of information technology services from developed countries to India is an example of comparative advantage shifting over time.[6] This shift was facilitated by India's growing pool of highly skilled and relatively low-wage labor, the development and growth of its telecommunication infrastructure, and government policies that liberalized trade in the 1990s.

In the Heckscher–Ohlin Model (also known as the factor-proportions theory), both capital and labor are variable factors of production. That is, each good can be produced with varying combinations of labor and capital. According to this model, differences in the relative endowment of these factors are the source of a country's comparative advantage. This model assumes that technology in each industry is the same among countries, but it varies between industries. According to the theory, a country has a comparative advantage in goods whose production is intensive in the factor with which it is relatively abundantly endowed, and would tend to specialize in and export that good. Capital is relatively more (less) abundant in a country if the ratio of its endowment of capital to labor is greater (less) than that of its trading partner.[7] This scenario means a country in which labor is relatively abundant would export relatively labor-intensive goods and import relatively capital-intensive goods. For example, because the manufacture of textiles and clothing is relatively labor intensive, they are exported by such countries as China and India where labor is relatively abundant.

Relative factor intensities in production can be illustrated with the following example. In 2002, capital per worker in the Canadian paper industry was C$118,777, whereas in the clothing manufacturing sector it was C$8,954.[8] These amounts indicate that manufacturing paper is more capital intensive than clothing production. Canada trades with Thailand and, being relatively capital abundant compared with Thailand, it exports relatively capital-intensive paper to Thailand and imports relatively labor-intensive clothing from Thailand.

Because the Heckscher–Ohlin model has two factors of production, labor and capital (unlike the Ricardian model that has only labor), it allows for the possibility of income redistribution through trade. The demand for an input is referred to as a *derived demand* because it is derived from the demand for the product it is used to produce. As a country opens up to trade, it has a favorable impact on the abundant factor, and a negative impact on the scarce factor. This result occurs because trade causes output prices to change; more specifically, the price of the export good increases and the price of the import good declines. These price changes affect the demand for factors used to produce the import and export goods, and hence affect the incomes received by each factor of production.

Changes in factor endowments can cause changes in the patterns of trade and can create profitable investment opportunities. For example, in 1967 Japan had a comparative advantage in unskilled-labor-intensive goods, such as textiles, apparel, and leather. Meier (1998) notes that by 1980, Japan had greatly increased its skilled labor and consequently had a comparative advantage in skill-intensive products, especially non-electrical machinery.

---

6 According to NASSCOM (India's prominent IT-BPO trade association), Indian firms offer a wide range of information technology services that include consulting, systems integration, IT outsourcing/managed services/hosting services, training, and support/maintenance. See www.nasscom.in.

7 Alternatively, factor abundance can be defined in terms of the relative factor prices that prevail in autarky. Under this definition, labor is more (less) abundant in a country if the cost of labor relative to the cost of capital is lower (higher) in that country.

8 Appleyard, Field, and Cobb (2010).

It is important to note that technological differences, as emphasized in the Ricardian trade model, and differences in factor abundance, as emphasized in the Heckscher–Ohlin model, are both important drivers of trade. They are complementary, not mutually exclusive. Tastes and preferences can also vary among countries and can change over time, leading to changes in trade patterns and trade flows.

5. BALANCE OF PAYMENTS: ACCOUNTS AND COMPONENTS

> ☐ describe the balance of payments accounts including their components

The **balance of payments** (BOP) is a double-entry bookkeeping system that summarizes a country's economic transactions with the rest of the world for a particular period of time, typically a calendar quarter or year. In this context, a transaction is defined as "an economic flow that reflects the creation, transformation, exchange, or extinction of economic value and involves changes in ownership of goods and/or financial assets, the provision of services, or the provision of labour and capital."[9] In other words, the BOP reflects payments for exports and imports as well as financial transactions and financial transfers. Analyzing the BOP is an important element in assessing a country's macroeconomic environment, its monetary and fiscal policies, and its long-term growth potential. Investors use data on trade and capital flows to evaluate a country's overall level of capital investment, profitability, and risk. The following section describes the balance of payments, the factors that influence it, and its impact on exchange rates, interest rates, and capital market transactions.

Balance of Payments Accounts

The BOP is a double-entry system in which every transaction involves both a debit and credit. In principle, the sum of all debit entries should equal the sum of all credit entries, and the net balance of all entries on the BOP statement should equal zero. In practice, however, this is rarely the case because the data used to record balance of payments transactions are often derived from different sources.

Debit entries reflect purchases of imported goods and services, purchases of foreign financial assets, payments received for exports, and payments (interest and principal) received from debtors. Credit entries reflect payments for imported goods and services, payments for purchased foreign financial assets, and payments to creditors (see Exhibit 6, Panel A). Put differently, a debit represents an increase in a country's assets (the purchase of foreign assets or the receipt of cash from foreigners) or a decrease in its liabilities (the amount owed to foreigners); a credit represents a decrease in assets (the sale of goods and services to foreigners or the payment of cash to foreigners) or an increase in liabilities (an amount owed to foreigners).

For example, as shown in Panel B of Exhibit 6, on 1 September Country A purchases $1 million of goods from Country B and agrees to pay for these goods on 1 December. On 1 September, Country A would record in its BOP a $1 million debit to reflect the value of the goods purchased (i.e., increase in assets) and a $1 million credit to reflect

---

9 IMF Balance of Payments Handbook, chapter II, page 6.

the amount owed to Country B. On 1 December, Country A would record in its BOP a $1 million debit to reflect a decrease in the amount owed (liability) to Country B and a $1 million credit to reflect the actual payment to Country B (decrease in assets).

From Country B's perspective, on 1 September it would record in its BOP a $1 million debit to reflect the amount owed by Country A and a $1 million credit to reflect the sale of goods (exports). On 1 December, Country B would record a $1 million debit to reflect the cash received from Country A and a $1 million credit to reflect the fact that it is no longer owed $1 million by Country A.

Exhibit 6: Basic Entries in a BOP Context

Panel A

DEBITS	CREDITS
Increase in Assets, Decrease in Liabilities	Decrease in Assets, Increase in Liabilities
- Value of imported goods and services - Purchases of foreign financial assets - Receipt of payments from foreigners - Increase in debt owed by foreigners - Payment of debt owed to foreigners	- Payments for imports of goods and services - Payments for foreign financial assets - Value of exported goods and services - Payment of debt by foreigners - Increase in debt owed to foreigners

Panel B

Country A	Debits	Credits
1 September	$1 million Goods purchased from Country B *(increase in real assets)*	$1 million Short-term liability for goods purchased from Country B *(increase in financial liabilities)*
1 December	$1 million Elimination of short-term liability for goods purchased from Country B *(decrease in financial liabilities)*	$1 million Payment for goods purchased from Country B *(decrease in financial assets)*

Country B	Debits	Credits
1 September	$1 million Short-term claim for goods delivered to Country A *(increase in financial assets)*	$1 million Goods delivered to Country A *(decrease in real assets)*
1 December	$1 million Receipt of payment for goods delivered to Country A *(increase in financial assets)*	$1 million Elimination of claim for goods delivered to Country A *(decrease in financial assets)*

Balance of Payments Components

The BOP is composed of the **current account** that measures the flow of goods and services, the **capital account** that measures transfers of capital, and the **financial account** that records investment flows. These accounts are further disaggregated into sub-accounts:

Current Account

The current account can be decomposed into four sub-accounts:

1. **Merchandise trade** consists of all commodities and manufactured goods bought, sold, or given away.
2. **Services** include tourism, transportation, engineering, and business services, such as legal services, management consulting, and accounting. Fees from patents and copyrights on new technology, software, books, and movies are also recorded in the services category.
3. **Income receipts** include income derived from ownership of assets, such as dividends and interest payments; income on foreign investments is included in the current account because that income is compensation for services provided by foreign investments. When a German company builds a plant in China, for instance, the services the plant generates are viewed as a service export from Germany to China equal in value to the profits the plant yields for its German owner.
4. **Unilateral transfers** represent one-way transfers of assets, such as worker remittances from abroad to their home country and foreign direct aid or gifts.

Capital Account

The capital account consists of two sub-accounts:

1. **Capital transfers** include debt forgiveness and migrants' transfers (goods and financial assets belonging to migrants as they leave or enter the country).[10] Capital transfers also include the transfer of title to fixed assets and the transfer of funds linked to the sale or acquisition of fixed assets, gift and inheritance taxes, death duties, uninsured damage to fixed assets, and legacies.
2. **Sales and purchases of non-produced, non-financial assets**, such as the rights to natural resources, and the sale and purchase of intangible assets, such as patents, copyrights, trademarks, franchises, and leases.

Financial Account

The financial account can be broken down in two sub-accounts: financial assets abroad and foreign-owned financial assets within the reporting country.

1. A country's assets abroad are further divided into official reserve assets, government assets, and private assets. These assets include gold, foreign currencies, foreign securities, the government's reserve position in the International Monetary Fund,[11] direct foreign investment, and claims reported by resident banks.
2. Foreign-owned assets in the reporting country are further divided into official assets and other foreign assets. These assets include securities issued by the reporting country's government and private sectors (e.g., bonds, equities, mortgage-backed securities), direct investment, and foreign liabilities reported by the reporting country's banking sector.

---

10 Immigrants bring with them goods and financial assets already in their possession. Hence, these goods are imported on grounds other than commercial transactions.

11 These are in effect official currency reserves held with the International Monetary Fund.

Balance of Payments: Accounts and Components

EXAMPLE 3

US Current Account Balance

1. Exhibit 7 shows a simplified version of the US balance of payments for 1970–2017.

Exhibit 7: US International Transactions Accounts Data

(Credits+, Debits–)	1970	1980	1990	2000	2009	2017
Current Account						
Exports of goods and services and income receipts	68,387	344,440	706,975	1,421,515	2,159,000	3,279,190
Exports of goods and services	56,640	271,834	535,233	1,070,597	1,570,797	2,351,072
Income receipts	11,747	72,606	171,742	350,918	588,203	928,118
Imports of goods and services and income payments	–59,901	–333,774	–759,290	–1,779,241	–2,412,489	–3,609,734
Imports of goods and services	–54,386	–291,241	–616,097	–1,449,377	–1,945,705	–2,903,349
Income payments	–5,515	–42,532	–143,192	–329,864	–466,783	–706,385
Unilateral current transfers, net	–6,156	–8,349	–26,654	–58,645	–124,943	–118,597
Capital Account						
Capital account transactions, net	...	...	–7,220	–1	–140	–24,746
Financial Account						
US-owned assets abroad, ex derivatives (increase/financial outflow (–))	–9,337	–86,967	–81,234	–560,523	–140,465	–1,182,749
Foreign-owned assets in the United States, ex derivatives (increase/financial inflow (+))	7,226	62,037	139,357	1,038,224	305,736	1,537,682
Financial derivatives, net	NA	NA	NA	NA	50,804	23,074
Statistical discrepancy (sum of above items with sign reversed)	–219	22,613	28,066	–61,329	162,497	–95,880

Based only on the information given, address the following:

1. Calculate the current account balance for each year.
2. Calculate the financial account balance for each year.
3. Describe the long-term change in the current account balance.
4. Describe the long-term change in the financial account balance.

Solutions to 1 and 2:

(Credits+, Debits–)	1970	1980	1990	2000	2009	2017
Current Account	2,330	2,317	–78,969	–416,371	–378,432	–449,141
Financial Account	–2,111	–24,930	58,123	477,701	216,075	378,007

Solution to 3:

The United States had a current account surplus until 1980. After 1990, the US current account had an increasing deficit as a result of strong import growth.

> **Solution to 4:**
>
> Mirroring the growing US current account deficit, the US financial account, after 1990, registered increasing net capital inflows in similar proportions to the deficit in the current account.

6. NATIONAL ECONOMIC ACCOUNTS AND THE BALANCE OF PAYMENTS

> explain how decisions by consumers, firms, and governments affect the balance of payments

In a closed economy, all output Y is consumed or invested by the private sector—domestic households and businesses—or purchased by the government. Letting Y denote GDP, C private consumption, I investment, and G government purchases of goods and services, the national income identity for a closed economy is given by:

$$Y = C + I + G \qquad (1)$$

Once foreign trade is introduced, however, some output is purchased by foreigners (exports) whereas some domestic spending is used for purchases of foreign goods and services (imports). The national income identity for an open economy is thus

$$Y = C + I + G + X - M \qquad (2)$$

where X denotes exports and M denotes imports.

For most countries, exports rarely equal imports. Net exports or the difference between exports and imports $(X - M)$ is the equivalent of the current account balance from a BOP perspective.[12] When a country's imports exceed its exports, the current account is in deficit. When a country's exports exceed its imports, the current account is in surplus. As the right side of Equation 2 shows, a current account surplus or deficit can affect GDP (and also employment). The balance of the current account is also important because it measures the size and direction of international borrowing.

In order for the balance of payments to balance, a deficit or surplus in the current account must be offset by an opposite balance in the sum of the capital and financial accounts. This requirement means that a country with a current account deficit has to increase its net foreign debts by the amount of the current account deficit. For example, the United States has run current account deficits for many years while accumulating net foreign liabilities: The current account deficit was financed by net capital imports (i.e., direct investments by foreigners), loans by foreign banks, and the sale of US equities and fixed-income securities to foreign investors. By the same token, an economy with a current account surplus is earning more for its exports than it spends for its imports. Japan, Germany, and China are traditional current account surplus countries accumulating substantial net foreign claims, especially against the United States. An economy with a current account surplus finances the current account deficit of its trading partners by lending to them—that is, granting

---

12 Strictly speaking, net exports as defined here are the trade balance rather than the current account balance because they exclude income receipts and unilateral transfers. This distinction arises because we have defined income Y as GDP rather than GNP. Because the trade balance is usually the dominant component of the current account, the terms "trade balance" and "current account" are often used interchangeably. We will do so here unless the distinction is important to the discussion.

bank loans and investing in financial and real assets. As a result, the foreign wealth of a surplus country rises because foreigners pay for imports by issuing liabilities that they will eventually have to redeem.

By rearranging Equation 2, we can define the current account balance from the perspective of the national income accounts as:

$$CA = X - M = Y - (C + I + G) \tag{3}$$

Only by borrowing money from foreigners can a country have a current account deficit and consume more output than it produces. If it consumes less output than it produces, it has a current account surplus and can (indeed must) lend the surplus to foreigners. International capital flows essentially reflect an *inter-temporal trade*. An economy with a current account deficit is effectively importing present consumption and exporting future consumption.

Let us now turn to the relationship between output Y and disposable income Y^d. We have to recognize that part of income is spent on taxes T, and that the private sector receives net transfers R in addition to (national) income. Disposable income Y^d is thus equal to income plus transfers minus taxes:

$$Y^d = Y + R - T \tag{4}$$

Disposable income, in turn, is allocated to consumption and saving so that we can write

$$Y^d = C + S_p \tag{5}$$

where S_p denotes private sector saving. Combining Equation 4 and Equation 5 allows us to write consumption as income plus transfers minus taxes and saving.

$$C = Y^d - S_p = Y + R - T - S_p \tag{6}$$

We can now use the right side of Equation 6 to substitute for C in Equation 3. With some rearrangement we obtain

$$CA = S_p - I + (T - G - R) \tag{7}$$

Because $(T - G - R)$ is taxes minus government spending and transfers, it is the government surplus, or put differently, government savings S_g. Equation 7 can therefore be restated as

$$S_p + S_g = I + CA \tag{8}$$

Equation 8 highlights an essential difference between open and closed economies: An open economy can use its saving for domestic investment or for foreign investment (i.e., by exporting its savings and acquiring foreign assets), while in a closed economy savings can only be used for domestic investment. Put another way, an open economy with promising investment opportunities is not constrained by its domestic savings rate in order to exploit these opportunities. As Equation 8 shows, it can raise investment by increasing foreign borrowing (a reduction in CA) without increasing domestic savings. For example, if India decides to build a network of high-speed trains, it can import all the required materials it needs from France and then borrow the funds, perhaps also from France, to pay for the materials. This transaction increases India's domestic investment because the imported materials contribute to the expansion in the country's capital stock. All else being equal, this transaction will also produce a current account deficit for India by an amount equal to the increase in investment. India's savings does not have to increase, even though investment increases. This example can be interpreted as an inter-temporal trade, in which India imports present consumption (when it borrows to fund current expenditure) and exports future consumption (when it repays the loan).

Rearranging Equation 8, we can write

$$S_p = I + CA - S_g \tag{9}$$

Equation 9 states that an economy's private savings can be used in three ways: (1) investment in domestic capital (I), (2) purchases of assets from foreigners (CA), and (3) net purchases (or redemptions) of government debt ($-S_g$).

Finally, we can rearrange Equation 8 again to illustrate the macroeconomic sources of a current account imbalance:

$$CA = S_p + S_g - I \tag{10}$$

A current account deficit tends to result from low private savings, high private investment, a government deficit ($S_g < 0$), or a combination of the three. Alternatively, a current account surplus reflects high private savings, low private investment, or a government surplus.

As outlined above, trade deficits can result from a lack of private or government savings or booming investments. If trade deficits primarily reflect high private or government consumption (i.e., scarce savings = $S_p + S_g$), the deficit country's capacity to repay its liabilities from future production remains unchanged. If a trade deficit primarily reflects strong investments (I), however, the deficit country can increase its productive resources and its ability to repay its liabilities.

We can also see from Equation 3 that a current account deficit tends to reflect a strong domestic economy (elevated consumer, government, and investment spending), which is usually accompanied by elevated domestic credit demand and high interest rates. In such an environment, widening interest rate differentials vis-à-vis other countries can lead to growing net capital imports and produce an appreciating currency. In the long run, however, a persistent current account deficit leads to a permanent increase in the claims held by other countries against the deficit country. As a result, foreign investors may require rising risk premiums for such claims, a process that appears to lead to a depreciating currency.

> **EXAMPLE 4**
>
> ### Historical Example: The United Kingdom Budget
>
> A financial newspaper had the following item:
>
> The UK's budget deficit is the highest in the G–20; in Europe, only Ireland borrows more. These are the stark facts facing Chancellor of the Exchequer George Osborne as he plans his first Budget tomorrow. He intends to tackle the problem even if that involves severe spending cuts and large tax increases.
>
> Source: *Financial Times*, 21 June 2010.
>
> 1. What are the likely consequences for the UK current account balance from the planned fiscal policy moves mentioned in the above article?
>
> ### Solution to 1:
>
> The combination of spending cuts and tax increases will, all else the same, lead to an improvement in the UK current account position.
>
> 2. Describe the impact spending cuts and tax increases are likely to have on UK imports.
>
> ### Solution to 2:
>
> UK imports are likely to be reduced by tax increases and spending cuts because government demand for foreign goods will fall and growth in private household income, which finances private imports, will be restricted as more household income goes to taxes.

EXAMPLE 5

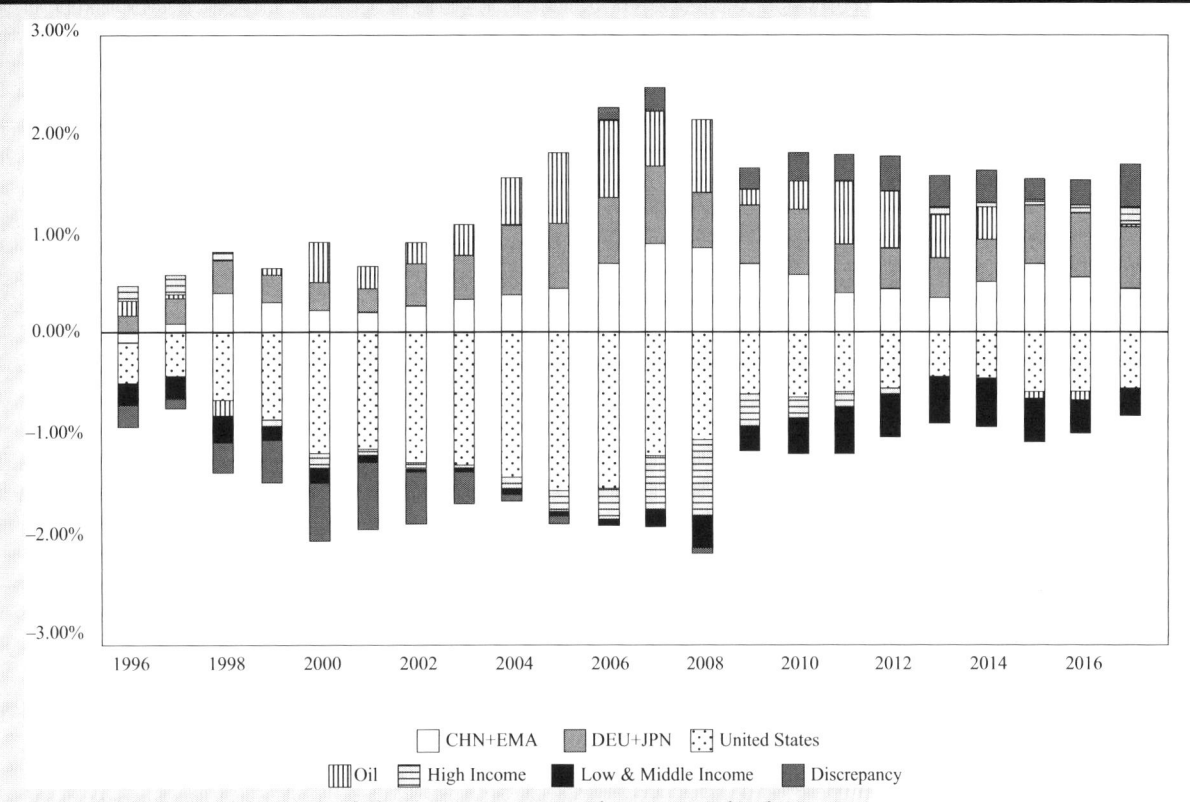

Exhibit 8: Global Imbalances (Current Account Balance in Percent of World GDP)

Legend: CHN+EMA, DEU+JPN, United States, Oil, High Income, Low & Middle Income, Discrepancy

Note: 1. CHN+EMA includes the following economies: Chinese mainland, Hong Kong SAR, Indonesia, South Korea, Malaysia, Philippines, Singapore, Thailand.

2. The Oil group consists of the 20 largest oil exporting countries in 2016—excluding the United States—as listed in the Economist Intelligence Unit World Factbook 2017.

3. The High Income as well as the Low and Middle Income groups' definitions include all countries that do not fall into any of the other categories.

Source: IMF *Balance of Payments Statistics Yearbook, 2018.*

As illustrated in Equation 10, current account deficits or surpluses reflect imbalances between national savings (including government savings) and investments. Current account deficits are often related to expansionary fiscal policy and government deficits. In the 1980s, for instance, the growing deficit in the US current account was widely seen as the consequence of tax cuts and rising defense spending adopted by the Reagan administration. Since the mid-1990s, however, the current account imbalances depicted in Exhibit 8 appear to reflect other, more complex factors. Exhibit 9 illustrates US net savings ($S-I$) for private domestic businesses, households and non-profits, and the government (i.e., federal, state, and local) from the first quarter of 1996 to the first quarter of 2018. The exhibit indicates that business sector net savings and government net savings as a percentage of GDP were near mirror-images between 1996 to 2008. During the technology bubble businesses invested heavily and ran progressively larger savings deficits while the government moved to a surplus. After the bubble burst the pattern reversed with businesses moving to net positive savings and the government fiscal balance deteriorating sharply. Meanwhile, the household sector gradually reduced its savings rate. After the global financial crisis in late 2008, households and businesses cut spending and increased savings sharply while the government deficit exploded to more than 12 percent of GDP. As the economy recovered from the financial crisis from 2012 onwards, government borrowing fell to five percent of GDP. Both households and business maintained a higher rate of saving during this period than before the financial crisis.

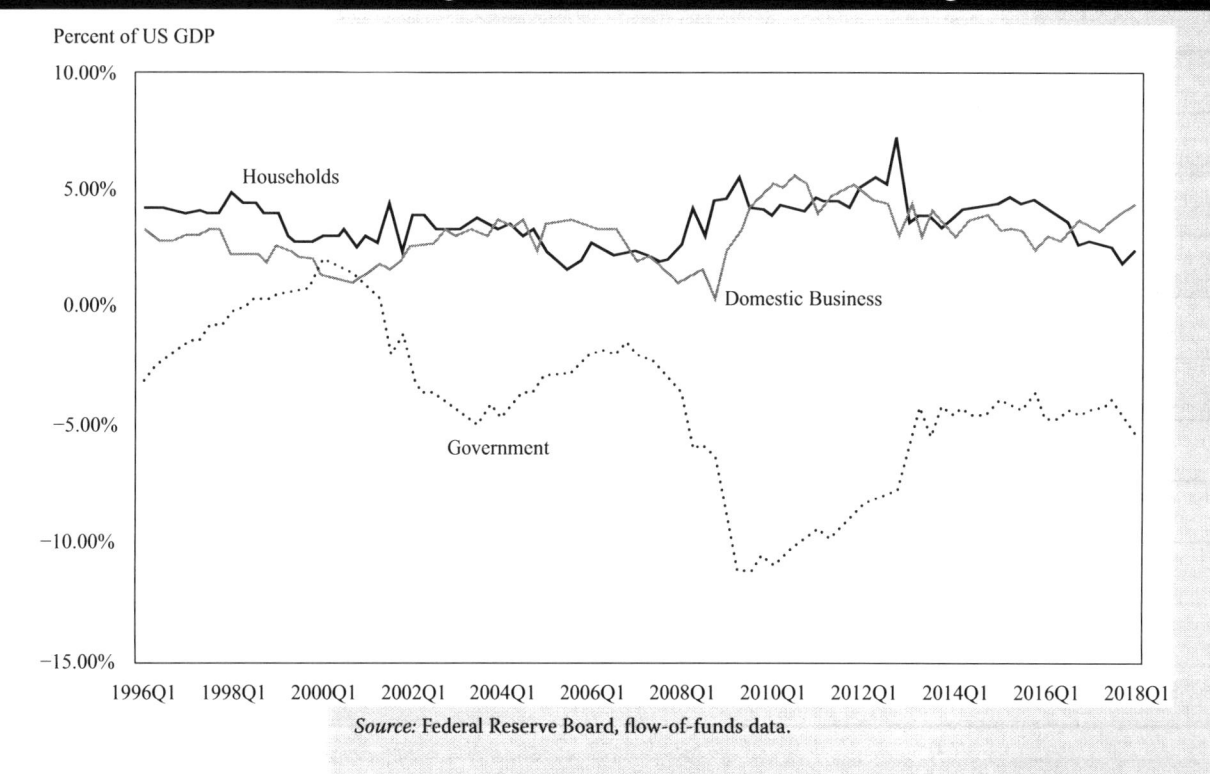

Exhibit 9: United States: Sectorial Saving–Investment Balance since 1996 (Net Savings in Percent of GDP)

Source: Federal Reserve Board, flow-of-funds data.

SUMMARY

This reading provides a framework for analyzing a country's trade and capital flows and their economic implications. It examines basic models that explain trade based on comparative advantage and provides a basis for understanding how international trade can affect the rate and composition of economic growth as well as the attractiveness of investment in various sectors.

- The benefits of trade include
    - gains from exchange and specialization;
    - gains from economies of scale as companies add new markets for their products;
    - greater variety of products available to households and firms; and
    - increased competition and more efficient allocation of resources.
- A country has an absolute advantage in producing a good (or service) if it is able to produce that good at a lower absolute cost or use fewer resources in its production than its trading partner. A country has a comparative advantage in producing a good if its *opportunity cost* of producing that good is less than that of its trading partner.

- Even if a country does not have an absolute advantage in the production of any good, it can gain from trade by producing and exporting the good(s) in which it has a comparative advantage and importing good(s) in which it has a comparative disadvantage.
- In the Ricardian model of trade, comparative advantage and the pattern of trade are determined by differences in technology between countries. In the Heckscher–Ohlin model of trade, comparative advantage and the pattern of trade are determined by differences in factor endowments between countries. In reality, technology and factor endowments are complementary, not mutually exclusive, determinants of trade patterns.
- Trade barriers prevent the free flow of goods and services among countries. Governments impose trade barriers for various reasons including: to promote specific developmental objectives, to counteract certain imperfections in the functioning of markets, or to respond to problems facing their economies.
- For purposes of international trade policy and analysis, a small country is defined as one that cannot affect the world price of traded goods. A large country's production and/or consumption decisions do alter the relative prices of trade goods.
- In a small country, trade barriers generate a net welfare loss arising from distortion of production and consumption decisions and the associated inefficient allocation of resources.
- Trade barriers can generate a net welfare gain in a large country if the gain from improving its terms of trade (higher export prices and lower import prices) more than offsets the loss from the distortion of resource allocations. However, the large country can only gain if it imposes an even larger welfare loss on its trading partner(s).
- A customs union extends the FTA by not only allowing free movement of goods and services among members but also creating a common trade policy against non-members.
- A common market incorporates all aspects of a customs union and extends it by allowing free movement of factors of production among members.
- An economic union incorporates all aspects of a common market and requires common economic institutions and coordination of economic policies among members.
- Members of a monetary union adopt a common currency.
- From an investment perspective, it is important to understand the complex and dynamic nature of trading relationships because they can help identify potential profitable investment opportunities as well as provide some advance warning signals regarding when to disinvest in a market or industry.
- The major components of the balance of payments are the
  - current account balance, which largely reflects trade in goods and services.
  - capital account balance, which mainly consists of capital transfers and net sales of non-produced, non-financial assets.
  - financial account, which measures net capital flows based on sales and purchases of domestic and foreign financial assets.
- Decisions by consumers, firms, and governments influence the balance of payments.

- Low private savings and/or high investment tend to produce a current account deficit that must be financed by net capital imports; high private savings and/or low investment, however, produce a current account surplus, balanced by net capital exports.
- All else the same, a government deficit produces a current account deficit and a government surplus leads to a current account surplus.
- All else the same, a sustained current account deficit contributes to a rise in the risk premium for financial assets of the deficit country. Current account surplus countries tend to enjoy lower risk premiums than current account deficit countries.

REFERENCES

Appleyard, Dennis, Alfred Field, Steven Cobb. 2010. International Economics. 7th edition. Boston: McGraw-Hill/Irwin.

Bernard, Andrew B., J. Bradford Jensen, Stephen J. Redding, Peter K. Schott. 2010. "Intrafirm Trade and Product Contractibility." American Economic Review, vol. 100, no. 2 (May): 444–448.

Hill, Charles W.L., G. Tomas M. Hult. 2019. International Business: Competing in the Global Marketplace. 12th edition. Boston: Irwin/McGraw-Hill.

Meier, Gerald M. 1998. The International Environment of Business: Competition and Governance in the Global Economy. New York: Oxford University Press.

World Bank. 2009. World Development Report 2009: Reshaping Economic Geography. Washington, DC: World Bank.

World Trade Organization. 2008. World Trade Report 2008: Trade in a Globalizing World. Geneva: World Trade Organization.

PRACTICE PROBLEMS

1. A country has a comparative advantage in producing a good if:

   A. it is able to produce the good at a lower cost than its trading partner.

   B. its opportunity cost of producing the good is less than that of its trading partner.

   C. its opportunity cost of producing the good is more than that of its trading partner.

2. Suppose Mexico exports vegetables to Brazil and imports flashlights used for mining from Brazil. The output per worker per day in each country is as follows:

	Flashlights	Vegetables
Mexico	20	60
Brazil	40	80

   Which country has a comparative advantage in the production of vegetables and what is the *most* relevant opportunity cost?

   A. Brazil: 2 vegetables per flashlight

   B. Mexico: 1.5 vegetables per flashlight

   C. Mexico: 1/3 flashlight per vegetable

3. Suppose three countries produce bananas and pencils with output per worker per day in each country as follows:

	Bananas	Pencils
Mexico	20	40
Brazil	30	90
Canada	40	160

   Which country has the greatest comparative advantage in the production of bananas?

   A. Canada

   B. Brazil

   C. Mexico

4. In the Ricardian trade model, a country captures more of the gains from trade if:

   A. it produces all products while its trade partner specializes in one good.

   B. the terms of trade are closer to its autarkic prices than to its partner's autarkic prices.

   C. the terms of trade are closer to its partner's autarkic prices than to its autarkic prices.

5. Germany has much more capital per worker than Portugal. In autarky each

country produces and consumes both machine tools and wine. Production of machine tools is relatively capital intensive whereas winemaking is labor intensive. According to the Heckscher–Ohlin model, when trade opens:

- **A.** Germany should export machine tools and Portugal should export wine.
- **B.** Germany should export wine and Portugal should export machine tools.
- **C.** Germany should produce only machine tools and Portugal should produce only wine.

6. According to the Heckscher–Ohlin model, when trade opens:
    - **A.** the scarce factor gains relative to the abundant factor in each country.
    - **B.** the abundant factor gains relative to the scarce factor in each country.
    - **C.** income is redistributed between countries but not within each country.

7. The sale of mineral rights would be captured in which of the following balance of payments components?
    - **A.** Capital account
    - **B.** Current account
    - **C.** Financial account

8. Patent fees and legal services are recorded in which of the following balance of payments components?
    - **A.** Capital account
    - **B.** Current account
    - **C.** Financial account

9. Which of the following *most likely* contributes to a current account deficit?
    - **A.** High taxes
    - **B.** Low private savings
    - **C.** Low private investment

10. Which of the following chronic deficit conditions is *least* alarming to the deficit country's creditors?
    - **A.** High consumption
    - **B.** High private investment
    - **C.** High government spending

SOLUTIONS

1. B is correct. Comparative advantage is present when the opportunity cost of producing a good is less than that of a trading partner.

2. C is correct. While Brazil has an absolute advantage in the production of both flashlights and vegetables, Mexico has a comparative advantage in the production of vegetables. The opportunity cost of vegetables in Mexico is ⅓ per flashlight, while the opportunity cost of vegetables in Brazil is ½ per flashlight.

3. C is correct. Mexico has the lowest opportunity cost to produce an extra banana. The opportunity cost is 2 pencils per banana in Mexico, 3 pencils per banana in Brazil, and 4 pencils per banana in Canada.

4. C is correct. A country gains if trade increases the price of its exports relative to its imports as compared to its autarkic prices; i.e., the final terms of trade are more favorable than its autarkic prices. If the relative price of exports and imports remains the same after trade opens, then the country will consume the same basket of goods before and after trade opens, and it gains nothing from the ability to trade. In that case, its trade partner will capture all of the gains. Of course, the opposite is true if the roles are reversed. More generally, a country captures more of the gains from trade the more the final terms of trade differ from its autarkic prices.

5. A is correct. In the Heckscher–Ohlin model a country has a comparative advantage in goods whose production is intensive in the factor with which it is relatively abundantly endowed. In this case, capital is relatively abundant in Germany so Germany has a comparative advantage in producing the capital-intensive product: machine tools. Portugal is relatively labor abundant and hence should produce and export the labor-intensive product: wine.

6. B is correct. As a country opens up to trade, it has a favorable impact on the abundant factor, and a negative impact on the scarce factor. This is because trade causes the output mix to change and therefore changes the relative demand for the factors of production. Increased output of the export product increases demand for the factor that is used intensively in its production, while reduced output of the import product decreases demand for the factor used intensively in its production. Because the export (import) product uses the abundant (scarce) factor intensively, the abundant factor gains relative to the scarce factor in each country.

7. A is correct. The capital account measures capital transfers and sale and purchase of non-produced, non-financial assets such as mineral rights and intangible assets.

8. B is correct. The current account measures the flows of goods and services (including income from foreign investments). Patent fees and legal services are both captured in the services sub-account of the current account.

9. B is correct. A current account deficit tends to result from low private saving, high private investment, a government deficit, or a combination of the three. Of the choices, only low private savings contributes toward a current account deficit.

10. B is correct. A current account deficit tends to result from low private saving, high private investment, low government savings, or a combination of the three. Of these choices, only high investments can increase productive resources and improve future ability to repay creditors.

LEARNING MODULE 7

Currency Exchange Rates

by William A. Barker, PhD, CFA, Paul D. McNelis, and Jerry Nickelsburg, PhD.

William A. Barker, PhD, CFA (Canada). Paul D. McNelis is at Gabelli School of Business, Fordham University (USA). Jerry Nickelsburg, PhD, is at the Anderson School of Management, University of California, Los Angeles (USA).

LEARNING OUTCOMES

Mastery	The candidate should be able to:
☐	define an exchange rate and distinguish between nominal and real exchange rates and spot and forward exchange rates
☐	calculate and interpret the percentage change in a currency relative to another currency
☐	describe functions of and participants in the foreign exchange market
☐	explain the effects of exchange rates on countries' international trade and capital flows

INTRODUCTION & THE FOREIGN EXCHANGE MARKET

☐	define an exchange rate and distinguish between nominal and real exchange rates and spot and forward exchange rates
☐	calculate and interpret the percentage change in a currency relative to another currency

Measured by daily turnover, the foreign exchange (FX) market—the market in which currencies are traded against each other—is by far the world's largest market. Current estimates put daily turnover at approximately USD5.1 trillion for 2016. This is about 10 to 15 times larger than daily turnover in global fixed-income markets and about 50 times larger than global turnover in equities.

The FX market is also a truly global market that operates 24 hours a day, each business day. It involves market participants from every time zone connected through electronic communications networks that link players as large as multibillion-dollar investment funds and as small as individuals trading for their own account—all brought together in real time. International trade would be impossible without the trade in currencies that facilitates it, and so too would cross-border capital flows that connect all financial markets globally through the FX market.

These factors make foreign exchange a key market for investors and market participants to understand. The world economy is increasingly transnational in nature, with both production processes and trade flows often determined more by global factors than by domestic considerations. Likewise, investment portfolio performance increasingly reflects global determinants because pricing in financial markets responds to the array of investment opportunities available worldwide, not just locally. All of these factors funnel through, and are reflected in, the foreign exchange market. As investors shed their "home bias" and invest in foreign markets, the exchange rate—the price at which foreign-currency-denominated investments are valued in terms of the domestic currency—becomes an increasingly important determinant of portfolio performance.

Even investors adhering to a purely "domestic" portfolio mandate are increasingly affected by what happens in the foreign exchange market. Given the globalization of the world economy, most large companies depend heavily on their foreign operations (for example, by some estimates about 30 percent of S&P 500 Index earnings are from outside the United States). Almost all companies are exposed to some degree of foreign competition, and the pricing for domestic assets—equities, bonds, real estate, and others—will also depend on demand from foreign investors. All of these various influences on investment performance reflect developments in the foreign exchange market.

This reading introduces the foreign exchange market, providing the basic concepts and terminology necessary to understand exchange rates as well as some of the basics of exchange rate economics.

2. MARKET FUNCTIONS

- [ ] define an exchange rate and distinguish between nominal and real exchange rates and spot and forward exchange rates
- [ ] describe functions of and participants in the foreign exchange market

FX markets facilitate international trade in goods and services, where companies and individuals need to make transactions in foreign currencies. This would cover everything from companies and governments buying and selling products in other countries, to tourists engaged in cross-border travel (for example, a German tourist selling euros and buying sterling for a visit to London). Although this is an important dimension of FX markets, and despite the growth of global trade in recent years, an even larger proportion of the daily turnover in FX markets is accounted for by capital market transactions, where investors convert between currencies for the purpose of moving funds into (or out of) foreign assets. These types of transactions cover the range from direct investments (for example, companies buying such fixed assets as factories) in other countries to portfolio investments (the purchase of stocks, bonds, and other financial assets denominated in foreign currencies). Because capital is extremely mobile in modern financial markets, this ebb and flow of money across international borders and currencies generates a huge and growing volume of FX transactions.

Regardless of the underlying motivation for the FX transaction, it will eventually require that one currency be exchanged for another in the FX market. In advance of that required transaction, market participants are exposed to the risk that the exchange

Market Functions

rate will move against them. Often they will try to reduce (hedge) this risk through a variety of FX instruments (described in more detail later). Conversely, market participants may form opinions about future FX movements and undertake speculative FX risk exposures through a variety of FX instruments in order to profit from their views.

The FX market provides a variety of products that provide the flexibility to meet this varied and complex set of financial goals. *Spot* transactions involve the exchange of currencies for immediate delivery. For most currencies, this corresponds to "T + 2" delivery, meaning that the exchange of currencies is settled two business days after the trade is agreed to by the two sides of the deal. (One exception is the Canadian dollar, for which spot settlement against the US dollar is on a T + 1 basis.) The exchange rate used for these spot transactions is referred to as the spot exchange rate, and it is the exchange rate that most people refer to in their daily lives (for example, this is the exchange rate usually quoted by the financial press, on the evening news, and so forth).

It is important to realize, however, that spot transactions make up only a minority of total daily turnover in the global FX market: The rest is accounted for by trade in outright forward contracts, FX swaps, and FX options.

Outright *forward contracts* (often referred to simply as forwards) are agreements to deliver foreign exchange at a future date at an exchange rate agreed upon today. For example, suppose that a UK-based company expects to receive a payment of 100 million euros in 85 days. Although it could convert these euros to British pounds with a spot transaction (the spot rate would be the GBP/EUR rate in 83 days, because of T + 2 settlement), this future spot rate is currently unknown and represents a foreign exchange risk to the company. The company can avoid this risk by entering into a transaction with a foreign exchange dealer to sell 100 million euros against the British pound for settlement 85 days from today at a rate—the forward exchange rate—agreed upon today.

As such, forward contracts are any exchange rate transactions that occur with currency settlement longer than the usual T + 2 settlement for spot delivery. Each of these contracts requires two specifications: the date at which the currencies are to be exchanged and the exchange rate to be applied on the settlement date. Accordingly, exchange rates for these transactions are called *forward exchange rates* to distinguish them from spot rates.

Dealers will typically quote forward rates for a variety of standard forward settlement dates (for example, one week, one month, or 90 days) on their dealing screens. In an over-the-counter (OTC) market, however, traders can arrange forward settlement at *any* future date they agree upon, with the forward exchange rate scaled appropriately for the specific term to settlement. Standard forward settlement dates (such as three months) are defined in terms of the spot settlement date, which is generally T + 2. For example, if today is 18 October and spot settlement is for 20 October, then a three-month forward settlement would be defined as 20 January of the following year. Note as well that these standard forward settlement dates may not always be good business days: 20 January could be a weekend or a holiday. In that case, the forward settlement date is set to the closest good business day. Traders always confirm the exact forward settlement date when making these types of trades, and the forward rate is scaled by the exact number of days to settlement.

In an OTC market, the size of the forward contracts can also be any size that the two counterparties agree upon. In general, however, liquidity in forward markets declines the longer the term to maturity and the larger the trade size. The concept of the forward exchange rate and exchange hedging is developed further in the next section.

Although the OTC market accounts for the majority of foreign exchange trades with future (i.e., greater than T + 2) settlement dates, there is also a deep, liquid market in exchange-traded *futures* contracts for currencies. Although there are technical differences between futures and forward contracts, the basic concept is the same: The price is set today for settlement on a specified future date. Futures contracts on currencies trade on several exchanges globally, but the majority of volume in exchange-traded currency futures contracts is found on the International Monetary Market (IMM) division of the Chicago Mercantile Exchange (CME). Futures contracts differ from OTC forward contracts in several important ways: They trade on exchanges (such as the CME) rather than OTC; they are only available for fixed contract amounts and fixed settlement dates; the exchanges demand that a fixed amount of collateral be posted against the futures contract trade; and this collateral is marked-to-market daily, with counterparties asked to post further collateral if their positions generate losses. On balance, futures contracts are somewhat less flexible than forward contracts. Nonetheless, they provide deep, liquid markets for deferred delivery with a minimum of counterparty (i.e., default) risk—a proposition that many FX traders find attractive. Accordingly, daily turnover in FX futures contracts is huge. As of 2010, the average daily trading volume of FX futures on the CME alone was estimated to be about USD140 billion, which is almost comparable in size to the interbank volume of spot transactions.

Because forward contracts eventually expire, existing speculative positions or FX hedges that need to be extended must be rolled prior to their settlement dates. This typically involves a spot transaction to offset (settle) the expiring forward contract and a new forward contract to be set at a new, more distant settlement date. The combination of an offsetting spot transaction and a new forward contract is referred to as an **FX swap**.[1]

An FX swap is best illustrated by an example. Suppose that a trader sells 100 million euros with settlement 95 days from today at a forward exchange rate (USD/EUR) of 1.2000. In 93 days, the forward contract is two days from settlement, specifically the T + 2 days to spot settlement. To roll the forward contract, the trader will engage in the following FX swap. First, the trader will need to buy 100 million euros spot, for which T + 2 settlement will fall on day 95, the same day as the settlement of the expiring forward contract. The purchase of the 100 million euros spot will be used to satisfy the delivery of the 100 million euros sold in the expiring forward contract. Because 100 million euros are being both bought and sold on day 95, there is no exchange of euros between counterparties on that day: The amounts net to zero. However, there will be an exchange of US dollars, reflecting the movement in exchange rates between the date the forward contract was agreed to (day 0) and day 93. Suppose that on day 93 the spot exchange rate for USD/EUR is 1.1900. This means that the trader will see a cash flow on day 95 of USD1,000,000. This is calculated as follows:

$$EUR100,000,000 \times (1.2000 - 1.1900) = USD1,000,000$$

The trader receives USD1,000,000 from the counterparty because the euro was *sold* forward to day 95 at a price of 1.2000; it was *bought* (on day 93) for spot settlement on day 95 at a price of 1.1900. This *price* movement in the euro indicates a profit to the trader, but because the euro *quantities* exchanged on day 95 net to zero (100,000,000 euros both bought and sold), this cash flow is realized in US dollars. The second leg of the FX swap is then to initiate a new forward sale of 100 million euros at the USD/EUR forward exchange rate being quoted on day 93. This renews the forward position (a forward sale of the euro) to a new date.

It is necessary to understand that (1) an FX swap consists of a simultaneous spot and forward transaction; (2) these swap transactions can extend (roll) an existing forward position to a new future date; and (3) rolling the position forward leads to a cash flow on settlement day. This cash flow can be thought of as a mark-to-market on the forward position. FX swaps are a large component of daily FX market turnover

---

1 Note that an "FX swap" is not the same as a "currency swap." An FX swap is simply the combination of a spot and a forward FX transaction (i.e., only two settlement dates—spot and forward—are involved). A currency swap is generally used for multiple periods and payments.

because market participants have to roll over existing speculative or hedging positions as the underlying forward contracts mature in order to extend the hedge or speculative position (otherwise, the position is closed out on the forward settlement date).

One other area where FX swaps are used in FX markets also bears mentioning: They are often used by market participants as a funding source (called swap funding). Consider the case of a UK-based firm that needs to borrow GBP100 million for 90 days, starting 2 days from today. One way to do this is simply to borrow 90-day money in GBP-denominated funds starting at T + 2. An alternative is to borrow in US dollars and exchange these for British pounds in the spot FX market (both with T + 2 settlement) and then sell British pounds 90 days forward against the US dollar. (Recall that the maturity of a forward rate contract is defined in terms of the spot settlement date, so the 90-day forward rate would be for settlement in 92 days from today.) The company has the use of GBP100 million for 90 days, starting on T + 2, and at the end of this period can pay off the US dollar loan at a known, pre-determined exchange rate (the 90-day forward rate). By engaging in simultaneous spot and forward transactions (i.e., an FX swap), the company has eliminated any FX risk from the foreign borrowing. The all-in financing rate using an FX swap will typically be close to that of domestic borrowing, usually within a few basis points. This near equivalence is enforced by an arbitrage relationship that will be described later. On large borrowing amounts, however, even a small differential can add up to substantial cost savings.

Another way to hedge FX exposures, or implement speculative FX positions, is to use options on currencies. FX options are contracts that, for an upfront premium or fee, give the purchaser the right, but not the obligation, to make an FX transaction at some future date at an exchange rate agreed upon today (when the contract is agreed to). The holder of an FX option will exercise the option only if it is advantageous to do so—that is, if the agreed upon exchange rate for the FX option contract is better than the FX rate available in the market at option expiry. As such, options are extremely flexible tools for managing FX exposures and account for a large percentage of daily turnover in the FX market.

Another concept to bear in mind is that spot, forward, swap, and option products are typically not used in isolation. Most major market participants manage their FX transactions and FX risk exposures through concurrent spot, forward, swap, and option positions. Taken together, these instruments (the building blocks of the FX market) provide an extremely flexible way for market participants to shape their FX risk exposures to match their operational mandate, risk tolerance, and market opinion. Moreover, FX transactions are often made in conjunction with transactions in other financial markets—such as equities, fixed income, and commodities. These markets have a variety of instruments as well, and market participants jointly tailor their *overall* position simultaneously using the building blocks of the FX market and these other markets.

EXAMPLE 1

Spot and Forward Exchange Rates

An investment adviser based in Sydney, Australia has a meeting with a local client who has diversified her domestic bond portfolio by adding investments in fixed-rate, long-term bonds denominated in HKD. Given that the client spends most of the year in Australia, she remains concerned about the foreign exchange risk of her foreign investments and asks the adviser how these might be managed. The investment adviser explains the difference between spot and forward exchange rates and their role in determining foreign exchange risk exposures. The investment adviser suggests the following investment strategy to the client: "You can exchange AUD for HKD in the spot exchange market, invest in a risk-free, one-year HKD-denominated zero coupon bond, and use a one-year forward contract for converting the proceeds back into AUD."

Spot exchange rate (AUD/HKD)	0.1714
One-year HKD interest rate	2.20%
One-year forward exchange rate (AUD/HKD)	0.1724

1. Which of the following statements is *most* correct? Over a one-year horizon, the exchange rate risk of the client's investment in HKD-denominated bonds is determined by uncertainty over:

    A. today's AUD/HKD forward rate.
    B. the AUD/HKD spot rate one year from now.
    C. the AUD/HKD forward rate one year from now.

Solution to 1:

B is correct. The exchange rate risk (for an unhedged investment) is defined by the uncertainty over future spot rates. In this case, the relevant spot rate is that which would prevail one year from now. Forward rates that would be in effect one year from now would be irrelevant, and the current forward rate is known with certainty.

2. To reduce the exchange rate risk of the Hong Kong SAR investment, the client should:

    A. sell AUD spot.
    B. sell AUD forward.
    C. sell HKD forward.

Solution to 2:

C is correct. The Australian-based investor owns HKD-denominated bonds, meaning that she is long HKD exposure. To hedge this exposure, she could enter into a forward contract to sell the HKD against the AUD for future delivery (that is, match a long HKD exposure in the cash market with a short HKD exposure in the derivatives market). The forward rate is established at the time the forward contract is entered into, eliminating any uncertainty about what exchange rate would be used to convert HKD-denominated cash flows back into AUD.

3. Over a one-year horizon, the investment proposed by the investment adviser is *most* likely:

    A. risk free.
    B. exposed to interest rate risk.
    C. exposed to exchange rate risk.

Solution to 3:

A is correct. The investment is risk free because the investment is based on a risk-free, one-year, zero coupon, HKD-denominated bond—meaning there is no default or reinvestment risk. The investment will mature in one year at par; there is no interest rate risk. The use of a forward contract to convert the HKD-denominated proceeds back to AUD eliminates any exchange rate risk.

4. To set up the investment proposed by the adviser, the client would need to:

   A. sell AUD spot; sell a one-year, HKD-denominated bond; and buy AUD forward.

   B. buy AUD spot; buy a one-year, HKD-denominated bond; and sell AUD forward.

   C. sell AUD spot; buy a one-year, HKD-denominated bond; and buy AUD forward.

Solution to 4:

C is correct. To create the investment, the client needs to convert AUD to HKD in the spot exchange market, invest in (buy) the one-year HKD bond, and sell the HKD forward/buy the AUD forward. Note that this process is directly comparable to the swap financing approach described in this section of the reading.

5. The return (in AUD) on the investment proposed by the investment adviser is *closest* to:

   A. 2.00 percent.

   B. 3.00 percent.

   C. 5.00 percent.

Solution to 5:

B is correct. Converting one AUD to HKD in the spot market gives the client (1/0.1714) = HKD5.83. Investing this for one year leads to 5.83 × (1.022) = HKD5.96. Selling this amount of HKD at the forward rate gives 5.96 × 0.1724 = AUD1.028 (rounding to three decimal places). This implies an AUD-denominated return of 2.8 percent which rounds up to 3 percent.

EXCHANGE RATES AND THE TRADE BALANCE: THE ELASTICITIES APPROACH

3

☐ explain the effects of exchange rates on countries' international trade and capital flows

The effectiveness of devaluation (in a fixed system) or depreciation (in a flexible system) of the currency for reducing a trade deficit depends on well-behaved demand and supply curves for goods and services. The condition that guarantees that devaluations improve the trade balance is called the Marshall–Lerner condition. The usual statement of this condition assumes that trade is initially balanced. We will present a generalization of the condition that allows for an initial trade imbalance and hence is more useful in addressing whether exchange rate movements will correct such imbalances.

Recall from microeconomics that the price elasticity of demand is given by:[2]

$$\varepsilon = -\frac{\%\ change\ in\ quantity}{\%\ change\ in\ price} = -\frac{\%\Delta Q}{\%\Delta P}$$

For example, a demand elasticity of 0.6 means that quantity demanded increases by 6 percent if price declines by 10 percent. Note that the elasticity of demand is defined so that it is a positive number. Because expenditure (R) equals price multiplied by quantity ($P \times Q$), by re-arranging the above expression to solve and substitute for $\%\Delta Q$, we can see that:

$$\%\ change\ in\ expenditure = \%\Delta R = \%\Delta P + \%\Delta Q = (1 - \varepsilon)\%\Delta P$$

From this we can see that an increase in price decreases expenditure if $\varepsilon > 1$, but it increases expenditure if $\varepsilon < 1$. By convention, if $\varepsilon > 1$ demand is described as being "elastic," while if $\varepsilon < 1$ demand is described as "inelastic."

The basic idea behind the Marshall–Lerner condition is that demand for imports and exports must be sufficiently price-sensitive so that increasing the relative price of imports increases the difference between export receipts and import expenditures. The generalized Marshall–Lerner condition is:

$$\omega_X \varepsilon_X + \omega_M(\varepsilon_M - 1) > 0$$

where ω_X and ω_M are the shares of exports and imports, respectively, in total trade (i.e., imports + exports) and ε_X and ε_M are the price elasticities of foreign demand for domestic country exports and domestic country demand for imports, respectively. Note that $(\omega_X + \omega_M) = 1$ and that an initial trade deficit implies $\omega_M > \omega_X$. If this condition is satisfied, a devaluation/depreciation of the domestic currency will move the trade balance toward surplus.

The first term in the generalized Marshall–Lerner condition reflects the change in export receipts assuming the domestic currency price of exports is unchanged (i.e., foreigners are billed in the domestic currency). It will be positive as long as export demand is not totally insensitive to price. Depreciation of the domestic currency makes exports cheaper in foreign currency and induces an increase in the quantity demanded by foreigners. This is reflected by the elasticity ε_X. There is no direct price impact on domestic currency export revenue because the domestic currency price is assumed to be unchanged. Hence, the percentage change in export revenue corresponding to a 1 percent depreciation of the currency is simply ε_X. The second term in the generalized Marshall–Lerner condition reflects the impact on import expenditures. Assuming that imports are billed in a foreign currency, the domestic currency price of imports rises as the domestic currency depreciates. The direct price effect increases import expenditures, while the induced reduction in the quantity of imports decreases import expenditures. The net effect depends on the elasticity of import demand, ε_M. Import expenditure declines only if import demand is elastic (i.e., $\varepsilon_M > 1$).

Examination of the generalized Marshall–Lerner condition indicates that more elastic demand—for either imports or exports—makes it more likely that the trade balance will improve. Indeed, if the demand for imports is elastic, $\varepsilon_M > 1$, then the trade balance will definitely improve. It should also be clear that the elasticity of import demand becomes increasingly important, and the export elasticity less important, as the initial trade deficit gets larger—that is, as ω_M increases. In the special case of initially balanced trade, $\omega_X = \omega_M$, the condition reduces to $(\varepsilon_X + \varepsilon_M > 1)$, which is the classic Marshall–Lerner condition.

Exhibit 1 illustrates the impact of depreciation on the trade balance. For ease of reference, we assume the domestic currency is the euro. A 10 percent depreciation of the euro makes imports 10 percent more expensive in euro terms. With an import elasticity of 0.65, this induces a 6.5 percent reduction in the quantity of imports. But

---
[2] See the Level I curriculum learning module Topics in Demand and Supply Analysis.

Exchange Rates and the Trade Balance: The Elasticities Approach

import expenditures increase by 3.5 percent [10% × (1 − 0.65)] or €21,000,000 because the drop in quantity is not sufficient to offset the increase in price. On the export side, the euro price of exports does not change but the foreign currency price of exports declines by 10 percent. This induces a 7.5 percent increase in the quantity of exports given an elasticity of 0.75. The euro value of exports therefore increases by 7.5 percent or €30,000,000. The net effect is a €9,000,000 improvement in the trade balance and a €51,000,000 increase in total trade.

Exhibit 1: Marshall–Lerner Condition with a 10 Percent Depreciation of Domestic Currency (€)

Assumptions	Exports	Imports
Demand elasticity	0.75	0.65
Percent price change		
In domestic currency (€)	0	10%
In foreign currency	−10%	0

Results	Initial value(€)	Change(€)
Exports	400,000,000	30,000,000
Imports	600,000,000	21,000,000
Trade balance	−200,000,000	9,000,000
Total trade	1,000,000,000	51,000,000

The balance of trade improves after the depreciation of the euro because the Marshall–Lerner condition is satisfied: The increase in the euro value of exports exceeds the increase in the value of imports. Based on the data in Exhibit 1, $\omega_M = 0.6$ (i.e., 600,000,000/1,000,000,000) and $\omega_X = 0.4$ (i.e., 1 − 0.6). Thus, the Marshall–Lerner equation is greater than zero:

$$\omega_X \varepsilon_X + \omega_M (\varepsilon_M - 1) = 0.4 \times 0.75 + 0.6(0.65 - 1) = 0.09$$

In practice, most countries import and export a variety of products. Hence, the overall price elasticities of their imports and exports reflect a composite of the products they trade. In conjunction with the Marshall–Lerner condition, our review of the factors that determine price elasticities suggests that exchange rate changes will be a more-effective mechanism for trade balance adjustment if a country imports and exports the following:

- Goods for which there are good substitutes
- Goods that trade in competitive markets
- Luxury goods, rather than necessities
- Goods that represent a large portion of consumer expenditures or a large portion of input costs for final producers

Note that each of these conditions is associated with higher demand elasticities (ε_X and ε_M).

Even when the Marshall–Lerner condition is satisfied, it is still possible that devaluation (in a fixed parity regime) or depreciation (in a floating regime) of the currency will initially make the trade balance worse before making it better. This effect, called the *J*-curve effect, is illustrated in Exhibit 2.

Exhibit 2: Trade Balance Dynamics: The *J*-Curve

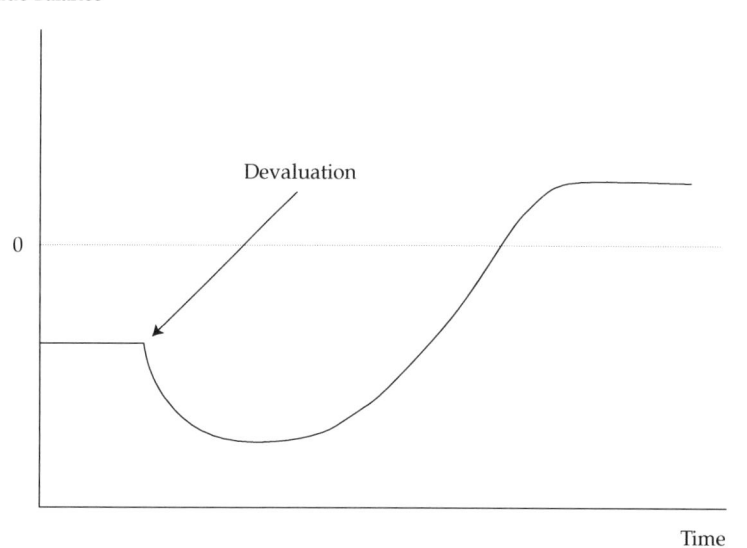

In the very short run, the *J*-curve reflects the order delivery lags that take place in import and export transactions. Imagine a clothing importer in Washington. Orders are placed in January for French spring fashions. Market forces cause the dollar to depreciate in February, but contracts were already signed for payment in euros. When the fashions arrive in March, more dollars have to go out to pay for the order signed in euros. Thus, the trade balance gets worse. However, after the depreciation, the clothing importer has to put in new orders for summer fashions. As a result of the currency depreciation, the French summer fashions are now more expensive, so the clothing store cuts the demand for imported clothes from France. The depreciation eventually improves the trade balance, even though it initially made it worse.

A *J*-curve pattern may also arise if short-term price elasticities do not satisfy the Marshall–Lerner condition but long-term elasticities do satisfy it. The trade balance may worsen initially and then gradually improve following a depreciation of the currency as firms and consumers adapt.

4 EXCHANGE RATES AND THE TRADE BALANCE: THE ABSORPTION APPROACH

☐ explain the effects of exchange rates on countries' international trade and capital flows

The elasticities approach focuses on the expenditure-switching effect of changing the relative prices of imports and exports. It is essentially a microeconomic view of the relationship between exchange rates and the trade balance. The absorption approach adopts an explicitly macroeconomic view of this relationship.

Recall from above that the trade balance is equal to the country's saving, including the government fiscal balance, minus its investment in new plants and equipment. Equivalently, it is equal to the difference between income (GDP) and domestic expenditure, or absorption. Thus, in order to move the trade balance toward surplus, a devaluation/depreciation of the domestic currency must increase income relative to expenditure or, equivalently, increase national saving relative to investment in physical capital.

If there is excess capacity in the economy, then by switching demand toward domestically produced goods and services, depreciation of the currency can increase output/income. Because some of the additional income will be saved, income rises relative to expenditure and the trade balance improves. If the economy is at full employment, however, the trade balance cannot improve unless domestic expenditure declines. If expenditure does not decline, then the depreciation will put upward pressure on domestic prices until the stimulative effect of the exchange rate change is negated by the higher price level and the trade balance reverts to its original level.

How might depreciation of the currency reduce domestic expenditure relative to income? The main mechanism is a wealth effect. A weaker currency reduces the purchasing power of domestic-currency-denominated assets (including the present value of current and future earned income). Households respond by reducing expenditure and increasing saving in order to rebuild their wealth. Of course, as real wealth is rebuilt, the effect on saving is likely to be reversed—resulting in only a temporary improvement in the trade balance. Thus, in the absence of excess capacity in the economy, currency depreciation is likely to provide only a temporary solution for a chronic trade imbalance. Lasting correction of the imbalance requires more fundamental changes in expenditure/saving behavior (e.g., a policy shift that improves the fiscal balance or an increase in saving relative to capital investment induced by an increase in real interest rates).

The absorption approach also reminds us that currency depreciation cannot improve the trade balance unless it also induces a corresponding change in the capital account. Not only must domestic saving increase, but that saving must also be willingly channeled into buying financial assets from foreigners. All else equal, this implies that foreign and domestic asset prices must change such that foreign assets become relatively more attractive and domestic assets relatively less attractive to both foreign and domestic investors.

EXAMPLE 2

Exchange Rates and the Trade Balance

An analyst at a foreign exchange dealing bank is examining the exchange rate for the Australian dollar (AUD), which is a freely floating currency. Currently, Australia is running a trade surplus with the rest of the world, primarily reflecting strong demand for Australian resource exports generated by rapid growth in emerging market economies in the Western Pacific region. In turn, Australia imports food and energy from a variety of foreign countries that compete with each other as well as with Australian producers of these products. The analyst uses data in the following table to estimate the effect of changes in the AUD exchange rate on Australia's balance of trade.

	Volume (AUD billions)	Demand Elasticity
Exports	200	0.3
Imports	180	0.6

The analyst's research report on this topic notes that the mix of products that Australia imports and exports seems to be changing and that this will affect the relation between the exchange rates and the trade surplus. The proportion of Australian exports accounted for by fine wines is increasing. These are considered a luxury good and must compete with increased wine exports from comparable-producing regions (such as Chile and New Zealand). At the same time, rising income levels in Australia are allowing the country to increase the proportion of its imports accounted for by luxury goods, and these represent a rising proportion of consumer expenditures. The analyst's report states: "Given the changing export mix, an appreciation of the currency will be more likely to reduce Australia's trade surplus. In contrast, the changing import mix will have the opposite effect."

1. Given the data in the table, an appreciation in the AUD will:

   A. cause the trade balance to increase.

   B. cause the trade balance to decrease.

   C. have no effect on the trade balance.

Solution to 1:

A is correct. As the AUD appreciates, the price of exports to *offshore buyers* goes up and they demand fewer of them; hence, the AUD-denominated revenue from exports decreases. (Although export demand is inelastic, or $\varepsilon_X < 1$, recall that the *Australian* price of these exports is assumed not to have changed, so the amount of export revenue received by Australia, in AUD terms, unambiguously declines as the quantity of exports declines.) Australian expenditure for imports also declines. Although the price of imports declines as the AUD appreciates, the Australians do not increase their import purchases enough to lead to higher expenditures. This is because import demand is also inelastic ($\varepsilon_M < 1$). This effect on import expenditure can be seen from: $\%\Delta R_M = (1 - \varepsilon_M)\%\Delta P_M$, where $\%\Delta P_M$ is negative (import prices are declining) and import demand is inelastic (so $(1 - \varepsilon_M) > 0$). With both import expenditures and export revenues declining, the net effect on the trade balance comes down to the relative size of the import and export weights (ω_M and ω_X, respectively). In this case, $\omega_X = 0.53$ (i.e., 200/380) and $\omega_M = 0.47$ (i.e., 180/380). Putting this into the Marshall–Lerner equation leads to:

$$\omega_X \varepsilon_X + \omega_M(\varepsilon_M - 1) = 0.53 \times 0.3 + 0.47(0.6 - 1) = -0.03$$

Because the Marshall–Lerner condition is not satisfied, exchange rate movements do not move the trade balance in the expected direction [i.e., appreciation (depreciation) of the currency does not decrease (increase) the trade balance]. However, note that with different import/export weights and the same elasticities, the Marshall–Lerner condition would be met. In particular, the condition would be met for any value of ω_X greater than 4/7 (≈ 0.571).

2. All else equal, an appreciation in the AUD will be *more* likely to reduce the trade surplus if the demand:

   A. elasticities for imports and exports increase.

   B. elasticity for exports and the export share in total trade decrease.

   C. elasticity for imports decreases and the import share in total trade increases.

Solution to 2:

A is correct. The basic intuition of the Marshall–Lerner condition is that in order for an exchange rate movement to rebalance trade, the demands for imports and exports must be sufficiently price-sensitive (i.e., they must have sufficiently high elasticities). However, the relative share of imports and exports in total trade must also be considered. The generalized Marshall–Lerner condition requires:

$$\omega_X \varepsilon_X + \omega_M (\varepsilon_M - 1) > 0$$

An increase in both ε_X and ε_M will clearly make this expression increase (A is correct). In contrast, a decrease in both ω_X and ε_X tends to make the expression smaller (B is incorrect).[3] If ε_M decreases and ω_M increases, import demand will respond less to an exchange rate movement and will have a larger role in determining the trade balance (C is incorrect).

3. All else equal, an appreciation in the AUD will be *more* likely to reduce the trade surplus if it leads to an increase in Australian:

   A. tax receipts.
   B. private sector investment.
   C. government budget surpluses.

Solution to 3:

B is correct. An Australian trade surplus means that Australia is spending less than it earns and is accumulating claims on foreigners. Equivalently, Australian saving, inclusive of both private saving and the government fiscal balance, is more than sufficient to fund Australian private sector investment. The relationship between the trade balance and expenditure/saving decisions is given by:

$$X - M = (S - I) + (T - G) > 0$$

For Australia's trade balance to decline, it must save less (S down), invest more (I up), decrease its fiscal balance ($T - G$ down), or some combination of these. Increasing tax receipts (T up) increases rather than decreases the fiscal balance, so answer A is incorrect. Similarly, answer C, increasing the government budget surplus, is incorrect. Increasing private investment (I up) does decrease the trade balance, so answer B is correct.

4. The report's statement about the effect of changing import and export mixes is *most* likely:

   A. correct.
   B. incorrect with respect to the import effect.
   C. incorrect with respect to the export effect.

Solution to 4:

B is correct. As Australian exports become more dominated by luxury goods that face highly competitive market conditions, the elasticity of export demand (ε_X) is likely to be increasing. Increasing export elasticity makes the trade surplus more responsive to an AUD appreciation (the increase in ε_X

---

[3] Because $\omega_M = 1 - \omega_X$ and $\varepsilon_M < 1$ in this example, a decrease in ω_X also decreases the second terms, $\omega_M(\varepsilon_M - 1)$, in the Marshall–Lerner condition.

will tend to increase the computed value for the Marshall–Lerner equation). Similarly, as Australian imports become more dominated by luxury goods that are an increasing proportion of household expenditure, import elasticity (ε_M) will most likely increase. This will also tend to increase the computed value for the Marshall–Lerner equation.

5. Suppose the Australian government imposed capital controls that prohibited the flow of financial capital into or out of the country. What impact would this have on the Australian trade balance?

   A. The trade surplus would increase.
   B. The trade balance would go to zero.
   C. The trade balance would not necessarily be affected.

Solution to 5:

B is correct. A trade deficit (surplus) must be exactly matched by an offsetting capital account surplus (deficit). Anything that impacts the trade balance must impact the capital account, and vice versa. If capital flows are prohibited, then both the capital account and the trade balance must be zero.

6. Suppose the Australian government imposed capital controls that prohibited the flow of financial capital into or out of the country. The impact on the trade balance, if any, would most likely take the form of:

   A. a decrease in private saving.
   B. a decrease in private investment.
   C. an increase in the government fiscal balance.

Solution to 6:

A is correct. The trade balance must go to zero. An increase in the fiscal balance implies an increase in the existing trade surplus, so answer C is incorrect. A decrease in private investment will also cause an increase in the trade surplus, so answer B is incorrect. A decrease in private saving will decrease the trade surplus as required, so answer A is correct: A decrease in saving will most likely reflect a decline in national income, especially the profit component, as export demand is choked off by the inability to extend credit to foreigners.

SUMMARY

Foreign exchange markets are crucial for understanding both the functioning of the global economy as well as the performance of investment portfolios. In this reading, we have described the diverse array of FX market participants and have introduced some of the basic concepts necessary to understand the structure and functions of these markets. The reader should be able to understand how exchange rates—both spot and forward—are quoted and be able to calculate cross exchange rates and forward rates. We also have described the array of exchange rate regimes that characterize foreign exchange markets globally and how these regimes determine the flexibility of

Exchange Rates and the Trade Balance: The Absorption Approach

exchange rates, and hence, the degree of foreign exchange rate risk that international investments are exposed to. Finally, we have discussed how movements in exchange rates affect international trade flows (imports and exports) and capital flows.

The following points, among others, are made in this reading:

- Measured by average daily turnover, the foreign exchange market is by far the largest financial market in the world. It has important effects, either directly or indirectly, on the pricing and flows in all other financial markets.

- There is a wide diversity of global FX market participants that have a wide variety of motives for entering into foreign exchange transactions.

- Individual currencies are usually referred to by standardized three-character codes. These currency codes can also be used to define exchange rates (the price of one currency in terms of another). There are a variety of exchange rate quoting conventions commonly used.

- Currencies trade in foreign exchange markets based on nominal exchange rates. An increase (decrease) in the exchange rate, quoted in indirect terms, means that the domestic currency is appreciating (depreciating) versus the foreign currency.

- The real exchange rate, defined as the nominal exchange rate multiplied by the ratio of price levels, measures the relative purchasing power of the currencies. An increase in the real exchange rate ($R_{d/f}$) implies a reduction in the relative purchasing power of the domestic currency.

- Given exchange rates for two currency pairs—A/B and A/C—we can compute the cross-rate (B/C) between currencies B and C. Depending on how the rates are quoted, this may require inversion of one of the quoted rates.

- Spot exchange rates are for immediate settlement (typically, T + 2), while forward exchange rates are for settlement at agreed-upon future dates. Forward rates can be used to manage foreign exchange risk exposures or can be combined with spot transactions to create FX swaps.

- The spot exchange rate, the forward exchange rate, and the domestic and foreign interest rates must jointly satisfy an arbitrage relationship that equates the investment return on two alternative but equivalent investments. Given the spot exchange rate and the foreign and domestic interest rates, the forward exchange rate must take the value that prevents riskless arbitrage.

- Forward rates are typically quoted in terms of forward (or swap) points. The swap points are added to the spot exchange rate in order to calculate the forward rate. Occasionally, forward rates are presented in terms of percentages relative to the spot rate.

- The base currency is said to be trading at a forward premium if the forward rate is above the spot rate (forward points are positive). Conversely, the base currency is said to be trading at a forward discount if the forward rate is below the spot rate (forward points are negative).

- The currency with the higher (lower) interest rate will trade at a forward discount (premium).

- Swap points are proportional to the spot exchange rate and to the interest rate differential and approximately proportional to the term of the forward contract.

- Empirical studies suggest that forward exchange rates may be unbiased predictors of future spot rates, but the margin of error on such forecasts is too large for them to be used in practice as a guide to managing exchange rate exposures. FX markets are too complex and too intertwined with other global financial markets to be adequately characterized by a single variable, such as the interest rate differential.

- Virtually every exchange rate is managed to some degree by central banks. The policy framework that each central bank adopts is called an exchange rate regime.

- A trade surplus (deficit) must be matched by a corresponding deficit (surplus) in the capital account. Any factor that affects the trade balance must have an equal and opposite impact on the capital account, and vice versa.

- A trade surplus reflects an excess of domestic saving (including the government fiscal balance) over investment spending. A trade deficit indicates that the country invests more than it saves and must finance the excess by borrowing from foreigners or selling assets to foreigners.

- The impact of the exchange rate on trade and capital flows can be analyzed from two perspectives. The elasticities approach focuses on the effect of changing the relative price of domestic and foreign goods. This approach highlights changes in the composition of spending. The absorption approach focuses on the impact of exchange rates on aggregate expenditure/saving decisions.

- The elasticities approach leads to the Marshall–Lerner condition, which describes combinations of export and import demand elasticities such that depreciation (appreciation) of the domestic currency will move the trade balance toward surplus (deficit).

- The idea underlying the Marshall–Lerner condition is that demand for imports and exports must be sufficiently price-sensitive so that an increase in the relative price of imports increases the difference between export receipts and import expenditures.

- In order to move the trade balance toward surplus (deficit), a change in the exchange rate must decrease (increase) domestic expenditure (also called absorption) relative to income. Equivalently, it must increase (decrease) domestic saving relative to domestic investment.

- If there is excess capacity in the economy, then currency depreciation can increase output/income by switching demand toward domestically produced goods and services. Because some of the additional income will be saved, income rises relative to expenditure and the trade balance improves.

- If the economy is at full employment, then currency depreciation must reduce domestic expenditure in order to improve the trade balance. The main mechanism is a wealth effect: A weaker currency reduces the purchasing power of domestic-currency-denominated assets (including the present value of current and future earned income), and households respond by reducing expenditure and increasing saving.

PRACTICE PROBLEMS

1. In order to minimize the foreign exchange exposure on a euro-denominated receivable due from a German company in 100 days, a British company would *most likely* initiate a:

   A. spot transaction.

   B. forward contract.

   C. real exchange rate contract.

2. A large industrialized country has recently devalued its currency in an attempt to correct a persistent trade deficit. Which of the following domestic industries is *most likely* to benefit from the devaluation?

   A. Luxury cars

   B. Branded prescription drugs

   C. Restaurants and live entertainment venues

3. A country with a persistent trade surplus is being pressured to let its currency appreciate. Which of the following *best* describes the adjustment that must occur if currency appreciation is to be effective in reducing the trade surplus?

   A. Domestic investment must decline relative to saving

   B. Foreigners must increase investment relative to saving

   C. Global capital flows must shift toward the domestic market

SOLUTIONS

1. B is correct. The receivable is due in 100 days. To reduce the risk of currency exposure, the British company would initiate a forward contract to sell euros/buy pounds at an exchange rate agreed to today. The agreed-upon rate is called the forward exchange rate.

2. A is correct. A devaluation of the domestic currency means domestic producers are cutting the price faced by their foreign customers. The impact on their unit sales and their revenue depends on the elasticity of demand. Expensive luxury goods exhibit high price elasticity. Hence, luxury car producers are likely to experience a sharp increase in sales and revenue due to the devaluation.

3. C is correct. The trade surplus cannot decline unless the capital account deficit also declines. Regardless of the mix of assets bought and sold, foreigners must buy more assets from (or sell fewer assets to) domestic issuers/investors.

Glossary

A priori probability A probability based on logical analysis rather than on observation or personal judgment.

Absolute advantage A country's ability to produce a good or service at a lower absolute cost than its trading partner.

Absolute dispersion The amount of variability present without comparison to any reference point or benchmark.

Absolute frequency The actual number of observations counted for each unique value of the variable (also called raw frequency).

Accelerated methods Depreciation methods that allocate a relatively large proportion of the cost of an asset to the early years of the asset's useful life.

Accounts payable Amounts that a business owes to its vendors for goods and services that were purchased from them but which have not yet been paid.

Accrued expenses Liabilities related to expenses that have been incurred but not yet paid as of the end of an accounting period—an example of an accrued expense is rent that has been incurred but not yet paid, resulting in a liability "rent payable." Also called *accrued liabilities*.

Addition rule for probabilities A principle stating that the probability that A or B occurs (both occur) equals the probability that A occurs, plus the probability that B occurs, minus the probability that both A and B occur.

Aggregate demand The quantity of goods and services that households, businesses, government, and non-domestic customers want to buy at any given level of prices.

Aggregate demand curve Inverse relationship between the price level and real output.

Aggregate income The value of all the payments earned by the suppliers of factors used in the production of goods and services.

Aggregate output The value of all the goods and services produced during a specified period.

Aggregate supply The quantity of goods and services producers are willing to supply at any given level of price.

Aggregate supply curve The level of domestic output that companies will produce at each price level.

Alternative hypothesis The hypothesis that is accepted if the null hypothesis is rejected.

Amortisation The process of allocating the cost of intangible long-term assets having a finite useful life to accounting periods; the allocation of the amount of a bond premium or discount to the periods remaining until bond maturity.

Amortised cost The historical cost (initially recognised cost) of an asset, adjusted for amortisation and impairment.

Annual percentage rate The cost of borrowing expressed as a yearly rate.

Annuity A finite set of level sequential cash flows.

Annuity due An annuity having a first cash flow that is paid immediately.

Arithmetic mean The sum of the observations divided by the number of observations.

Assets Resources controlled by an enterprise as a result of past events and from which future economic benefits to the enterprise are expected to flow.

Autarkic price The price of a good or service in an autarkic economy.

Autarky Countries seeking political self-sufficiency with little or no external trade or finance. State-owned enterprises control strategic domestic industries.

Available-for-sale Under US GAAP, debt securities not classified as either held-to-maturity or held-for-trading securities. The investor is willing to sell but not actively planning to sell. In general, available-for-sale debt securities are reported at fair value on the balance sheet, with unrealized gains included as a component of other comprehensive income.

Average fixed cost Total fixed cost divided by quantity produced.

Average product Measures the productivity of inputs on average and is calculated by dividing total product by the total number of units for a given input that is used to generate that output.

Average total cost Total cost divided by quantity produced.

Average variable cost Total variable cost divided by quantity produced.

Back-testing The process that approximates the real-life investment process, using historical data, to assess whether an investment strategy would have produced desirable results.

Backfill Bias A problem whereby certain surviving hedge funds may be added to databases and various hedge fund indexes only after they are initially successful and start to report their returns. Also see *survivorship bias*.

Balance of payments A double-entry bookkeeping system that summarizes a country's economic transactions with the rest of the world for a particular period of time, typically a calendar quarter or year.

Balance of trade deficit When the domestic economy is spending more on non-domestic goods and services than non-domestic economies are spending on domestic goods and services.

Balance sheet The financial statement that presents an entity's current financial position by disclosing resources the entity controls (its assets) and the claims on those resources (its liabilities and equity claims), as of a particular point in time (the date of the balance sheet). Also called *statement of financial position* or *statement of financial condition*.

Bar chart A chart for plotting the frequency distribution of categorical data, where each bar represents a distinct category and each bar's height is proportional to the frequency of the corresponding category. In technical analysis, a bar chart that plots four bits of data for each time interval—the high, low, opening, and closing prices. A vertical line connects the high and low prices. A cross-hatch left indicates the opening price and a cross-hatch right indicates the closing price.

Barter economy An economy where economic agents as house-holds, corporations, and governments "pay" for goods and services with another good or service.

Bernoulli random variable A random variable having the outcomes 0 and 1.

Bernoulli trial An experiment that can produce one of two outcomes.

Bimodal A distribution that has two most frequently occurring values.

Binomial random variable The number of successes in n Bernoulli trials for which the probability of success is constant for all trials and the trials are independent.

Binomial tree The graphical representation of a model of asset price dynamics in which, at each period, the asset moves up with probability p or down with probability $(1 - p)$.

Bottom-up analysis An investment selection approach that focuses on company-specific circumstances rather than emphasizing economic cycles or industry analysis.

Box and whisker plot A graphic for visualizing the dispersion of data across quartiles. It consists of a "box" with "whiskers" connected to the box.

Broad money Encompasses narrow money plus the entire range of liquid assets that can be used to make purchases.

Bubble line chart A line chart that uses varying-sized bubbles to represent a third dimension of the data. The bubbles are sometimes color-coded to present additional information.

Capital account A component of the balance of payments account that measures transfers of capital.

Capital consumption allowance A measure of the wear and tear (depreciation) of the capital stock that occurs in the production of goods and services.

Capital deepening investment Increases the stock of capital relative to labor.

Capital stock The accumulated amount of buildings, machinery, and equipment used to produce goods and services.

Cash flow additivity principle The principle that dollar amounts indexed at the same point in time are additive.

Cash flow from operating activities The net amount of cash provided from operating activities.

Cash flow from operations a cash profit measure over a period for an issuer's primary business activities. It includes cash from customers as well as interest and dividends received from financial investments, less cash paid to employees and suppliers as well as taxes paid to governments and interest paid to lenders.

Categorical data Values that describe a quality or characteristic of a group of observations and therefore can be used as labels to divide a dataset into groups to summarize and visualize (also called **qualitative data**).

Central banks The dominant bank in a country, usually with official or semi-official governmental status.

Central limit theorem The theorem that states the sum (and the mean) of a set of independent, identically distributed random variables with finite variances is normally distributed, whatever distribution the random variables follow.

Classified balance sheet A balance sheet organized so as to group together the various assets and liabilities into subcategories (e.g., current and noncurrent).

Closed economy An economy that does not trade with other countries; an *autarkic economy*.

Clustered bar chart See *grouped bar chart*.

Coefficient of variation The ratio of a set of observations' standard deviation to the observations' mean value.

Combination A listing in which the order of the listed items does not matter.

Combination Formula (Binomial Formula) The number of ways that we can choose r objects from a total of n objects, when the order in which the r objects are listed does not matter, is $_nC_r = \binom{n}{r} = \frac{n!}{(n-r)!r!}$.

Comparative advantage A country's ability to produce a good or service at a lower relative cost, or opportunity cost, than its trading partner.

Complement The event not-S, written S^C, given the event S. Note that $P(S) + P(S^C) = 1$.

Complements Goods that tend to be used together; technically, two goods whose cross-price elasticity of demand is negative.

Compounding The process of accumulating interest on interest.

Comprehensive income All changes in equity other than contributions by, and distributions to, owners; income under clean surplus accounting; includes all changes in equity during a period except those resulting from investments by owners and distributions to owners. Comprehensive income equals net income plus other comprehensive income.

Conditional probability The probability of an event given (conditioned on) another event.

Confidence level The complement of the level of significance.

Confusion matrix A grid used for error analysis in classification problems, it presents values for four evaluation metrics including true positive (TP), false positive (FP), true negative (TN), and false negative (FN).

Consumer surplus The difference between the value that a consumer places on units purchased and the amount of money that was required to pay for them.

Contingency table A table of the frequency distribution of observations classified on the basis of two discrete variables.

Continuous data Data that can be measured and can take on any numerical value in a specified range of values.

Continuous random variable A random variable for which the range of possible outcomes is the real line (all real numbers between $-\infty$ and $+\infty$) or some subset of the real line.

Contra account An account that offsets another account.

Convergence The tendency for differences in output per capita across countries to diminish over time. In technical analysis, the term describes the case when an indicator moves in the same manner as the security being analyzed.

Core inflation Refers to the inflation rate calculated based on a price index of goods and services except food and energy.

cost averaging <u>The periodic investment of a fixed amount of money.</u>

Coupon rate The interest rate promised in a contract; this is the rate used to calculate the periodic interest payments.

Credit analysis The evaluation of credit risk; the evaluation of the creditworthiness of a borrower or counterparty.

credit risk the expected economic loss under a potential borrower default over the life of the contract

Critical values Values of the test statistic at which the decision changes from fail to reject the null hypothesis to reject the null hypothesis.

Cross-price elasticity of demand The percentage change in quantity demanded for a given percentage change in the price of another good; the responsiveness of the demand for Product A that is associated with the change in price of Product B.

Cross-sectional data A list of the observations of a specific variable from multiple observational units at a given point in time. The observational units can be individuals, groups, companies, trading markets, regions, etc.

Cumulative absolute frequency   Cumulates (i.e., adds up) in a frequency distribution the absolute frequencies as one moves from the first bin to the last bin.

Cumulative distribution function   A function giving the probability that a random variable is less than or equal to a specified value.

Cumulative frequency distribution chart   A chart that plots either the cumulative absolute frequency or the cumulative relative frequency on the y-axis against the upper limit of the interval and allows one to see the number or the percentage of the observations that lie below a certain value.

Cumulative relative frequency   A sequence of partial sums of the relative frequencies in a frequency distribution.

Current account   A component of the balance of payments account that measures the flow of goods and services.

Current assets   Assets that are expected to be consumed or converted into cash in the near future, typically one year or less. *Also called liquid assets.*

Current cost   With reference to assets, the amount of cash or cash equivalents that would have to be paid to buy the same or an equivalent asset today; with reference to liabilities, the undiscounted amount of cash or cash equivalents that would be required to settle the obligation today.

Current liabilities   Short-term obligations, such as accounts payable, wages payable, or accrued liabilities, that are expected to be settled in the near future, typically one year or less.

Cyclical companies   Companies with sales and profits that regularly expand and contract with the business cycle or state of economy.

Data   A collection of numbers, characters, words, and text—as well as images, audio, and video—in a raw or organized format to represent facts or information.

Data snooping   The practice of determining a model by extensive searching through a dataset for statistically significant patterns.

Data table   see **two-dimensional rectangular array**.

Days of inventory on hand   An activity ratio equal to the number of days in the period divided by inventory turnover over the period.

Dealing securities   Securities held by banks or other financial intermediaries for trading purposes.

Deciles   Quantiles that divide a distribution into 10 equal parts.

default risk premium   n extra return that compensates investors for the possibility that the borrower will fail to make a promised payment at the contracted time and in the contracted amount.

Defensive companies   Companies with sales and profits that have little sensitivity to the business cycle or state of the economy.

Deferred income   A liability account for money that has been collected for goods or services that have not yet been delivered; payment received in advance of providing a good or service.

Deferred revenue   A liability account for money that has been collected for goods or services that have not yet been delivered; payment received in advance of providing a good or service.

Deferred tax assets   A balance sheet asset that arises when an excess amount is paid for income taxes relative to accounting profit. The taxable income is higher than accounting profit and income tax payable exceeds tax expense. The company expects to recover the difference during the course of future operations when tax expense exceeds income tax payable.

Degree of confidence   The probability that a confidence interval includes the unknown population parameter.

Degrees of freedom   The number of independent variables used in defining sample statistics, such as variance, and the probability distributions they measure.

Demand curve   Graph of the inverse demand function. A graph showing the demand relation, either the highest quantity willingly purchased at each price or the highest price willingly paid for each quantity.

Demand function   A relationship that expresses the quantity demanded of a good or service as a function of own-price and possibly other variables.

Dependent   With reference to events, the property that the probability of one event occurring depends on (is related to) the occurrence of another event.

Depreciation   The process of systematically allocating the cost of long-lived (tangible) assets to the periods during which the assets are expected to provide economic benefits.

Descriptive statistics   The study of how data can be summarized effectively.

Diluted shares   The number of shares that would be outstanding if all potentially dilutive claims on common shares (e.g., convertible debt, convertible preferred stock, and employee stock options) were exercised.

Diminishing balance method   An accelerated depreciation method, i.e., one that allocates a relatively large proportion of the cost of an asset to the early years of the asset's useful life.

Diminishing marginal productivity   When each additional unit of an input, keeping the other inputs unchanged, increases output by a smaller increment.

Direct format   With reference to the cash flow statement, a format for the presentation of the statement in which cash flow from operating activities is shown as operating cash receipts less operating cash disbursements. Also called *direct method*.

Direct method   See *direct format*.

Direct write-off method   An approach to recognizing credit losses on customer receivables in which the company waits until such time as a customer has defaulted and only then recognizes the loss.

Discount   To reduce the value of a future payment in allowance for how far away it is in time; to calculate the present value of some future amount. Also, the amount by which an instrument is priced below its face value.

Discouraged worker   A person who has stopped looking for a job or has given up seeking employment.

Discrete data   Numerical values that result from a counting process; therefore, practically speaking, the data are limited to a finite number of values.

Discrete random variable   A random variable that can take on at most a countable number of possible values.

Dispersion   The variability of a population or sample of observations around the central tendency.

Double declining balance depreciation   An accelerated depreciation method that involves depreciating the asset at double the straight-line rate. This rate is multiplied by the book value of the asset at the beginning of the period (a declining balance) to calculate depreciation expense.

Down transition probability   The probability that an asset's value moves down in a model of asset price dynamics.

Downside risk Risk of incurring returns below a specified value.

Dutch Book Theorem A result in probability theory stating that inconsistent probabilities create profit opportunities.

Economic costs All the remuneration needed to keep a productive resource in its current employment or to acquire the resource for productive use; the sum of total accounting costs and implicit opportunity costs.

Economic profit Equal to accounting profit less the implicit opportunity costs not included in total accounting costs; the difference between total revenue (TR) and total cost (TC). Also called *abnormal profit* or *supernormal profit*.

Effective annual rate An interest rate with a periodicity of one.

Effective interest rate The borrowing rate or market rate that a company incurs at the time of issuance of a bond.

Elastic Said of a good or service when the magnitude of elasticity is greater than one.

Elasticity The percentage change in one variable for a percentage change in another variable; a general measure of how sensitive one variable is to a change in the value of another variable.

Elasticity of demand A measure of the sensitivity of quantity demanded to a change in a product's own price: $\%\Delta Q^D/\%\Delta P$.

Elasticity of supply A measure of the sensitivity of quantity supplied to a change in price: $\%\Delta Q^S/\%\Delta P$.

Empirical probability The probability of an event estimated as a relative frequency of occurrence.

Employed The number of people with a job.

Equity Ownership interest in an entity. A residual claim on the assets of an entity after more senior claims, such as debt, have been satisfied. Also known as *net assets*.

Estimate The particular value calculated from sample observations using an estimator.

Estimator An estimation formula; the formula used to compute the sample mean and other sample statistics are examples of estimators.

Event Any outcome or specified set of outcomes of a random variable.

Exhaustive An index construction strategy that selects every constituent of a universe.

Expected inflation The level of inflation that economic agents expect in the future.

Expenses Outflows of economic resources or increases in liabilities that result in decreases in equity (other than decreases because of distributions to owners); reductions in net assets associated with the creation of revenues.

Exports Goods and services that an economy sells to other countries.

Externalities This term refers to situations where the production or consumption of goods and services creates costs or benefits for others that are not reflected in the prices charged for them. In other words, externalities include the consumption, production, and investment decisions of firms (and individuals) that affect people not directly involved in the transactions. Externalities can be either negative or positive.

Face value The amount of principal on a bond, also known as par value.

Fair value A market-based measure of an investment based on observable or derived assumptions to determine a price that market participants would use to exchange an asset or liability in an orderly transaction at a specific time.

False discovery approach An adjustment in the *p*-values for tests performed multiple times.

False discovery rate The rate of Type I errors in testing a null hypothesis multiple times for a given level of significance.

Finance lease A type of lease which is more akin to the purchase or sale of the underlying asset.

Financial account A component of the balance of payments account that records investment flows.

Financial flexibility The ability to react and adapt to financial adversity and opportunities.

Financing activities Activities related to obtaining or repaying capital to be used in the business (e.g., equity and long-term debt).

First-degree price discrimination Where a monopolist is able to charge each customer the highest price the customer is willing to pay.

Fiscal policy The use of taxes and government spending to affect the level of aggregate expenditures.

Fisher effect The thesis that the real rate of interest in an economy is stable over time so that changes in nominal interest rates are the result of changes in expected inflation.

Foreign direct investment Direct investment by a firm in one country (the source country) in productive assets in a foreign country (the host country).

Foreign portfolio investment Shorter-term investment by individuals, firms, and institutional investors (e.g., pension funds) in foreign financial instruments such as foreign stocks and foreign government bonds.

Fractile A value at or below which a stated fraction of the data lies. Also called quantile.

Fractional reserve banking Banking in which reserves constitute a fraction of deposits.

Free trade When there are no government restrictions on a country's ability to trade.

Frequency distribution A tabular display of data constructed either by counting the observations of a variable by distinct values or groups or by tallying the values of a numerical variable into a set of numerically ordered bins (also called a one-way table).

Frequency polygon A graph of a frequency distribution obtained by drawing straight lines joining successive points representing the class frequencies.

Future value (FV) The amount to which a payment or series of payments will grow by a stated future date.

FX swap The combination of a spot and a forward FX transaction.

Gains Asset inflows not directly related to the ordinary activities of the business.

GDP deflator A gauge of prices and inflation that measures the aggregate changes in prices across the overall economy.

Geometric mean A measure of central tendency computed by taking the *n*th root of the product of *n* non-negative values.

Goodwill An intangible asset that represents the excess of the purchase price of an acquired company over the value of the net assets acquired.

Gross domestic product The market value of all final goods and services produced within the economy during a given period (output definition) or, equivalently, the aggregate income earned by all households, all companies, and the government within the economy during a given period (income definition).

Gross margin Sales minus the cost of sales (i.e., the cost of goods sold for a manufacturing company).

Gross profit Sales minus the cost of sales (i.e., the cost of goods sold for a manufacturing company).

Gross profit margin The ratio of gross profit to revenues.

Grouped bar chart A bar chart for showing joint frequencies for two categorical variables (also known as a **clustered bar chart**).

Grouping by function With reference to the presentation of expenses in an income statement, the grouping together of expenses serving the same function, e.g. all items that are costs of goods sold.

Grouping by nature With reference to the presentation of expenses in an income statement, the grouping together of expenses by similar nature, e.g., all depreciation expenses.

Growth investors With reference to equity investors, investors who seek to invest in high-earnings-growth companies.

harmonic mean A type of weighted mean computed as the reciprocal of the arithmetic average of the reciprocals.

Headline inflation Refers to the inflation rate calculated based on the price index that includes all goods and services in an economy.

Heat map A type of graphic that organizes and summarizes data in a tabular format and represents it using a color spectrum.

Histogram A chart that presents the distribution of numerical data by using the height of a bar or column to represent the absolute frequency of each bin or interval in the distribution.

Historical cost In reference to assets, the amount paid to purchase an asset, including any costs of acquisition and/or preparation; with reference to liabilities, the amount of proceeds received in exchange in issuing the liability.

Hypothesis A proposed explanation or theory that can be tested.

Hypothesis testing The process of testing of hypotheses about one or more populations using statistical inference.

Implicit price deflator for GDP A gauge of prices and inflation that measures the aggregate changes in prices across the overall economy.

Implicit selection bias One type of selection bias introduced through the presence of a threshold that filters out some unqualified members.

Imports Goods and services that a domestic economy (i.e., house-holds, firms, and government) purchases from other countries.

Income Increases in economic benefits in the form of inflows or enhancements of assets, or decreases of liabilities that result in an increase in equity (other than increases resulting from contributions by owners).

Income elasticity of demand A measure of the responsiveness of demand to changes in income, defined as the percentage change in quantity demanded divided by the percentage change in income.

Income tax payable The income tax owed by the company on the basis of taxable income.

Increasing marginal returns When the marginal product of a resource increases as additional units of that input are employed.

Independent With reference to events, the property that the occurrence of one event does not affect the probability of another event occurring. With reference to two random variables X and Y, they are independent if and only if $P(X,Y) = P(X)P(Y)$.

Indirect format With reference to cash flow statements, a format for the presentation of the statement which, in the operating cash flow section, begins with net income then shows additions and subtractions to arrive at operating cash flow. Also called *indirect method*.

Indirect method See *indirect format*.

Inelastic Said of a good or service when the magnitude of elasticity is less than one. Insensitive to price changes.

Inferior goods A good whose consumption decreases as income increases.

Inflation The percentage increase in the general price level from one period to the next; a sustained rise in the overall level of prices in an economy.

inflation premium An extra return that compensates investors for expected inflation.

Inflation uncertainty The degree to which economic agents view future rates of inflation as difficult to forecast.

Input productivity The amount of output produced by workers in a given period of time—for example, output per hour worked; measures the efficiency of labor.

Intangible assets Assets without a physical form, such as patents and trademarks.

Interest Payment for lending funds.

Interest rate A rate of return that reflects the relationship between differently dated cash flows; a discount rate.

Interest rate effect The effect through which price level changes, through demand for money, impact interest rate, which in turn impacts investment and consumption.

Interquartile range The difference between the third and first quartiles of a dataset.

Interval With reference to grouped data, a set of values within which an observation falls.

Inventory investment Net change in business inventory.

Inventory turnover An activity ratio calculated as cost of goods sold divided by average inventory.

Inverse demand function A restatement of the demand function in which price is stated as a function of quantity.

Investing activities Activities associated with the acquisition and disposal of property, plant, and equipment; intangible assets; other long-term assets; and both long-term and short-term investments in the equity and debt (bonds and loans) issued by other companies.

Investment property Property used to earn rental income or capital appreciation (or both).

Joint frequencies The entry in the cells of the contingency table that represent the joining of one variable from a row and the other variable from a column to count observations.

Joint probability The probability of the joint occurrence of stated events.

Labor force Everyone of working age (ages 16 to 64) who either is employed or is available for work but not working.

Labor productivity The quantity of goods and services (real GDP) that a worker can produce in one hour of work.

Law of demand The principle that as the price of a good rises, buyers will choose to buy less of it, and as its price falls, they will buy more.

Law of diminishing marginal returns The observation that a variable factor's marginal product must eventually fall as more of it is added to a fixed amount of the other factors.

Law of diminishing returns The smallest output that a firm can produce such that its long run average costs are minimized.

Level of significance The probability of a Type I error in testing a hypothesis.

Liabilities Present obligations of an enterprise arising from past events, the settlement of which is expected to result in an outflow of resources embodying economic benefits; creditors' claims on the resources of a company.

LIFO reserve The difference between the reported LIFO inventory carrying amount and the inventory amount that would have been reported if the FIFO method had been used (in other words, the FIFO inventory value less the LIFO inventory value).

Line chart A type of graph used to visualize ordered observations. In technical analysis, a plot of price data, typically closing prices, with a line connecting the points.

Linear interpolation The estimation of an unknown value on the basis of two known values that bracket it, using a straight line between the two known values.

Liquidity a characteristic of an asset or a liability that reflects its nearness to cash or settlement.

liquidity premium An extra return that compensates investors for the risk of loss relative to an investment's fair value if the investment needs to be converted to cash quickly.

Long-lived assets Assets that are expected to provide economic benefits over a future period of time, typically greater than one year. Also called *long-term assets*.

Look-ahead bias A bias caused by using information that was unavailable on the test date.

Losses Asset outflows not directly related to the ordinary activities of the business.

Macroeconomics The branch of economics that deals with aggregate economic quantities, such as national output and national income.

Marginal cost The cost of producing an additional unit of a good.

Marginal frequencies The sums determined by adding joint frequencies across rows or across columns in a contingency table.

Marginal product Measures the productivity of each unit of input and is calculated by taking the difference in total product from adding another unit of input (assuming other resource quantities are held constant).

Marginal propensity to consume The proportion of an additional unit of disposable income that is consumed or spent; the change in consumption for a small change in income.

Marginal propensity to save The proportion of an additional unit of disposable income that is saved (not spent).

Marginal revenue The change in total revenue divided by the change in quantity sold; simply, the additional revenue from selling one more unit.

Marginal value curve A curve describing the highest price consumers are willing to pay for each additional unit of a good.

Market rate of interest The rate demanded by purchasers of bonds, given the risks associated with future cash payment obligations of the particular bond issue.

Market-oriented investors With reference to equity investors, investors whose investment disciplines cannot be clearly categorized as value or growth.

maturity premium An extra return that compensates investors for the increased sensitivity of the market value of debt to a change in market interest rates as maturity is extended.

Mean absolute deviation With reference to a sample, the mean of the absolute values of deviations from the sample mean.

Measure of central tendency A quantitative measure that specifies where data are centered.

Measure of value A standard for measuring value; a function of money.

Measures of location Quantitative measures that describe the location or distribution of data. They include not only measures of central tendency but also other measures, such as percentiles.

Median The value of the middle item of a set of items that has been sorted into ascending or descending order (i.e., the 50th percentile).

Medium of exchange Any asset that can be used to purchase goods and services or to repay debts; a function of money.

Microeconomics The branch of economics that deals with markets and decision making of individual economic units, including consumers and businesses.

Modal interval With reference to grouped data, the interval containing the greatest number of observations (i.e., highest frequency).

Mode The most frequently occurring value in a distribution.

Monetarists Economists who believe that the rate of growth of the money supply is the primary determinant of the rate of inflation.

Monetary policy Actions taken by a nation's central bank to affect aggregate output and prices through changes in bank reserves, reserve requirements, or its target interest rate.

Money A generally accepted medium of exchange and unit of account.

Money creation The process by which changes in bank reserves translate into changes in the money supply.

Money multiplier Describes how a change in reserves is expected to affect the money supply; in its simplest form, 1 divided by the reserve requirement.

Money neutrality The thesis that an increase in the money supply leads in the long-run to an increase in the price level, while leaving real variables like output and employment unaffected.

Multi-step format With respect to the format of the income statement, a format that presents a subtotal for gross profit (revenue minus cost of goods sold).

Multinational corporation A company operating in more than one country or having subsidiary firms in more than one country.

Multinomial formula (general formula for labeling problems) The number of ways that n objects can be labeled with k different labels, with n_1 of the first type, n_2 of the second type, and so on, with $n_1 + n_2 + ... + n_k = n$, is given by $\frac{n!}{n_1! n_2! ... n_k!}$.

Multiple testing problem The risk of getting statistically significant test results when performing a test multiple times.

Multiplication rule for counting If one task can be done in n_1 ways, and a second task, given the first, can be done in n_2 ways, and a third task, given the first two tasks, can be done in n_3 ways, and so on for k tasks, then the number of ways the k tasks can be done is $(n_1)(n_2)(n_3) ... (n_k)$.

Multiplication rule for independent events The rule that when two events are independent, the joint probability of A and B equals the product of the individual probabilities of A and B.

Multiplication rule for probability The rule that the joint probability of events A and B equals the probability of A given B times the probability of B.

Multivariate distribution A probability distribution that specifies the probabilities for a group of related random variables.

Glossary

Multivariate normal distribution A probability distribution for a group of random variables that is completely defined by the means and variances of the variables plus all the correlations between pairs of the variables.

Mutually exclusive Indicates that only one event can occur at a time.

***n* Factorial** For a positive integer *n*, the product of the first *n* positive integers; 0 factorial equals 1 by definition. *n* factorial is written as *n*!.

Narrow money The notes and coins in circulation in an economy, plus other very highly liquid deposits.

Natural rate of unemployment Effective unemployment rate, below which pressure emerges in labor markets.

Net book value The remaining (undepreciated) balance of an asset's purchase cost. For liabilities, the face value of a bond minus any unamortized discount, or plus any unamortized premium.

Net exports The difference between the value of a country's exports and the value of its imports (i.e., value of exports minus imports).

Net realisable value Estimated selling price in the ordinary course of business less the estimated costs necessary to make the sale.

Net revenue Revenue after adjustments (e.g., for estimated returns or for amounts unlikely to be collected).

Node Each value on a binomial tree from which successive moves or outcomes branch.

Nominal data Categorical values that are not amenable to being organized in a logical order. An example of nominal data is the classification of publicly listed stocks into sectors.

Nominal GDP The value of goods and services measured at current prices.

Nominal risk-free interest rate The sum of the real risk-free interest rate and the inflation premium.

Non-accelerating inflation rate of unemployment Effective unemployment rate below which pressure emerges in labor markets.

Non-current assets Assets that are expected to benefit the company over an extended period of time (usually more than one year).

Non-current liabilities Obligations that broadly represent a probable sacrifice of economic benefits in periods generally greater than one year in the future.

Non-renewable resources Finite resources that are depleted once they are consumed; oil and coal are examples.

Normal goods Goods that are consumed in greater quantities as income increases.

Normal profit The level of accounting profit needed to just cover the implicit opportunity costs ignored in accounting costs.

Null hypothesis The hypothesis that is tested.

Numerical data Values that represent measured or counted quantities as a number. Also called **quantitative data**.

Objective probabilities Probabilities that generally do not vary from person to person; includes a priori and empirical probabilities.

Observation The value of a specific variable collected at a point in time or over a specified period of time.

Odds against *E* The reciprocal of odds for *E*.

Odds for *E* The probability of *E* divided by 1 minus the probability of *E*.

One-dimensional array The simplest format for representing a collection of data of the same data type.

One-sided hypothesis test A test in which the null hypothesis is rejected only if the evidence indicates that the population parameter is greater than or less than the hypothesized parameter; occurs when the alternative hypothesis is stated either as greater than or less than the hypothesized population parameter.

Open economy An economy that trades with other countries.

Operating activities Activities that are part of the day-to-day business functioning of an entity, such as selling inventory and providing services.

Operating cash flow The net amount of cash provided from operating activities.

Operating profit A company's profits on its usual business activities before deducting taxes. Also called *operating income*.

Opportunity cost The value that investors forgo by choosing a particular course of action; the value of something in its best alternative use.

Ordinal data Categorical values that can be logically ordered or ranked.

Ordinary annuity An annuity with a first cash flow that is paid one period from the present.

Other comprehensive income Items of comprehensive income that are not reported on the income statement; comprehensive income minus net income.

Out-of-sample test A test of a strategy or model using a sample outside the period on which the strategy or model was developed.

Outcome A possible value of a random variable.

Own price The price of a good or service itself (as opposed to the price of something else).

Own-price elasticity of demand The percentage change in quantity demanded for a percentage change in good's own price, holding all other things constant.

Owners' equity The excess of assets over liabilities; the residual interest of shareholders in the assets of an entity after deducting the entity's liabilities. Also called *shareholders' equity* or *shareholders' funds*.

p-Value The smallest level of significance at which the null is rejected.

Paired comparisons test See *test of the mean of the differences*.

Panel data A mix of time-series and cross-sectional data that contains observations through time on characteristics of across multiple observational units.

Per capita real GDP Real GDP divided by the size of the population, often used as a measure of a country's average standard of living.

Percentiles Quantiles that divide a distribution into 100 equal parts that sum to 100.

Perfectly elastic When the quantity demanded or supplied of a given good is infinitely sensitive to a change in the value of a specified variable (e.g., price).

Perfectly inelastic When the quantity demanded or supplied of a given good is completely insensitive to a change in the value of a specified variable (e.g., price).

Permutation An ordered listing.

Permutation formula The number of ways that we can choose *r* objects from a total of *n* objects, when the order in which the *r* objects are listed does matter, is $_nP_r = \frac{n!}{(n-r)!}$.

Perpetuity A perpetual annuity, or a set of never-ending level sequential cash flows, with the first cash flow occurring one period from now. A bond that does not mature.

Point estimate A single numerical estimate of an unknown quantity, such as a population parameter.

Population All members of a specified group.

Potential GDP The maximum amount of output an economy can sustainably produce without inducing an increase in the inflation rate. The output level that corresponds to full employment with consistent wage and price expectations.

Power of a test The probability of correctly rejecting the null—that is, rejecting the null hypothesis when it is false.

Precautionary money balances Money held to provide a buffer against unforeseen events that might require money.

Prepaid expense A normal operating expense that has been paid in advance of when it is due.

Present value (PV) The present discounted value of future cash flows: For assets, the present discounted value of the future net cash inflows that the asset is expected to generate; for liabilities, the present discounted value of the future net cash outflows that are expected to be required to settle the liabilities.

Principal The amount that an issuer agrees to repay the debtholders on the maturity date.

Probability A number between 0 and 1 describing the chance that a stated event will occur.

Probability density function A function with non-negative values such that probability can be described by areas under the curve graphing the function.

Probability distribution A distribution that specifies the probabilities of a random variable's possible outcomes.

Probability function A function that specifies the probability that the random variable takes on a specific value.

Production function Provides the quantitative link between the levels of output that the economy can produce and the inputs used in the production process.

Productivity The amount of output produced by workers during a given period—for example, output per hour worked measures the efficiency of labor.

Profit The return that owners of a company receive for the use of their capital and the assumption of financial risk when making their investments.

Profit and loss (P&L) statement A financial statement that provides information about a company's profitability over a stated period of time. Also called the *income statement*.

Promissory note A written promise to pay a certain amount of money on demand.

Property, plant, and equipment Tangible assets that are expected to be used for more than one period in either the production or supply of goods or services, or for administrative purposes.

Qualitative data see **categorical data**.

Quantile A value at or below which a stated fraction of the data lies. Also referred to as a fractile.

Quantitative data see **numerical data**.

Quantity equation of exchange An expression that over a given period, the amount of money used to purchase all goods and services in an economy, $M \times V$, is equal to monetary value of this output, $P \times Y$.

Quantity theory of money Asserts that total spending (in money terms) is proportional to the quantity of money.

Quartiles Quantiles that divide a distribution into four equal parts.

Quintiles Quantiles that divide a distribution into five equal parts.

Quoted interest rate A quoted interest rate that does not account for compounding within the year. Also called *stated annual interest rate*.

Random variable A quantity whose future outcomes are uncertain.

Range The difference between the maximum and minimum values in a dataset.

Raw data Data available in their original form as collected.

Real exchange rate effect The effect through which changing price level impacts real exchange rate which in turn impacts net exports and aggregate demand.

Real GDP The value of goods and services produced, measured at base year prices.

Real income Income adjusted for the effect of inflation on the purchasing power of money. Also known as the *purchasing power of income*. If income remains constant and a good's price falls, real income is said to rise, even though the number of monetary units (e.g., dollars) remains unchanged.

Real interest rate Nominal interest rate minus the expected rate of inflation.

real risk-free interest rate The single-period interest rate for a completely risk-free security if no inflation were expected.

Realizable (settlement) value With reference to assets, the amount of cash or cash equivalents that could currently be obtained by selling the asset in an orderly disposal; with reference to liabilities, the undiscounted amount of cash or cash equivalents expected to be paid to satisfy the liabilities in the normal course of business.

Recession A period during which real GDP decreases (i.e., negative growth) for at least two successive quarters, or a period of significant decline in total output, income, employment, and sales usually lasting from six months to a year.

Relative dispersion The amount of dispersion relative to a reference value or benchmark.

Relative frequency The absolute frequency of each unique value of the variable divided by the total number of observations of the variable.

Renewable resources Resources that can be replenished, such as a forest.

Rent Payment for the use of property.

Reserve requirement The requirement for banks to hold reserves in proportion to the size of deposits.

Revaluation model Under IFRS, the process of valuing long-lived assets at fair value, rather than at cost less accumulated depreciation. Any resulting profit or loss is either reported on the income statement and/or through equity under revaluation surplus.

Revenue The amount charged for the delivery of goods or services in the ordinary activities of a business over a stated period; the inflows of economic resources to a company over a stated period.

Rule of 72 The principle that the approximate number of years necessary for an investment to double is 72 divided by the stated interest rate.

Sales Generally, a synonym for revenue; "sales" is generally understood to refer to the sale of goods, whereas "revenue" is understood to include the sale of goods or services.

Sample A subset of a population.

Sample mean The sum of the sample observations divided by the sample size.

Sample selection bias Bias introduced by systematically excluding some members of the population according to a particular attribute—for example, the bias introduced when data availability leads to certain observations being excluded from the analysis.

Sample standard deviation The positive square root of the sample variance.
Sample statistic A quantity computed from or used to describe a sample.
Sample variance The sum of squared deviations around the mean divided by the degrees of freedom.
Scatter plot A two-dimensional graphical plot of paired observations of values for the independent and dependent variables in a simple linear regression.
Scatter plot matrix A tool for organizing scatter plots between pairs of variables, making it easy to inspect all pairwise relationships in one combined visual.
Screening The application of a set of criteria to reduce a set of potential investments to a smaller set having certain desired characteristics.
Second-degree price discrimination When the monopolist charges different per-unit prices using the quantity purchased as an indicator of how highly the customer values the product.
Shareholders' equity Total assets minus total liabilities.
Simple interest The interest earned each period on the original investment; interest calculated on the principal only.
Single-step format With respect to the format of the income statement, a format that does not subtotal for gross profit (revenue minus cost of goods sold).
Speculative demand for money The demand to hold speculative money balances based on the potential opportunities or risks that are inherent in other financial instruments. Also called *portfolio demand for money*.
Speculative money balances Monies held in anticipation that other assets will decline in value.
Stacked bar chart An alternative form for presenting the frequency distribution of two categorical variables, where bars representing the sub-groups are placed on top of each other to form a single bar. Each sub-section is shown in a different color to represent the contribution of each sub-group, and the overall height of the stacked bar represents the marginal frequency for the category.
Stagflation The combination of a high inflation rate with a high level of unemployment and a slowdown of the economy.
Standard deviation The positive square root of the variance; a measure of dispersion in the same units as the original data.
Standard normal distribution The normal density with mean (μ) equal to 0 and standard deviation (σ) equal to 1.
Standardizing A transformation that involves subtracting the mean and dividing the result by the standard deviation.
Stated annual interest rate A quoted interest rate that does not account for compounding within the year. Also called *quoted interest rate*.
Statement of changes in equity (statement of owners' equity) A financial statement that reconciles the beginning-of-period and end-of-period balance sheet values of shareholders' equity; provides information about all factors affecting shareholders' equity. Also called *statement of owners' equity*.
Statement of financial condition The financial statement that presents an entity's current financial position by disclosing resources the entity controls (its assets) and the claims on those resources (its liabilities and equity claims), as of a particular point in time (the date of the balance sheet).
Statement of financial position The financial statement that presents an entity's current financial position by disclosing resources the entity controls (its assets) and the claims on those resources (its liabilities and equity claims), as of a particular point in time (the date of the balance sheet).
Statement of operations A financial statement that provides information about a company's profitability over a stated period of time.
Statistic A summary measure of a sample of observations.
Statistically significant A result indicating that the null hypothesis can be rejected; with reference to an estimated regression coefficient, frequently understood to mean a result indicating that the corresponding population regression coefficient is different from zero.
Store of wealth Goods that depend on the fact that they do not perish physically over time, and on the belief that others would always value the good.
Straight-line method A depreciation method that allocates evenly the cost of a long-lived asset less its estimated residual value over the estimated useful life of the asset.
Structured data Data that are highly organized in a pre-defined manner, usually with repeating patterns.
Subjective probability A probability drawing on personal or subjective judgment.
Substitutes Said of two goods or services such that if the price of one increases the demand for the other tends to increase, holding all other things equal (e.g., butter and margarine).
Survivorship bias Relates to the inclusion of only current investment funds in a database. As such, the returns of funds that are no longer available in the marketplace (have been liquidated) are excluded from the database. Also see *backfill bias*.
Sustainable rate of economic growth The rate of increase in the economy's productive capacity or potential GDP.
Tag cloud see *word cloud*.
Target semideviation A measure of downside risk, calculated as the square root of the average of the squared deviations of observations below the target (also called target downside deviation).
Technology The process a company uses to transform inputs into outputs.
Terms of trade The ratio of the price of exports to the price of imports, representing those prices by export and import price indexes, respectively.
Test of the mean of the differences A statistical test for differences based on paired observations drawn from samples that are dependent on each other.
Third-degree price discrimination When the monopolist segregates customers into groups based on demographic or other characteristics and offers different pricing to each group.
Time value of money The principles governing equivalence relationships between cash flows with different dates.
Time-period bias The possibility that when we use a time-series sample, our statistical conclusion may be sensitive to the starting and ending dates of the sample.
Time-series data A sequence of observations for a single observational unit of a specific variable collected over time and at discrete and typically equally spaced intervals of time (such as daily, weekly, monthly, annually, or quarterly).
Top-down analysis An investment selection approach that begins with consideration of macroeconomic conditions and then evaluates markets and industries based upon such conditions.
Total comprehensive income The change in equity during a period resulting from transaction and other events, other than those changes resulting from transactions with owners in their capacity as owners.

Total cost The summation of all costs, for which costs are classified as fixed or variable.

Total factor productivity A scale factor that reflects the portion of growth unaccounted for by explicit factor inputs (e.g., capital and labor).

Total fixed cost The summation of all expenses that do not change as the level of production varies.

Total invested capital The sum of market value of common equity, book value of preferred equity, and face value of debt.

Total probability rule A rule explaining the unconditional probability of an event in terms of probabilities of the event conditional on mutually exclusive and exhaustive scenarios.

Total variable cost The summation of all variable expenses.

Trade payables Amounts that a business owes to its vendors for goods and services that were purchased from them but which have not yet been paid.

Trade protection Government policies that impose restrictions on trade, such as tariffs and quotas.

Trade surplus (deficit) When the value of exports is greater (less) than the value of imports.

Trading securities Under US GAAP, a category of debt securities held by a company with the intent to trade them. Also called *held-for-trading securities*.

Transactions money balances Money balances that are held to finance transactions.

Tree-Map Another graphical tool for displaying categorical data. It consists of a set of colored rectangles to represent distinct groups, and the area of each rectangle is proportional to the value of the corresponding group.

Trimmed mean A mean computed after excluding a stated small percentage of the lowest and highest observations.

Trimodal A distribution that has the three most frequently occurring values.

Two-dimensional rectangular array A popular form for organizing data for processing by computers or for presenting data visually. It is comprised of columns and rows to hold multiple variables and multiple observations, respectively (also called a **data table**).

Two-sided hypothesis test A test in which the null hypothesis is rejected in favor of the alternative hypothesis if the evidence indicates that the population parameter is either smaller or larger than a hypothesized value; occurs when the alternative hypothesis is stated as not equal to the hypothesized population parameters.

Type I error The error of rejecting a true null hypothesis; a false positive.

Type II error The error of not rejecting a false null hypothesis; false negative.

Underemployed A person who has a job but has the qualifications to work a significantly higher-paying job.

Unearned revenue A liability account for money that has been collected for goods or services that have not yet been delivered; payment received in advance of providing a good or service. Also called *deferred revenue* or *deferred income*.

Unemployed People who are actively seeking employment but are currently without a job.

Unemployment rate The ratio of unemployed to the labor force.

Unexpected inflation The component of inflation that is a surprise.

Unimodal A distribution with a single value that is most frequently occurring.

Unit elastic An elasticity with a magnitude of negative one. Also called *unitary elastic*.

Unit labor cost The average labor cost to produce one unit of output.

Unit normal distribution The normal density with mean (μ) equal to 0 and standard deviation (σ) equal to 1.

Units-of-production method A depreciation method that allocates the cost of a long-lived asset based on actual usage during the period.

Univariate distribution A distribution that specifies the probabilities for a single random variable.

Unstructured data Data that do not follow any conventionally organized forms.

Up transition probability The probability that an asset's value moves up.

Value investors With reference to equity investors, investors who are focused on paying a relatively low share price in relation to earnings or assets per share.

Variable A characteristic or quantity that can be measured, counted, or categorized and that is subject to change (also called a field, an attribute, or a feature).

Variable costs Costs that fluctuate with the level of production and sales.

Variance The expected value (the probability-weighted average) of squared deviations from a random variable's expected value.

Visualization The presentation of data in a pictorial or graphical format for the purpose of increasing understanding and for gaining insights into the data.

Voluntarily unemployed A person voluntarily outside the labor force, such as a jobless worker refusing an available vacancy.

Wealth effect An increase (decrease) in household wealth increases (decreases) consumer spending out of a given level of current income.

Weighted mean An average in which each observation is weighted by an index of its relative importance.

Winsorized mean A mean computed after assigning a stated percentage of the lowest values equal to one specified low value and a stated percentage of the highest values equal to one specified high value.

Word cloud A visual device for representing textual data, which consists of words extracted from a source of textual data. The size of each distinct word is proportional to the frequency with which it appears in the given text (also known as **tag cloud**).

Working capital The difference between current assets and current liabilities.

World price The price prevailing in the world market.

Printed in Poland
by Amazon Fulfillment
Poland Sp. z o.o., Wrocław